Antonov An-12

The Soviet Hercules

Yefim Gordon
and Dmitriy Komissarov

MIDLAND

An imprint of
Ian Allan Publishing

Antonov An-12: The Soviet Hercules
© 2007 Yefim Gordon and Dmitriy Komissarov

ISBN (10) 1 85780 255 1
ISBN (13) 978 1 85780 255 9

Published by Midland Publishing
4 Watling Drive, Hinckley, LE10 3EY, England
Tel: 01455 254 490   Fax: 01455 254 495
E-mail: midlandbooks@compuserve.com

Midland Publishing is an imprint of
Ian Allan Publishing Ltd

Worldwide distribution (except North America):
Midland Counties Publications
4 Watling Drive, Hinckley, LE10 3EY, England
Telephone: 01455 254 450   Fax: 01455 233 737
E-mail: midlandbooks@compuserve.com
www.midlandcountiessuperstore.com

North American trade distribution:
Specialty Press Publishers & Wholesalers Inc.
39966 Grand Avenue, North Branch, MN 55056, USA
Tel: 651 277 1400   Fax: 651 277 1203
Toll free telephone: 800 895 4585
www.specialtypress.com

Design concept and layout by
Polygon Press Ltd (Moscow, Russia)
Line drawings by Aleksandr & Konstantin Krasnikov
Colour artwork by the late Sergey Yershov

This book is illustrated with photos by A. Dotsenko,
Victor Drushlyakov, Yefim Gordon, Yuriy Kirsanov,
Dmitriy Komissarov, Sergey Krivchikov, Dmitriy
Petrochenko, Dmitriy Pichoogin, Sergey Popsuyevich,
Sergey Sergeyev, the late Sergey Skrynnikov, the late
Boris Vdovenko, Aidan Curley, Peter Davison, Waclaw
Holys, Chris Lofting, Martin Novak, ITAR-TASS, the
Swedish Air Force, as well as from the archives of the
Antonov Aviation Scientific & Technical Complex,
Yefim Gordon, Sergey & Dmitriy Komissarov, the
Russian Aviation Research Trust and the Internet.

Printed in England by Ian Allan Printing Ltd
Riverdene Business Park, Molesey Road,
Hersham, Surrey, KT12 4RG

Visit the Ian Allan Publishing website at:
www.ianallanpublishing.com

Contents

Introduction 3

1. Birth of an Airlifter 15
2. A Versatile Antonov 23
3. An-12 Anatomy 61
4. Beyond the Great Wall 75
5. At War and At Work 89
6. The *Cub* Worldwide 97

Line Drawings 138
Colour Artwork 142

Title page: Civil-configured An-12BP RA-12959 (c/n 8345510) displays the polar version of Aeroflot's 1973-standard livery on approach to Moscow-Sheremet'yevo. This page: Caught by the camera as the landing gear begins to extend, Ukrainian Air Force An-12BK '21 Blue' (c/n 7345208) makes a smoky final approach. This aircraft later became UR-11348 with Busol Airline.

Front cover: '16 Yellow', a Russian Navy/North Fleet Air Arm An-12PS SAR aircraft (c/n 7344702), completes the gear retraction sequence as it takes off from Severomorsk-1 AB. Note the polar bear nose art.
Rear cover, top: Russian Air Force An-12BK '51 Red' (c/n 8345801) with RusAF titles; bottom: An-12BK RA-12137 (c/n 6344410) on finals to Chkalovskaya AB.

Introduction

The Antonov An-12 transport belongs to the category of outstanding aircraft. It came on the scene at exactly the right time; it was a fairly sophisticated design by the standards of the day and was manufactured in sufficient numbers. Easy to fly and undemanding in operation, it earned world renown both for the Antonov design bureau and for the Soviet aircraft industry in general. From the mid-1960s onwards there was not a single major event in the history of the Soviet Union, and later Russia, in which the An-12 was not involved. It served in a multitude of roles ranging from military transport duties to development of sparsely populated areas and polar research, taking part in many armed conflicts. For several decades this machine, along with its American counterpart (the Lockheed C-130 Hercules), remained a mainstay of the world's transport aviation, civil and military alike.

The An-12 has been operated by the air forces and airlines of many nations and has earned a reputation as a thoroughly efficient and reliable means of transport. To this day it can be seen at numerous airbases and airports both in and outside the Commonwealth of Independent States (CIS). Quite a few airlines still operate this relatively cheap aircraft. The type's longevity testifies well to the qualities of an aircraft that first took to the skies nearly half a century ago.

Surprisingly, the Soviet Union, which was the first to establish airborne troops as a separate arm of its armed forces, had no dedicated military transport aircraft until the end of the 1950s. This role was filled by heavy bombers and airliners adapted for the purpose. During the Great Patriotic War, transport and troopship duties were performed mainly by converted Tupolev TB-3 bombers of pre-war vintage and PS-84 (Lisunov Li-2) passenger aircraft; the latter type was a licence-built Douglas DC-3 derivative (see Red Star Vol. 27). Later they were superseded by the Tupolev Tu-4D (a conversion of the Tu-4 strategic bomber adapted for transport and paradropping tasks; see Red Star Vol. 7) and the Ilyushin IL-12D (a purpose-built military assault transport version of the IL-12B twin-engined airliner; see Red Star Vol. 25). To be sure, large assault gliders, such as the Tsybin Ts-25 and Yakovlev Yak-14 were also constructed, but they could not obviate the need for transport aircraft and take over their role completely.

The Tu-75 assault transport aircraft – again a derivative of the Tu-4 – was designed, built and tested by Andrey Nikolayevich Tupolev's OKB-156, but series production failed to materialise. Shortly after the beginning of flight tests the sole prototype crashed, killing the crew of four. (OKB – *opytno-konstrooktorskoye byuro* – experimental design

Above: The Tu-75 assault transport was derived from the Tu-4 bomber, combining the latter's wings, tail surfaces and powerplant with a new fuselage incorporating a cargo cabin.

Above: This three-quarters rear view shows the Tu-75's tail gunner's station. The actual cannon barbette was never fitted.

The cabin of the Tu-75 in troop carrier configuration with the additional centreline seats in place.

Three views of a Tu-4D transport fitted with underwing cargo pods. which were suitable for transporting jeeps and field guns.

bureau; the number is a code allocated for security reasons.)

Several other projects for dedicated transport aircraft were under development at the end of the 1940s. Thus, in 1944-48 a design bureau led by Robert Lyudvigovich Bartini worked on the T-108 and T-117 piston-engined military transport aircraft and on the T-200 heavy transport aircraft featuring a compound powerplant (with piston engines as the main powerplant assisted by turbo-jets). Implementation of these projects, however, proved to be impracticable because the Bartini OKB was closed down by then.

The situation changed in the early 1950s when the USA was already operating the twin-boom Fairchild C-119 Flying Boxcar dedicated military transport on a mass scale, the more conventional Fairchild C-123 Provider had entered production, and the Lockheed Company had begun development of a new-generation machine – the turboprop-powered C-130 Hercules.

A new military doctrine evolved in the USSR with due regard to the changing world political situation contained a requirement for increased troop mobility; to this end, plans were made for modernising and expanding transport aviation to meet the exigencies of contemporary warfare. On 17th April 1953, having studied a TsAGI report on assembly of the two YC-130 prototypes, Marshal Dmitriy F. Ustinov (the then Minister of Defence Industry of the USSR) wrote on the title page: 'To Comrade Khrunichev. Must confer with you'. (Note: TsAGI = Tsentrahl'nyy aero- i ghidrodi-namicheskiy institoot – the Central Aero- and Hydrodynamics Institute named after Nikolay Ye. Zhukovskiy. Mikhail V. Khrunichev was then Minister of Aircraft Industry; Ustinov later became Minister of Defence, a post which he held until his death in office.) This served as the first official go-ahead for the work that eventually resulted in the creation of a Soviet dedicated transport aircraft powered by turboprop engines. Several design

teams, including the design bureaux led by Oleg Konstantinovich Antonov, Vladimir Mikhaïlovich Myasishchev and A. N. Tupolev were asked to develop projects of dedicated turboprop-powered transport aircraft. There was no contest as such, but in the end it was the Antonov OKB that received this task from the Government.

Within a short period the Antonov OKB – then based at aircraft factory No.153 in Novosibirsk and called OKB-153 – succeeded in evolving its own concept of transport machines. Since then the aircraft created by the Antonov design team have featured the characteristic high-wing layout with wing-mounted engines. (When asked in a television interview in 1984 why all of his aircraft except the An-2 utility biplane were high-wing designs, Oleg K. Antonov responded with a question: 'Have you ever seen a low-wing bird?') Placing the engines and propellers high above the ground reduced the risk of foreign object damage, enhanced the lift/drag ratio and operational safety. Ground vehicles could freely move about under the high wings, which made it possible to park the aircraft closer to each other on the airfield. Moreover, the wings housing the fuel tanks remained intact in the event of a belly landing, which reduced the risk of a fire breaking out. Another key point of the concept was the ability to transport bulky cargoes and operate from semi-prepared airstrips.

An-8: Antonov's First Turboprop

The first steps toward a new-generation military transport embodying these features were taken in December 1951 when OKB-153 prepared an advanced development project (ADP) of a twin-turboprop aircraft provisionally designated DT-5/8 (DT = desahntno-trahnsportnyy [samolyot] – assault transport aircraft). The machine had a maximum payload of 8 tons (17,640 lb); it was provided with a large rear cargo door allowing troops and materiel to be paradropped. The powerplant consisted of two 5,163-ehp TV-2 turboprops (toorbovintovoy [dvigatel'] – turboprop engine) created by Nikolay D. Kuznetsov's OKB-276 in 1947-1950 – virtually the only turboprop engine available in the USSR at that time. (OKB-276 is now the Samara Scientific & Technical Complex named after Nikolay D. Kuznetsov.)

On 11th December 1953 the Soviet Council of Ministers issued directive No.2922-1251 requiring the Antonov OKB – which, after moving to Kiev, was renamed GSOKB-473 (Gosoodarstvennoye soyooznoye opytno-konstrooktorskoye byuro – State All-Union Design Bureau, meaning that the OKB had national importance) – to design and build a twin-turboprop transport aircraft. The directive, backed up by order No.278 issued by the

Above: The almost completed prototype of the Bartini T-117 transport. It never received its intended Shvetsov ASh-82 radial engines and was eventually scrapped without ever being flown.

Right: The T-117's cargo cabin was wide enough to accommodate two GAZ-67B jeeps side by side.

Below right: A GAZ-67B is driven into the T-117's cargo cabin via the rear loading door and ramps.

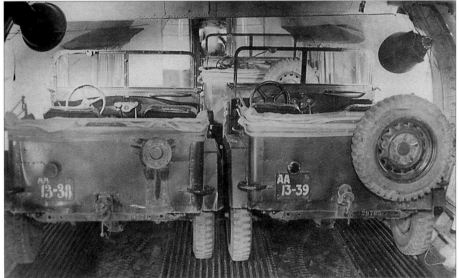

Ministry of Aircraft Industry (MAP – *Ministerstvo aviatsionnoy promyshlennosti*) on 23rd December, set forth the basic specifications for the aircraft.

Hence GSOKB-473 started work on a new version of the project bearing the in-house designation '*izdeliye* P' (product P); engineer A. Ya. Belolipetskiy led the actual design effort. The aircraft was powered by TV-2T engines (a refined version of the TV-2 developed with assistance from Aleksandr G. Ivchenko's OKB-478) driving AV-58 four-bladed reversible-pitch propellers. The TV-2T had a take-off rating of 6,250 ehp (some documents quote it as 6,500 ehp). Note that '*Izdeliye* such-and-such' was/is a commonly used code for Soviet/Russian military hardware items. OKB-478 is now ZMKB 'Progress' (*Zaporozhskoye motorno-konstrooktorskoye byuro* – the 'Progress' Zaporozhye Engine Design Bureau).

The slab-sided fuselage was capacious enough to accommodate bulky military equipment, such as artillery pieces of up to 122 mm (4.8 in) calibre, 120-mm (4.7-in) and 160-mm (6.3-in) mortars towed by GAZ-63 four-wheel-drive lorries, two ASU-57 self-propelled guns, a D-211 bulldozer, a ZiS-151 6x6 lorry, and BTR-40 or BTR-152 armoured personnel carriers. Alternatively, the cargo hold

Two views of the An-8 (*izdeliye* P) full-scale mock-up at GSOKB-473's prototype construction facility in Kiev. Note the alternative powerplants (a TV-2F turboprop to port and an AL-7 turbojet to starboard), the external tanks and the rear loading ramp/door which was not incorporated on the actual aircraft.

accommodated up to 60 troops with full kit or 40 paratroopers. The pressurised crew section was partly protected with armour and included an extensively glazed navigator's station in the extreme nose, with a panoramic navigation/ground mapping radar in a teardrop-shaped radome below it. For self-defence the aft fuselage incorporated a pressurised compartment for a tail gunner with a powered turret mounting two 23-mm (.90 cal-ibre) Afanas'yev/Makarov AM-23 cannons with a 1,000-rpm rate of fire.

The tricycle undercarriage retracted aft, the four-wheel main gear bogies rotating aft through 180° in the process to stow in neat lateral fairings. As compared to other aircraft the *izdeliye* P had a very narrow wheel track (in relation to the wingspan) – just a little more than half the recommended one. Nevertheless, this feature was deemed acceptable.

At that time the OKB did not have the production facilities, resources and experience to take on such a complex task; all three components had to be gained as soon as possible. Hence the OKB began actively recruiting aircraft engineers, including large numbers of fresh graduates of the Khar'kov Aviation Institute. The Kiev-based aircraft factory No.473 placed one of its buildings at the OKB's disposal for use as a prototype production facility. Also, GSOKB-473 engineers were allowed to study the design features of the Tu-16 twin-turbojet medium bomber and the IL-28 twin-turbojet tactical bomber – both in the form of drawings and on the actual production lines. Antonov also received assistance from Bartini, who had already accumulated some experience in designing dedicated transport aircraft. Learning fast, the Antonov OKB managed to avoid many mistakes and save a lot of time when designing the *izdeliye* P.

The design features of the aircraft posed a number of tough problems which necessitated a large amount of theoretical research and experiments. A matter of particular complexity was the design of the rear fuselage incorporating the large cargo hatch which weakened the structure. The designers had to make sure the fuselage would withstand the loads created by the empennage. Tests of scaled-strength models were undertaken, using specially evolved calculation methods;

this made it possible to optimise the weight of the design. To study the mutual influence of the aircraft and the cargoes paradropped by it, flight tests were conducted, using scale models of the *izdeliye* P's fuselage suspended under an actual aircraft. New high-lift devices (double-slotted flaps with a fixed second slot) and a special heavy-duty undercarriage giving rough-field capability were developed.

The ADP was completed in July 1954, and on 26th October 1954 the mock-up review commission headed by Air Major-General V. I. Lebedev examined the full-scale mock-up. The latter was presented with alternative powerplants: a TV-2T turboprop on the port wing and a 6,830-kgp (15,060-lbst) Lyul'ka AL-7 turbojet under the starboard wing. The commission gave a thumbs-up, and construction of the first prototype got under way. The new machine, by then bearing the official designation An-8, was ceremonially rolled out in early February 1956 – incidentally, on Chief Designer Oleg K. Antonov's 50th birthday.

On 11th February 1956 the An-8 made its maiden flight from Kiev-Svyatoshino (the factory airfield of plant No.473), piloted by a crew from the Flight Research Institute named after Mikhail M. Gromov (LII – *Lyotno-issledovatel'skiy institoot*); the crew was captained by Yakov I. Vernikov (Hero of the Soviet Union). Manufacturer's flight tests initially proceeded in Kiev, later at the LII airfield in Zhukovskiy near Moscow. On 18th August 1956 the aircraft made its public debut when the first prototype took part in the annual Aviation Day display at Moscow's Tushino airfield together with other new Soviet aviation hardware. After this the NATO's Air Standards Co-ordinating Committee (ASCC) allocated to it the reporting name *Camp* to the An-8.

Manufacturer's tests were completed on 2nd October. Then the An-8 was transferred to the Red Banner State Research Institute of the Air Force (GK NII VVS – *Gosoodarstvennyy krasnoznamyonnyy naoochno-issledovatel'skiy institoot Voyenno-vozdooshnykh seel*) for State acceptance trials, which were completed on 27th November 1956; the final protocol of the State commission was endorsed on 15th December. The machine demonstrated commendable performance. It could carry up to 11 tons (24,250 lb) of cargo, which could be conventionally unloaded after landing or paradropped. Nevertheless, the State commission chose not to recommend the An-8 for series production and service in as-was configuration – for several reasons. Among other things, the trials revealed unsatisfactory spinning characteristics, directional stability and control problems, shimmy oscillations on the nose gear unit and poor controllability during landing in crosswinds exceeding 6 m/sec (12 kts). Self-induced oscillations in all three axes occurred during straight and level flight, making piloting difficult and causing pilot fatigue.

The main reason for the thumbs-down, however, was the poor functioning of the TV-2T engines caused by the low stability of their gas dynamics at altitudes in excess of 6,000 m (19,690 ft). Starting of the powerplant was unreliable and its operation at high altitude unstable; this was compounded by the engine's low service life. The experimental design features incorporated in this engine made it impossible to eliminate these shortcomings. A new powerplant was urgently sought, but the only alternatives were the new 4,000-ehp Kuznetsov NK-4 or Ivchenko AI-20 turboprops, with which the aircraft would be clearly underpowered. A four-engined version of *izdeliye* P was proposed, but the idea was rejected. Under these circumstances Chief Designer Aleksandr G. Ivchenko suggested replacing the TV-2T with an uprated version of the AI-20. After studying the behaviour of this engine in contingency mode OKB-478 stated that it was possible to create an uprated version, the AI-20D (*dorabotannyy* – updated) delivering 5,500 ehp for take-off. Ivchenko's proposal was accepted, and on 4th April 1957 the Council of Ministers issued directive No.373-184 prescribing that the shortcomings noted on the prototype An-8 be eliminated and the aircraft be re-engined with AI-20Ds, whereupon the machine was to be put into production at aircraft factory No.84 in Tashkent.

In July-October 1957 the Antonov OKB was busy modifying the An-8 prototype. Apart from AI-20D engines driving AV-68D four-bladed reversible-pitch propellers, the area of the vertical and horizontal tail was increased, the wing leading-edge slats were deleted, some local structural reinforcements were made, and anti-spin strakes were installed on the upper rear fuselage. The modifications cut the aircraft's empty weight by 3 tons (6,610 lb), which was mainly due to the installation of lighter engines.

Series production of the An-8 military airlifter started in 1957 and lasted until 1961 when the type was supplanted by the An-12 on the Tashkent production line. Since the An-8 was radically different in its design from the IL-14 which plant No.84 had been manufacturing previously, new production techniques were introduced for the stamping and forging of large structural members, for extrusion of long sections, chemical milling of skin panels and so on. In keeping with a State Committee for Aviation Hardware (GKAT – *Gosoodarstvennyy komitet po aviatsionnoy tekhnike*) order dated 29th July 1959, a branch office of GSOKB-473 was set up at the Tashkent aircraft factory to support series production of the An-8. (Note: GKAT was the name of the former MAP in 1956-65. It was, in fact, a demotion from ministry status due to the Soviet leader Nikita S. Khrushchov's predilection towards missile systems to the detriment of manned aviation. Later, when Leonid I. Brezhnev became head of state, the Ministry of Aircraft Industry was reinstated.)

Despite a lot of bench and flight testing, the AI-20D engine would not deliver the advertised power rating. However, the Tashkent plant was already completing the first production An-8 airframes. Therefore, MAP and the Air Force took the joint decision to introduce the An-8 into service with the engines derated to 5,180 ehp. The take-off weight was limited to 38 tons (83,800 lb) versus the initial 42 tons (92,600 lb) for the TV-2T powered version. Derating the engines impaired the performance considerably. Suffice it to say that the maximum payload was limited to 8 tons (17,640 lb), although the normal payload of 5 tons (11,000 lb) remained unchanged. The top speed, range and service ceiling also deteriorated; the inadequate power-to-weight ratio precluded the continuation of take-off from unpaved runways in the event of an engine failure.

The first production An-8 was rolled out in August 1958; at the end of the year it was flown by the plant's test crew. It differed from the prototype by introducing changes in the undercarriage control system, the fuel tank vents, the pressurisation and de-icing systems. In addition, the fuselage skin was reinforced in the propellers' plane of rotation and the maximum rudder deflection angle was reduced.

On 30th October 1959 the An-8's State acceptance trials were successfully completed. That same year the aircraft achieved initial operational capability with the Soviet Air Force. Later, in the 1970s, when sufficient numbers of newer military transports became available, the An-8s were progressively transferred to MAP and other ministries to cater for their transport needs.

Overall An-8 production in Tashkent totalled 151. Apart from the baseline transport version, specialised versions were evolved over the years. These included the experimental An-8T (*toplivovoz* – fuel carrier) optimised for transporting all kinds of automotive, aircraft and rocket fuels. Depending on the mission, it could be fitted with two 5,300-litre (1,166-Imp gal) tanks for petroleum products, or a 5,000-litre (1,100-Imp gal) reservoir for oxidisers based on nitric acid, or a liquid oxygen reservoir. At least one An-8 was converted for radiation intelligence duties by fitting two RR8311-100 standardised air sampling pods under the tail gunner's station (no separate designation is known). It was used for monitoring radiation levels in the wake of nuclear tests. Another production *Camp* was

Above: An as-yet uncoded production An-8 powered by Ivchenko AI-20D engines.

Above: Soviet Airborne Forces (VDV) troopers board an An-8 coded '11 Red'. Oddly enough, the aircraft has had the tail turret removed and the tail gunner's station glazing faired over.

fitted experimentally with two solid-propellant rocket boosters with a view to increasing the maximum TOW to 42 tons (92,590 lb) while retaining the standard An-8's rate of climb during take-off with one engine inoperative. Designated An-8RU (s *raket*nymi *oosko-rit*elyami – with rocket boosters), the aircraft entered flight test in 1964 but the programme was abandoned after the crash of the sole prototype.

Other versions of the An-8 never left the drawing board. These were the An-8M anti-submarine warfare aircraft (the M stood for either *modifitseerovannyy*, modified, or *morskoy*, naval or maritime) developed in 1958; the An-8Sh navigator trainer (*shtoormanskiy* – for navigators) and the An-8PS maritime search and rescue aircraft (*poiskovo-spasahtel'nyy* – SAR, used attributively), both developed in 1959; and an airliner derivative called '*izdeliye* N' designed as early as 1955, with an all-new pressurised fuselage of circular cross-section accommodating a maximum of 57 passengers.

An-10 – the ill-starred progenitor

The *izdeliye* N project inspired the designers to develop a bigger, four-engined airliner. This aircraft, said Oleg K. Antonov, should be created in such a way that it would be easy to evolve a military transport from it. His belief was that a single project should be developed in two versions differing only in the rear fuselage design and equipment fit. This approach speeded up the design process and production entry considerably, reducing the expenses involved; it also facilitated crew conversion and simplified operation. In addition, an airliner sharing a heavy-duty under-carriage with a military transport could operate from a wider network of airports, including ill-equipped and unpaved provincial airfields which were still common in those

Another Soviet Air Force An-8, '92 Red'; unusually, the tactical code is carried on the nose. This is an early-production aircraft, as indicated by the lack of the APU.

days, which would endow local air services with the same level of comfort as on trunk routes. Finally, should war become imminent, the airliners could be easily converted into transports by simply substituting the 'civil' rear fuselage with the 'military' one.

The idea appealed to the Soviet leader Nikita S. Khrushchov, who visited the Antonov OKB in 1955. Soon afterwards, on 30th December 1955, the *izdeliye* N was abandoned and the Council of Ministers issued a directive requiring Chief Designer Oleg K. Antonov to develop the 85-seat An-10 airliner and the An-12 military transport. These were 'twin brothers', two versions of the same basic design. The same directive required engine designers Nikolay D. Kuznetsov and Aleksandr G. Ivchenko to develop the NK-4 and TV-20 (later renamed AI-20) turboprop engines which were intended, among other things, to be installed on his new IL-18 airliner – a direct competitor of the An-10.

In effect, for the first time in the post-war years, a contest was organised in the USSR for the best civil airliner. Each of the contenders had its 'selling points': the Il-18's advantage lay in its low fuel consumption when operated on trunk routes, whereas the An-10 was expected to operate from a wider network of airfields, serving medium-haul routes 500-2,000 km (310-1,240 miles) long, and to have a military transport version.

The An-10, allocated the in-house designation '*izdeliye* U' and the popular name *Ookraïna* (the Ukraine), was superficially similar to the *izdeliye* N, featuring a circular-section pressurised fuselage with a glazed navigator's station and a chin radome (a characteristic feature of many Soviet aircraft developed in the 1950s and early 1960s) and a conventional tail unit augmented by a ventral fin. The four engine nacelles adhered to the underside of the wings, as on the An-8. Unlike the latter, the four-wheel main landing gear bogies retracted inwards rather than aft.

N. S. Troonchenkov and V. N. Ghel'prin were appointed chief project engineers for the An-10 and the An-12 respectively. The general arrangement team was headed by N. A. Nechayev, the fuselage design team by S. D. Yel'mesev, the wing design team by A. A. Batoomov and the undercarriage team by N. P. Smirnov. A. M. Kondrat'yev was responsible for the development of hydraulic systems, I. A. Pashinin and M. S. Gal'perin for the electrical equipment, V. A. Danil'chenko for the avionics. All cabin equipment was developed in-house by a special team headed by N. A. Pogorelov.

The fact that GSOKB-473 was located on Ukrainian soil had major consequences for the An-10 and An-12 programmes, affecting the choice of the engine for these aircraft. The 4,000-ehp NK-4 turboprop developed by

Above: The cargo cabin of an An-8 occupied by paratroopers. Note the longitudinal steel cables to which the paratroopers' static lines are hooked up.

OKB-276 in Kuibyshev, Russia (now renamed back to Samara), seemed very promising; it had high specific performance characteristics. On the other hand, the identically rated TV-20 (AI-20) developed by OKB-478 (which was located in the southern Ukrainian town of Zaporozhye), albeit less advanced, relied on proven technical features. For some reason an opinion prevails that, thanks to Ivchenko's wisely cautious conservative approach, his engine was superior to that of his rival in reliability and operational safety. However, to this day no documentary proof has been found of the NK-4's alleged 'unreliability'.

In the Antonov OKB each of the two engine types had its supporters and opponents. Some aviation historians believe that Antonov, being in two minds, took the decision that the first prototype of the An-10 should be powered by NK-4s and the first prototype of the An-12 by TV-20 (AI-20) engines. However, this was not the case. There is documentary evidence that the Chief Designer intended to fit Kuznetsov turboprops to the first two An-12s, and only subsequent aircraft of this type were to be powered by Ivchenko

engines. A certain part in this matter was also played by the Central Committee of the Communist Party of the Ukraine. Their reasoning was simple: since the aircraft was being created in the Ukraine, its engines should also be 'Ukrainian'. Understandably, Antonov, whose enterprise was situated in Kiev and depended to a large extent on the goodwill of the Ukrainian leaders, could not ignore this 'opinion'. Thus, the AI-20 engine was launched on a long and successful service career.

In May 1956 the ADP of *izdeliye* U was submitted for approval, and the full-size mock-up was endorsed five months later. The An-10 prototype registered CCCP-У1957 (that is, SSSR-U1957 in Cyrillic characters, the U referring to *izdeliye* U and the digits denoting the year) entered flight test on 7th March 1957 with captain Yakov I. Vernikov (LII) and co-pilot I. Ye. Davydov (GSOKB-473) at the controls. As noted above, the aircraft was powered by NK-4 engines driving AV-60 four-bladed propellers which had passed bench testing ahead of the AI-20.

The machine incorporated many unusual features for an airliner, including the large

CCCP-У1957 (that is, SSSR-U1957 in Cyrillic characters), the prototype of the An-10 airliner. Note the *Ookraïna* (the Ukraine) titles – in Ukrainian, not Russian instead of Aeroflot titles.

Above: Passengers wait to board an early An-10 *sans suffixe* via the rear entry door, while mailbags are loaded through the forward entry door. The aircraft is still in original configuration with endplate fins.

Above: A Soviet Air Force An-10A, wearing the type's basic Aeroflot red/white colours but no tactical code, comes in to land. The aircraft has the ultimate tail treatment with twin ventral fins and no endplate fins.

allowing you to listen to the radio without disturbing your fellow passengers.

For take-off at maximum all-up weight the aircraft needed an airstrip no more than 700-800 m (2,300-2,625 ft) long – even if it was unpaved. The landing run was even shorter, being just 500-600 m (1,640-1,970 ft). Besides, the An-10's navigation suite and flight instrumentation were advanced by the day's standards. The pressurised and air-conditioned cabin enabled cruise flight at high altitudes, ensuring comfort and proper conditions for the crew and passengers.

The manufacturer's flight test programme was completed by I. Ye. Davydov and V. A. Kalinin. The tests revealed poor directional stability. Hence the prototype was soon fitted with a taller vertical tail; when this proved insufficient, large hexagonal endplate fins were added to the stabiliser tips.

In July 1957 the An-10 prototype was presented to journalists and the general public at Moscow-Vnukovo airport. That same year the airliner entered series production at aircraft factory No.64 in Voronezh, Russia. By the end of the year the plant had manufactured three aircraft; these were powered by NK-4 engines because the definitive AI-20 engines were still unavailable. Starting in 1958, production An-10s were fitted with AI-20As driving AV-68 propellers. The Ivchenko engines had a longer service life and compared favourably to the Kuznetsov engine in terms of weight, ease of production and in some other respects.

State acceptance trials of the An-10, which began in January 1959, were conducted by GK NII VVS and included high-alpha and stalling tests. Proceeding from the results of the trials, which were completed in June 1959, the new aircraft – the first Soviet turboprop airliner – was formally recommended for series production (which had long since begun!).

fuselage diameter (4.1 m; 13 5½ in), the high-set wings with a span of 38 m (124 ft 8 in) and the short fuselage-mounted landing gear. In those years only two other airliners – the Soviet Tu-114 *Rossiya* (Russia; see Red Star Vol. 31) and the British Saunders-Roe

Princess flying boat – could boast such a wide fuselage. The An-10's comfortable cabin featured carpeted floors and interior decor based on ethnic Ukrainian motifs; the seats incorporated ashtrays, individual reading lamps and even sockets for headphones

Some Soviet Air Force An-10TS transports, like these examples pictured at an unpaved airfield, wore an overall silver finish. The nearest aircraft is coded '19 Blue'.

Most of the defects revealed during the trials could be easily rectified in production; however, two of them required additional and rather lengthy research. Firstly, when the aircraft reached Mach 0.62 a rather dangerous buffeting arose; hence the pilots were forbidden to exceed this speed, even though the available engine power allowed the An-10 to fly faster. Secondly, longitudinal instability manifested itself during landing approach. As the An-10 came in for landing with the flaps extended, even an insignificant but abrupt 'push' of the control column would cause the nose to 'fall through' and the pilot had to be extra careful at this crucial stage of the flight.

On 27th April 1959 the An-10 performed its first route-proving flight; exactly a month later the aircraft took off on a publicity tour which took it from Kiev to Moscow, Tbilisi, Sochi/Adler (the two cities share the same airport), Khar'kov and thence back to Kiev. The type's first revenue service (from Moscow-Vnukovo to Simferopol') took place on 22nd July 1959. On 10th September of the same year, after successfully completing operational trials, the new aircraft officially entered service with Aeroflot, the sole Soviet airline.

The pilots of the Ukrainian Civil Aviation Directorate (CAD) were the first to master the An-10. Following suit, several other Aeroflot directorates in the Russian Federative Soviet Socialist Republic and other Soviet republics simultaneously started operating the machine on medium-haul routes.

The aircraft quickly won favour thanks to its large cargo-carrying capacity and good field performance. As noted earlier, the machine was well suited for operation from unpaved airstrips, which was a major asset in the Soviet Union. In 1959 even Kiev-Borispol', the Ukrainian capital's main airport, had no paved runway – to say nothing of other cities big and small where paved runways were at best under construction. The An-10 could operate in a mixed cargo/passenger configuration (52 passengers, 1,040 kg/2,290 lb of baggage and 9,080 kg/20,020 lb of cargo) or, if need be, in pure cargo configuration, carrying 15 tons (33,070 lb) of cargo; the aircraft could be reconfigured very quickly in field conditions. On shorter trunk routes with intensive passenger traffic this versatility made it possible to venture on the concept of an 'airbus' able to land on any more or less suitable airfield. Not infrequently, tickets were sold on the spot (right in the cabin) and the airliner took off after all the seats had been sold. Low fares (the price of the airline ticket was on a par with the price of a railway ticket in a sleeping car for the same distance), together with the machine's initially high profitability, fuelled hopes for the whole concept to prove economically viable.

Above: The Soviet Air Force used the An-10, including silver-painted An-10TS '18 Blue', chiefly as a troopship for transporting and paradropping personnel.

Above: Paradropping took place via the An-10's standard baggage door. This aircraft is coded '20 Blue'.

A string of parachutists leaves an An-10TS as it passes overhead.

Above: As the An-8 was phased out by the Soviet Air Force, the aircraft found use with industrial enterprises. CCCP-13323 (c/n 0E 3430) belonged to the Kaluga Engine Production Association. The red tips of the propeller spinners are squadron markings left over from its Air Force days.

According to calculations, the seat-mile costs of the 85-seat An-10 were considerably lower than those of the turbojet-powered 50-seat Tu-104A, mainly thanks to the former type's higher seating capacity. However, the introduction of the stretched Tu-104B seating up to 100 passengers negated this advantage – in fact, the Tu-104B proved to be more economical than the Antonov machine. It should be noted that the Tu-104B's high fuel efficiency manifested itself only at high altitudes, deteriorating markedly at medium and low altitudes. Conversely, the An-10 offered high fuel efficiency both at medium and at relatively low altitudes.

It may be said now that the considerable structural commonality of the An-10 and its transport derivative, the An-12, was a liability in certain respects. For example, early production An-12s had their centre fuselage structure hermetically sealed (as on the pressurised An-10), even though the freight hold was unpressurised – with an attendant increase in manufacturing costs and complexity. In turn, owing to the low placement of the cabin floor (on the same level as the freighter's cargo floor), the An-10 featured excessive passenger cabin volume at the expense of baggage stowage. All this incurred a weight penalty, especially in the case of the airliner. The An-10's payload/TOW ratio was appreciably lower as compared to the IL-18; Sergey V. Il'yushin considered the concept of the An-10/An-12 'twins' to be flawed for this very reason. Nevertheless, Oleg K. Antonov consciously put up with these weight penalties, regarding them an acceptable price to pay for the advantages described above. From the present-day point of view this attitude is extremely vulnerable,

but in the days when the country had plentiful supplies of kerosene and any project was judged mainly as to whether it was conducive to 'speeding up progress' (and bolstering the nation's defences – don't let's forget the Cold War), the concept looked very attractive and even economically sound – after all, it made it possible to create powerful military transport assets by manufacturing innocuous-looking passenger aircraft.

In 1958 the An-10 was awarded the Major Gold Medal and a diploma at the World Exhibition in Brussels. In 1960-61 the An-10 made demonstration trips to many countries of the world. (In 1961 it was accompanied by the IL-18. Not one of these trips resulted in an An-10 sale; conversely, the IL-18 attracted numerous export orders.) When the An-10's existence became known to the West, the airliner received the reporting name *Cat*.

Most of the industry-operated An-8s retained basic Air Force grey colours with the addition of a blue cheatline and sometimes, as in the case of CCCP-69319 (c/n 0A 3420), Aeroflot titles. This aircraft, which belonged to the Orenburg helicopter factory, has been upgraded with a TG-16 APU in the port main gear fairing.

In December 1959 the original An-10 with no suffix letter to the designation (or *sans suffixe*, as we will call it hereinafter) was superseded on the production line by the improved An-10A. The first 'As were still powered by AI-20A engines but these were replaced by 4,250-ehp AI-20Ks on later examples. The An-10A was built in two versions which initially seated 89 and 100 passengers respectively. Later the seating capacity was increased to 117-118 and then to 132 by changing the cabin layout and reducing the seat pitch (contrary to allegations by some authors, the An-10A did not have a stretched fuselage, differing from the previous version only in cabin window and baggage door placement). The maximum payload was increased to 14.5 tons (31,970 lb).

The An-10's production run was rather modest, totalling 104 machines (including the Kiev-built prototype and the static test airframe; the exact proportion of An-10s and An-10As is unknown). Of these, three aircraft were built in 1957, sixteen aircraft in 1958, 39 more in 1959 and 46 in 1960.

Originally the An-10A had the same 'triple tails' as the initial version. In 1962, however, the An-10As (and some An-10s *sans suffixe*) received an upgrade – the endplate fins were deleted and the single ventral fin gave place to two splayed ventral fins. They were mounted in an area where separation of the turbulent airflow occurred. As a result, the ventral fins not only had a positive effect on the aerodynamics but also caused unpleasant vibration of the aircraft. The effect of this modification was felt immediately. Flight tests conducted by GK NII VVS between 5th and

Above: The nose of an Aeroflot An-10A wearing the type's original red/white livery with 'feathers' aft of the flightdeck glazing. A blue/white scheme was introduced later.

CCCP-11185 (c/n 0402002) was the one-off An-10B development aircraft operated by the Antonov OKB. It had the definitive tail unit, as well as the extra baggage door ahead of the starboard main gear unit (just visible in this view) that became standard on the An-10A. Kiev-Svyatoshino was still unpaved at the time.

30th September 1961 showed that the onset of Mach buffet was delayed until Mach 0.702. There was an improvement of longitudinal stability under high G loads during landing approach.

A civil cargo version of the An-10A intended for carrying various small cargoes with an all-up weight of 16,300 kg (35,940 lb) was designated An-10AS (the meaning of the S suffix remains unknown). The freighter lacked passenger seats and cabin partitions but featured a reinforced cargo floor incorporating tie-down cleats. The conversion to An-10AS standard was effected by Aeroflot divisions operating the An-10A.

The type also saw service with the Soviet Air Force's transport arm (VTA – *Voyenno-trahnsportnaya aviahtsiya*) To suit the needs of the latter GSOKB-473 developed a version designated An-10TS (*trahnsportno-sanitarnyy* – transport/ambulance, used attributively). The aircraft had a payload of 14,500 kg (31,970 lb) and was capable of paradropping personnel through the standard cargo door on the starboard side of the rear fuselage. 45 examples were in service by July 1965; interestingly, only ten of them were operated full-time by the VTA while the remaining 38 were loaned to the Ministry of Civil Aviation so as to ensure the most profitable use of the aircraft. Some of the An-10TSs used by Aeroflot were fitted out for passenger transportation.

A single An-10A (CCCP-11185) retained by the Antonov OKB as a 'dogship' for testing new features was converted into a 132-seater designated An-10B. The additional seating capacity was obtained without stretching the fuselage – merely by installing seven-abreast seating instead of the standard six-abreast arrangement and increasing the number of seat rows from seven to nine in the centre cabin. The aircraft also featured increased fuel tankage extending the range to 2,000 km (1,240 miles) with a payload of 14,500 kg (31,970 lb). Previously the An-10B designation had been allocated to an unbuilt version featuring a new avionics suite and a 118-seat cabin layout.

Other projected versions of the An-10 included the An-10V (alias An-16) featuring a new fuselage of increased cross-section and 6 m (19 ft 8 in) greater length accommodating 175 passengers, mostly seven-abreast, in four cabins. The tail unit was revised, featuring a moderately sweptback vertical tail. Confusingly, the designation An-16 is also quoted for another proposed version of the An-10 developed in 1957, which was to carry 130 passengers over a distance of 2,000 km (1,240 miles). The increase in the seating capacity was to be achieved by inserting a 3-m (9 ft 10¾ in) cylindrical plug in the fuselage. The project was not implemented.

In January 1960 Chief Designer Oleg K.

Antonov proposed a reworked version designated An-10D; it was to incorporate a lot of new features which would place it on a par with the world's best airliners in its class. Among other things, it had new inner wing panels of approximately 1 m (3 ft) greater span allowing the engines to be moved away from the fuselage, thus reducing cabin noise levels. The inner wings were to house extra fuel tankage increasing the range to 3,650 km (2,270 miles) – or even 4,400 km (2,735 miles) if integral fuel tanks in the detachable outer wings were added. The seating capacity was to be increased to 124 (in a tourist-class layout) for flights of up to three hours' duration. It was hoped to increase the speed (and thereby improve the fuel efficiency) by fitting new propellers with fibreglass blades. The An-10D was expected to be some 30% more efficient than the baseline version; however, the project did not progress further than the drawing board.

The fate of the An-10 turned out to be an unlucky one. Firstly, during the early years the aircraft was plagued by poor reliability. In the course of An-10/An-10A operations up to 1961 no fewer than 670 defects were revealed and rectified.

Secondly, the airliner suffered form serious longitudinal stability and control problems which led to several fatal accidents. On final approach, when the speed was reduced to about 280-290 km/h (174-180 mph) and the aircraft was quite close to the ground, it would often drop its nose abruptly, entering a dive. At low altitude and given the reduced elevator authority (compounded by the suddenness of the phenomenon and limited time available for taking a decision), this often led to accidents. This was the case on 16th November 1959 when Ukrainian CAD An-10 *sans suffixe* CCCP-11167 dived into the ground 1 km (3,280 ft) short of L'vov airport, killing all on board, and on 26th February 1960 when An-10 CCCP-11180 crashed at the same location – again with no survivors. In the latter case the cause was eventually traced to tailplane icing – an especially dangerous phenomenon, given the aerodynamic peculiarities of high-wing turboprop aircraft equipped with powerful high-lift devices. Consequently the entire fleet was retrofitted with a highly effective stabiliser de-icing system.

During the first five years of operation the An-10 carried more than 10 million passengers and more than 500,000 tons (1,102,290 lb) of cargo. By 1967 the *Cat* was operated on more than 90 domestic air routes; new services were inaugurated every year, and by 1971 the type had carried 35 million passengers and one million tons (2,204,585 lb) of cargo. Thus the An-10 ranked first among Aeroflot's types as far as the passenger turnover was concerned. Everything seemed

to be going nicely when suddenly disaster struck again. On 18th May 1972 a Ukrainian CAD An-10A (CCCP-11215) crashed near Khar'kov-Sokol'nikovo airport, killing all 114 passengers and eight crew. The tragedy provoked a tremendous public outcry – not least because the victims of the crash included a well-known female reporter and a popular actor.

The cause was found fairly quickly; the 'tin kickers' discovered fatigue cracks in the wing centre-section stringers that had caused the wing to disintegrate. Considering that the crashed aircraft was a late-production example, a fleet-wide check was mounted and the same defect was promptly discovered on other An-10s as well. By then some 70 An-10s were in service with Aeroflot's East Siberian, North Caucasian, Komi, Volga, Moldavian and Ukrainian CADs and the Ul'yanovsk Higher Flying School. As a result, on 27th August 1973 the Ministry of Civil Aviation issued order No.032 withdrawing the An-10 from Aeroflot service. 42 high-time aircraft were struck off charge and scrapped; another 25 An-10As in reasonably good condition were transferred to the Air Force and various MAP enterprises. Thus the An-10 gained the distinction of being the first turboprop airliner to be flown in the USSR, the first Soviet turboprop airliner to reach production and service – and the first such aircraft to be phased out.

True, this was not the end of the road for the An-10 just yet. Moreover, new versions continued appearing. In response to an order from the Airborne Troops (VDV – *Vozdooshno-desahntnyye voyska*), in 1970 a single An-10A registered CCCP-11854 was converted into an airborne command post intended for combat control and for maintaining communications with various headquarters and ground control posts. This mission could be performed with the aircraft airborne or on the ground. The passenger cabin accommodated a 'war room' and secure communications equipment operators' workstations. Designated An-10KP (*komahndnyy poonkt* – command post), CCCP-11854 served with the Group of Soviet Forces in Germany, operating from the Soviet airbase at Sperenberg near Berlin, until it was withdrawn from use as time-expired.

Whist we are on the subject of the An-10, it deserves mention that in 1961 a world speed record for turboprop-powered aircraft was established on this aircraft. On 22nd April 1961 pilot A. Mitronin performed a flight on a 500-km (310.5-mile) closed circuit, clocking an average speed of 730.6 km/h (437.3 mph). This result was quite commendable for a turboprop airliner at the time, bearing in mind that the cruising speed of aircraft in this class averaged 560-650 km/h (348-404 mph).

Chapter 1

Birth of an Airlifter

Except for the choice of the engine type, few major problems were encountered in designing the An-12, which received the in-house designation *izdeliye* T (meaning *trahnsportnyy samolyot* – transport aircraft). The general arrangement, basic structural design features and principal systems and equipment of the new Antonov 'twins' (the An-10 and An-12) had been verified on the An-8. The first available photos of their American counterpart – the Lockheed YC-130A Hercules – confirmed to the Antonov engineers that the choice of the four-engined layout and the upswept rear fuselage with rear loading doors had been the correct one.

The detail design work on the An-12 took just 11 months to complete. Unusually, the prototype was built not by the prototype manufacturing facility of GSOKB-473 in Kiev but by the Irkutsk aircraft factory No.39, which had been selected to build the transport. Actually the term 'production prototype' would be more appropriate in this case. The An-10 and the initial version of the An-12 had such a high degree of commonality (86% for

the airframe and 100% for the powerplant) that production could begin right away, with no need to master new manufacturing techniques, and for all practical purposes the first An-12 prototype powered by NK-4 engines was also the first production aircraft.

Even though the airliner enjoyed priority over the transport, the An-10's general arrangement, overall dimensions, fuselage cross-section and the wing, tail unit and landing gear design had been selected in such a way as to ensure the possibility of manufacturing the commercial and military versions on the same production line. In fact, it was even suggested that, should war become imminent, the An-10 fleet could be quickly converted into An-12s *by replacing the entire rear fuselage*! This was made possible – in theory at least – by a production break aft of the wings. Paraphrasing a well-known saying, what a man hath joined together another man can always set apart. Getting ahead of our story, we may say now that the idea of converting An-10s into An-12s was thwarted by the difference in the two types' mission equip-

ment and by the progressive improvement of the transport, which was manufactured by three different plants into the bargain. As production progressed, the An-10 and An-12 drifted steadily farther apart as far as the design was concerned. For instance, after the first 100 or so aircraft had been built the pressure sealing of the An-12's fuselage structure in the freight hold area was deleted, leaving only a small pressurised area at the front. The Voronezh aircraft factory did convert at least one An-10 into an An-12 to prove the feasibility of the idea – but that was it.

Up to fuselage frame 41 the An-12's airframe was identical to that of the production An-10 *sans suffixe*. The upswept aft fuselage was new, being similar to that of the An-8; the flat underside incorporated a large cargo hatch closed by an upward-hinged rear door and two forward door segments split fore and aft which opened inwards and upwards to lie flat against the sides of the freight hold. The tail surfaces were similar to those of the An-10 but the vertical tail had a much deeper fin fillet; the latter blended into a 'superstructure'

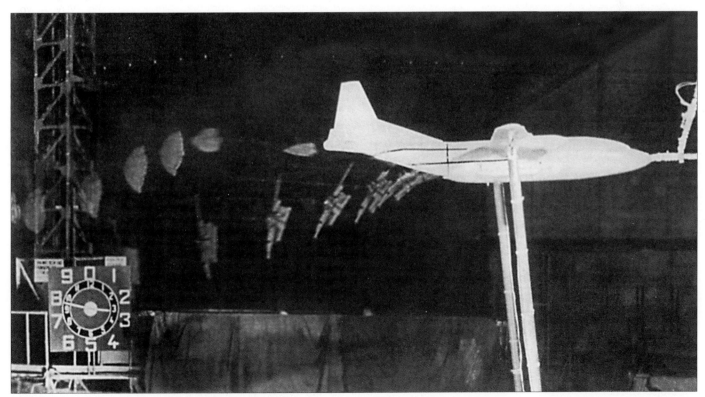

This multi-exposure shot taken by a special high-speed camera shows a wind tunnel test undertaken by TsAGI with the objective of exploring the behaviour of items paradropped by the An-12, using parachute extraction.

Above and below: The uncoded first production prototype An-12 (c/n 7900101) shortly after being rolled out in Irkutsk in December 1957. The flightdeck glazing design development paralleled that of the An-10: the first An-12s had triangular sliding direct vision windows and large trapezoidal windows further aft.

Above: This three-quarters rear view shows the tail gunner's station. Note the triple aerials of the PDSP-2 tactical navigation system under the nose and wings.
Below: Head-on view of the same aircraft. The lack of anhedral on the outer wings is clearly visible, as is the narrow wheel track.

incorporating a glazed tail gunner's station with a DB-65U powered turret mounting two 23-mm (.90 calibre) Afanas'yev/Makarov AM-23 cannons.

The mock-up review commission concluded its work on the *izdeliye* T on 22nd July 1957, by which time prototype construction was well advanced. Commonality notwithstanding, it took all of 18 months to complete the first An-12, which received the construction number 7900101 (that is, year of manufacture 1957, aircraft factory No.39 (the first digit is omitted for security reasons to confuse hypothetical spies), production batch 001, 01st aircraft in the batch). Wearing Soviet Air Force insignia but no tactical code, the first production prototype took off from the factory airfield (Irkutsk-2) at 14:37 hours local time on 16th December 1957, with many of the plant's employees watching. The aircraft was flown by captain Yakov I. Vernikov (Hero of the Soviet Union), a LII test pilot, and co-pilot G. I. Lysenko who had recently been transferred to GSOKB-473 from NII GVF. The test crew also included navigator P. I. Oovarov, flight engineer I. M. Morozov, radio operator M. G. Yoorov and tail gunner V. G. Zhilkin.

(Note: Unlike western military aircraft, which have *serial numbers* allowing positive identification, since 1955 Soviet/CIS military aircraft usually have two-digit *tactical codes* which, as a rule, are simply the aircraft's number in the unit operating it, making positive identification impossible. Three- or four-digit tactical codes are usually worn by development aircraft only, in which case they still tie in with the c/n or manufacturer's designation. Also, some military transport aircraft have three-digit tactical codes which are the last three of the former civil registration – many Soviet/Russian Air Force transports were/are quasi-civilian.)

In its maiden flight the aircraft became airborne a little earlier than anticipated. Retracting the flaps and throttling back to nominal power, the crew initiated a climb. All at once vibration was felt in the forward fuselage; Vernikov chose to abort the mission and land. During the nine-minute first flight the An-12 had reached an altitude of 880 m (2,890 ft) and a speed of 340 km/h (211 mph).

The cause of the vibration was nothing more serious than a nosewheel well door that had opened on its own accord (as is normally

the case, the landing gear was not retracted during the first flight, and the An-12's wheel well doors were designed to close when the gear was down). There had been no danger for the aircraft and crew; yet Vernikov, who had been appointed captain only a few days earlier, had not had time to study the aircraft thoroughly, and his decision to return to base was a prudent one. From the second test flight onwards Lysenko was assigned as project test pilot.

The strengths and weaknesses of the An-12 came to light almost immediately as the flight tests continued. Pilots who flew the new transport were impressed by its unusually high power-to-weight ratio and good aerodynamics, as well as by the sheer dimensions of the machine. On the other hand, the initial test flights were performed with no payload and the unladen aircraft accelerated quickly during take-off, reaching rotation speed before the pilots knew it, which led to an overly high unstick speed. Because of the powerful gyroscopic force created by the four propellers (which turned clockwise when seen from the front) the starboard main gear bogie absorbed a higher load than the port one;

Top and above: This uncoded An-12 with no anhedral on the outer wings appears to be the second production prototype (c/n 8900102) as originally flown; note the two windows to starboard in the forward cabin, whereas the first prototype had three.

Above: The second prototype at a later stage of the trials with anhedral outer wings. Here, two 45-mm field guns are wheeled into the cabin, using the detachable loading ramps.

Right: For paradropping suitability tests An-12 c/n 8900102 had large grid-like photo calibration markings applied to the rear fuselage. Before drops of actual hardware could be ventured, a mock-up of a field gun on a pallet was dropped.

Below right: Test drops of personnel from the An-12.

hence the An-12 tended to swing to the right during the take-off run. Countering this propensity by differential braking was impossible because of the relatively narrow landing gear track; the problem was cured by introducing nose gear steering operated by the rudder pedals on the second prototype (c/n 8900102). This aircraft, too, was powered by NK-4s and wore no tactical code; it sported large grid-shaped photo calibration markings on the rear fuselage sides.

During landing the An-12 was quite a handful: the aircraft literally refused to land with the engines running at flight idle, and retarding the throttles to ground idle would produce a braking effect, causing an excessively high sink rate. Hence the landing procedure demanded a lot of concentration and skill, and heavy landings were a common occurrence. In the sixth test flight one of the throttle levers jammed as the flight engineer retarded the throttles sharply at the moment of flareout. Banking abruptly, the aircraft struck the ground with one wingtip, then banked the other way and touched down on the runway shoulder – mercifully suffering no further damage. After this incident the flight tests were suspended and a special landing technique was developed for the An-12, requiring the inner engines to be set at ground idle and the outer engines at flight idle for final approach.

Early test flights also revealed poor lateral and longitudinal stability, which was reme-

died by increasing the anhedral on the outer wing panels. The rear fuselage structure proved insufficiently rigid and when the cargo doors were opened in flight for the first time they could not be closed again because the fuselage had flexed under the aerodynamic loads, deforming the cargo hatch aperture. The An-12 landed safely with the doors open; measures were subsequently taken to stiffen the rear fuselage.

The An-12 completed manufacturer's flight tests in just eight months; in comparison, the An-8 and An-10 had taken more than a year and two years respectively to do so. The test programme included never-exceed speed (V_{NE}) trials and engine failure simulations during which the aircraft landed with one or two engines shut down. A third aircraft (c/n 8900103) had joined the two prototypes by August 1958 when the tests were completed;

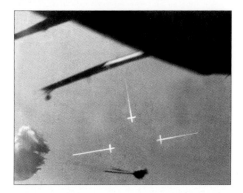

this was the first An-12 with the definitive AI-20 powerplant.

Aircrew training proceeded in parallel, and the process was sometimes accompanied by spills. On one occasion factory test pilot Yeliferov applied the port wheel brakes sharply during take-off to keep the aircraft

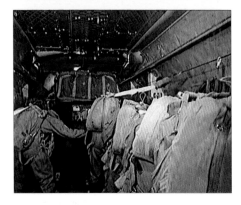

from straying off the runway centreline. With loud bangs, two of the four tyres on the port main gear bogie blew, showering fragments of rubber all over the runway. On landing the pilot was a bit overenthusiastic with the brakes again and ruined the other two port side tyres; the aircraft banked, making a tremendous racket as the wheel rims struck sparks from the concrete runway, but no disastrous consequences ensued.

A rather funny episode was caused by the aircraft's hydraulic system design. The An-12 had two independent hydraulic systems, port and starboard, both of which could operate the landing gear. After retracting the landing gear on take-off, using the port system, the captain forgot to set the gear control lever neutral. During the landing approach the co-pilot (the very same pilot Yeliferov) extended the landing gear by means of the starboard hydraulic system – again neglecting to set the lever neutral. A hardware conflict ensued, the two systems fighting each other as valves popped and hydraulic lines vibrated. The starboard system won and the gear extended normally, but no sooner had the aircraft touched down than the port system took over and the gear started retracting. Luckily the pilots realised what had happened and took corrective action in the nick of time; the An-12 came to a standstill 'on bent knees', as one Russian author later put it.

In late August 1958 An-12 c/n 7900101, captained by G. I. Lysenko, was ferried from Irkutsk to Tret'yakovo airfield near the town of Lookhovitsy, Moscow Region. (This airfield was then a test facility; later Tret'yakovo became the factory airfield of the Lookhovitsy Machinery Plant forming part of the Moscow Aircraft Production Association.) The airport and ATC authorities along the route had heard on the grapevine that a new aircraft type was coming their way. Hence the crew was bombarded with questions from curious ATC officers which Lysenko had to avoid answering – politely but firmly – so as not to disclose sensitive information. Near Gor'kiy (now renamed back to Nizhniy Novgorod) the An-12 was even 'intercepted' by a flight of fighters whose pilots were eager to have a close look.

Top left: Test and development work on paradropping techniques continued for quite a while. Here an An-12 flies with the cargo doors open, ready to perform a test drop.

Second from top: Paratroopers board an An-12 via the entry door.

Centre left: A BMD armoured fighting vehicle prepared for paradropping; note the roller tracks on which it moves and the drogue parachute pack.

Above left and left: The troopers sit in the front half of the main cabin, ready to follow the BMD.

Six months later the first prototype was due to be transferred to GK NII VVS for State acceptance trials; yet these plans were foiled by a crash landing at Moscow's now-defunct Central airfield named after Mikhail V. Frunze (aka Moscow-Khodynka) where the An-12 arrived for a demonstration to the military top brass. The airfield is located in downtown Moscow, a mere 6 km (3.75 miles) from the Kremlin, and runway approaches are over a built-up area with lots of tall obstacles, which means a lot of pilot skill is required to operate into and out of Khodynka. This flight was no exception. The crew captain G. I. Lysenko maintained the minimum recommended speed during final approach. As the aircraft passed the perimeter fence at an altitude of 25 m (80 ft), he throttled back the Nos. 2 and 3 engines as prescribed by the manual; however, the aircraft lost speed and landed hard with a slight right bank, undershooting by 65 m (213 ft). The starboard main gear unit collapsed and the aircraft groundlooped, the No.4 propeller striking the ground; some structural damage was also incurred. Sure enough, the accident investigation board quickly found the cause and made appropriate recommendations, but the aircraft was temporarily out of action.

The second prototype had to be flown from Irkutsk to LII's airfield in Zhukovskiy, Moscow Region, so that the trials could continue. An-12 c/n 8900102 was used, for the first time in Soviet practice, to investigate the stalling and spinning characteristics of a heavy aircraft; the tests showed that there was a delay between the stall and the onset of the spin – a few precious seconds during which the pilots could (and should) take corrective action and recover.

In late 1958 GK NII VVS took delivery of an early-production An-12 (tactical code unknown, c/n 8900305) which also participated in Stage A of the State acceptance trials; these were duly completed in June 1959. This aircraft was flown by project test pilots I. K. Goncharov and A. K. Degtyar', with I. V. Orlitskiy as project engineer. Interestingly, part of the trials programme was performed in Kiev at the Antonov OKB's flight test facility. The State commission gave a thumbs-up, recommending the An-12 for Soviet Air Force service.

Yet the top command of the VVS and the leaders of the Soviet Ministry of Defence were far from unanimous in their appraisal of the new airlifter. Debates as to whether the Armed Forces needed this aircraft raged among the military top brass; the anti-An-12 lobby asserted that the cheaper An-8, which also required less metal to build, would cater for all of the Soviet Army's transport needs in the foreseeable future. Eventually, however, the sceptics were put to shame; subsequent

Above: This uncoded production An-12 in a non-standard colour scheme with a thin black cheatline was used by GK NII VVS for trials. Note the redesigned flightdeck glazing with rectangular windows.

Right and below right: A field gun is paradropped on a PGS-500 pallet with crushable shock absorbers.

events showed that the decision to launch large-scale production of the An-12 had been right. The aircraft could carry a much wider range of loads than the An-8 and outperformed it by a considerable margin; besides, it had a considerable upgrade potential. Small wonder that the An-12 became the mainstay of the Soviet Air Force's military airlift component for many years to come.

Stage B of the State acceptance trials, which lasted from October 1959 to April 1960, involved paradropping of personnel and materiel near Boozovaya settlement. Apart from G. I. Lysenko, test pilots Yuriy V. Koorlin (who later became the Antonov OKB's chief test pilot) and I. Ye. Davydov flew as crew captains at this stage.

In the Soviet Union, the An-12 was manufactured by three major aircraft factories – No.39 in Irkutsk, No.64 in Voronezh (Pridacha airfield) and No.84 named after the famous test pilot Valeriy P. Chkalov in Tashkent (Tashkent-Vostochnyy, that is, Tashkent-East airfield). Total Soviet production amounted to 1,275 copies – 155 aircraft built in Irkutsk (December 1957 to December 1961), 290 in Voronezh (June 1961 to mid-1968) and 830 in Tashkent (mid-1961 to late 1972). Apart from that, the An-12 was built in China (Chinese production still continues and is described in Chapter 4).

A note must be made here on construction numbers. Each of the three factories had its own c/n system(s), explained as follows:

System 1: An-12A CCCP-69321 manufactured on 31st August 1961, c/n 1901708:
1   – year of manufacture (1961);
9   = Irkutsk aircraft factory No.39;
017 – batch number;

08   – number of the aircraft in the batch (five per batch in Batches 1-5, ten per batch in Batches 6-19).

System 2: An-12A CCCP-11916 manufactured on 31st July 1962, c/n 2400901:
2   – year of manufacture (1962);
4   = Voronezh aircraft factory No.64;
009 – batch number;
01   – number of the aircraft in the batch (six per batch in Batches 1-16, twelve per batch from Batch 17 onwards, except Batches 29 and 31 (the final batch) which were 'baker's dozens').

The year of manufacture was usually omitted on Voronezh-built examples after 1962. Thus, An-12B CCCP-11008 manufactured on 19th February 1965 is c/n 402612 (the 12th and last aircraft in batch 026), although An-12B CCCP-11117 is c/n 5402707.

System 3: An-12BP CCCP-12959 manufactured on 31st March 1968, c/n 8345510:

An-12B CCCP-29110 was used for soggy runway tests. However the odd-looking fairings on the wings in line with the engine nacelles suggest it may have been fitted with boundary layer control (blown flaps).

8 – year of manufacture (1968);

34 = Tashkent aircraft factory No.84 (34 was a code – originally the number of an unbuilt aircraft factory whose site plant No.84 had taken up after evacuation from Moscow in 1941);

55 – production batch number;

10 – number of the aircraft in the batch (ten per batch).

In 1970 the Tashkent aircraft factory started using two-digit year designators. Thus, An-12BP CCCP-12995 manufactured on 31st August 1970 is c/n 00347402, Yugoslav Air Force An-12BP 73312/YU-AID manufactured on 19th December 1971 is c/n 01348010 and An-12BP CCCP-11128 manufactured on 31st May 1972 is c/n 02348203.

Grey-painted Soviet/CIS Air Force An-12s, regardless of manufacturer, have the c/n stencilled on the starboard side of the nose and tail, and sometimes under the wing leading edge at the roots. Civil and quasi-civil examples in Aeroflot colours carry the c/n on the tail only; interestingly, truly civil aircraft usually have it on the port side while quasi-civil examples often carry it on the starboard side. Only the last four digits were sometimes stencilled on export An-12s (except Voronezh-built examples).

System 4 (Irkutsk-built export aircraft only): Iraqi Air Force An-12B '507', c/n 024012:

024 – a code for the An-12?

012 – sequential number of the exported aircraft.

Some Soviet aircraft delivered to foreign customers by the Aviaexport All-Union Agency (the sole national exporter of aircraft in those days) received special 'Aviaexport c/ns' meant to conceal the year of manufacture, plant number, batch number and the number of the aircraft in the batch so as to avoid indicating how many had been built. However, only a dozen An-12s received c/ns under this system. Such aircraft also had fuselage numbers or line numbers indicating the batch and the number of the machine in it; thus, Indian Air Force An-12 BL533 (c/n 024002) was f/n 1601 – that is, under the normal system it would have been c/n 1901601.

As noted earlier, the An-12 was formally included into the VVS inventory in 1959 after completing Stage A of the State acceptance trials. Much later a handful of An-12s were delivered to the air forces of two Warsaw Pact nations – Czechoslovakia and Poland (Bulgaria had a number of civil An-12s but of course these could be operated on behalf of the Air Force if need arose).

In recognition of their part in the development of the An-12, GSOKB-473 Chief Designer (later General Designer) Oleg K. Antonov and other leading engineers involved in the project – A. Ya. Belolipetskiy, V. N. Ghel'prin, Ye. K. Senchuk and Ye. A. Shakhatooni – were awarded the prestigious Lenin Prize by decree of the Soviet government.

An-12 reassembly after an overhaul.

A Versatile Antonov

An-12 Military Transport

The initial production version with no suffix letter, which entered production at the Irkutsk aircraft factory No.39 in 1958, was powered by 4,000-ehp AI-20A engines driving AV-68I propellers. The aircraft could carry 60 paratroopers or 91 troops with full kit, or 20 tons (44,090 lb) of cargo. Paradropping was typically performed at 250-300 km/h (155-186 mph) and an altitude of 600-1,000 m (1,970-3,280 ft).

In addition to the defensive armament (two AM-23 cannons with 360 rounds per gun), the An-12 had bomb armament. The rear fuselage incorporated a DYa-SS-AT bomb cassette holding six 10-kg (22-lb) TsOSAB-10 flare/marker bombs; two beam-type bomb cradles were mounted inside the rear portions of the main landing gear fairings and two more externally beneath the forward portions of these fairings – again for carrying flare bombs. The An-12 could be used for setting up minefields in case of need, carrying up to ten mines of similar dimensions to 1,500-kg (3,306-lb) FAB-1500 bombs or 20 mines of similar dimensions to 500-kg (1,102-lb) FAB-500 bombs. NKPB-7 and AIP-32 bomb sights

were provided for precision paradropping and, if necessary, bomb-aiming.

Note: DYa-SS = *derzhahtel' yashchichnyy sredstv signalizahtsiï* – 'box-type rack for signal means'; KD = *kassetnyy derzhahtel'* – cassette-type rack; TsOSAB = *tsvetnaya oriyenteerno-signahl'naya aviabomba* – coloured marker/signal flare bomb; FAB = *foogahsnaya aviabomba* – high-explosive bomb; NKPB = *nochnoy kollimahtornyy pritsel bombardirovochnyy* – night-capable collimator bomb sight; AIP = *aviatsionnyy infrakrahsnyy pritsel* – aircraft-mounted infra-red sight (the AIP-32 was an OPB-1R optical bomb sight with an IR imaging adapter).

8-mm (0⅝₆-in) sheets of APBL-1 steel armour were installed beneath the pilots' seats on both sides of the flightdeck for protection against AA shell fragments (*aviatsionnaya bronya protivo'oskolochnaya listovaya* – anti-shell fragment sheet armour for aviation applications). Also, the pilots' seats featured 16-mm (0⅝ in) armoured seat backs and 25-mm (0⅚₄ in) armoured headrests. The tail gunner was protected by bulletproof glass

panels, 135 mm (5⅚₆ in) thick at the rear and 112 mm (4¹³⁄₃₂ in) thick at the sides.

The An-12 could operate from tactical dirt or grass strips with a bearing strength of 8-9 kg/cm² (114-128 lb/sq in). Early production aircraft had a take-off weight of 54 tons (119,050 lb), including 10.8 tons (23,810 lb) of fuel, and could paradrop a 14.5-ton (31,970-lb) load. The aircraft was capable of sustained level flight at up to 5,000 m (16,400 ft) even with two engines inoperative.

The basic military transport version had an RBP-2 ground mapping radar (**rahdiolokatsionnyy bombardirovochnyy pritsel** – radar bomb sight; NATO codename *Toad Stool*) in a small teardrop-shaped chin radome and a PDSP-2S Proton-M radio navigation system for precise navigation to the drop zone (*parashootno-desahntnaya sistema privodnaya*). Vertical cameras, including those for detailed and night photography, could be installed – mostly for 'post-strike reconnaissance' (that is, evaluating the accuracy of the drop).

Originally the ASCC assigned the reporting name *Cat-B* to the An-12, but then thought better of it and renamed it *Cub* – this was a

A fine shot showing the anhedral wings of the production An-12.

Above and below: Silver-painted An-12A CCCP-75617 was one of several examples with non-standard registrations in the 75xxx block normally allocated to the IL-18 airliner (instead of the usual 11xxx or 12xxx); these were probably Air Force aircraft operating outside the USSR. The absence of the APU is clearly visible.

An-12A '04 Blue' (c/n 8900203) on display at the Central Russian Air Force Museum in Monino, with An-10A CCCP-11213 visible in the background.

separate design after all. This was later changed to *Cub-A* when special mission versions were identified.

An-12A Military Transport

The first attempt to improve the baseline transport resulted in the An-12A, which entered production in Voronezh (plant No.64) and Tashkent (plant No.84) in 1961. The main changes concerned the powerplant and the fuel system. The An-12A was powered by 4,250-ehp AI-20K engines. Four additional fuel cells were installed in the inner wing panels close to the engines, increasing the total number to 26; the overall fuel capacity was now 15,440-16,600 litres (3,396-3,652 Imp gal; different sources quote different figures). The result was a 600-km (370-mile) increase in the aircraft's range.

The nose landing gear was fitted with reinforced 900 x 300 mm (35.43 x 11.81 in) K2-92/I non-braking wheels. The freight hold featured an overhead gantry crane with a lifting capacity of 2,100 kg (4,630 lb). The original seven 12SAM-28 DC batteries were augmented by ten more to ensure trouble-free engine starting; the batteries were housed in the starboard main landing gear fairing and in a bay beneath the rear portion of the freight hold. Main electric power was supplied by eight STG-12TMO starter-generators. An oxygen system with twelve permanently installed 12-litre (2.64 Imp gal) bottles was fitted, and two toilets were provided; thus, unlike the An-12 *sans suffixe*, the A model had an adequate oxygen supply for maximum-range flight at any altitude not only for the crew but for the 'passengers' as well.

The avionics and equipment received an upgrade as well. Among other things, the An-12A had an AP-28D1 autopilot, an ARK-5 Amur (a river in the Soviet Far East; pronounced like the French word *amour*) automatic direction finder, a KS-6G automatic heading reference system (*koorso**va**ya sis**tema**), a DAK-DB-5 remote compass (*distantsionnyy astro**kom**pas*), an NI-50BM-1 navigation display (*navigatsi**o**nnyy indi**kah**tor*), an RSBN-2 Svod (Dome) short-range radio navigation system, an SP-50 *Materik* (Continent) instrument landing system, an MRP-56P marker beacon receiver (***mar**kernyy **rah**diopri**yom**nik*), an SP-1M astrosextant, an RV-2 radio altimeter (***rah**diovyso**tomer***) and a Proton-M radio navigation system. Communications equipment included a 1RSB-70 HF

Above: A Polish Army BRDM-1 scout vehicle passes behind a Soviet Air Force An-12B coded '05 Blue' during a Warsaw Pact exercise. Note the TG-16 APU in the rear portion of the port main gear fairing.

communications radio, a Gheliy (Helium) back-up HF comms radio, an RSIU-5 UHF command radio, an SPU-7 intercom, Kedr-S (Cedar-S) and DP-3 radios. The aircraft was fitted with an SRO-2M IFF transponder, an SOD-57M air traffic control transponder and a Sirena-3 radar warning receiver. The main gear fairings housed AFA-42/20, AFA-42/50 or AFA-42/75 day cameras or an NAFA-MK-25 camera and FotAB-100-80 flare bombs for night operations. (Note: ARK = *avtomatich-eskiy* **rah**dio**kom**pas – ADF; RSBN = **rah**dio-sis**tema** **blizh**ney navi**gah**tsiï – SHORAN; SP = [sis**tema**] sle**poy** po**sah**dki – blind landing system; AFA = **a**ero**fotoa**ppa**raht** – aerial camera; NAFA = noch**noy** **a**ero**fotoa**ppa**raht** – aerial camera for night operations; FotAB = fotogra**fich**eskaya **a**via**bom**ba – 'photo bomb', = flare bomb for aerial photography.)

The An-12A remained in production until 1962, the Voronezh aircraft factory producing

A regiment of red-coded Soviet Air Force An-12Bs prepares to make a landing assault during a major exercise (note the open cargo doors).

Above: Many Soviet Air Force An-12s were quasi-civil, and some of them, including An-12B CCCP-11965 (c/n 2400703), retained the basic overall grey Air Force colours with *very* unobtrusive Aeroflot titles and logo. Note the 1960s-style 'flying' presentation of the Soviet flag.

Most of the quasi-civil An-12s wore Aeroflot's full livery. This machine seen in 1992, however, was truly civil; An-12B CCCP-11375 (c/n 402405) belonged to the Komi Civil Aviation Directorate. Note the odd combination of the Russian flag and the old Soviet prefix. It crashed in Slavgorod on 20th August 1993 as RA-11375.

Above: An-12BP LZ-SFS is one of several operated by the Bulgarian carrier Air Sofia. Like the other An-12s operated by this airline, it has had the radar removed, giving the machine a strange look.

Although it wore Iraqi Airways titles and logo, An-12BP YI-AFJ (c/n 8345910) was actually an Iraqi Air Force aircraft.

at least eight batches (some sources say up to and including c/n 401604) while the one in Tashkent built six batches (up to and including CCCP-12978, c/n 2340610). Early production An-12As up to and including CCCP-11804 (c/n 2400806) retained the original wing centre section structure, with a resulting TOW limit of 54 tons (119,050 lb) and a payload limit of 13 tons (28,660 lb). Subsequent aircraft introduced a beefed-up wing centre section, allowing the maximum TOW to be increased to 61 tons (134,480 lb) and the payload to 20 tons (44,090 lb).

An-12B Military Transport

The next version, which entered production in 1962, was the extended-range An-12B. Development of this version began in 1960. The An-12B was powered by AI-20M engines (*moderni**zee**rovannyy* – upgraded) which had the same take-off rating as the K model but incorporated measures enhancing reliability. The aft portion of the port main gear fairing housed a TG-16 auxiliary power unit (APU) developed by the Kazan' Machinery Design Bureau (now the Aviamotor Joint-Stock Co.), which served for self-contained engine starting and provided electric power up to an altitude of 1,000 m (3,280 ft). (TG = *toor**bo**ghene**rahtor** – lit. 'turbo generator'. This specific reference to the generator is because the TG-16 had no provisions for using bleed air for engine starting, since the engines were started electrically.)

To extend range the detachable outer wing panels incorporated integral fuel tanks holding 1,390 litres (305.8 Imp gal) each, giving a total fuel capacity of 18,240 litres (4,012.8 Imp gal); some sources say 1,600 litres (352 Imp gal) and 19,500 litres (4,290 Imp gal) respectively. Thus, while the B suffix to the designation could be simply in alphabetical sequence, it may just as easily stand for *[dopol**nitel'nyye**] **bah**ki* – extra tanks. The additional tankage required the wing centre section to be further reinforced.

The rudder featured a larger trim tab. The APU installation required the rear pair of bomb cradles in the main gear fairings to be deleted. A separate workstation was provided for the flight engineer. Finally, the existing BL-52 cargo handling winches (*borto**va**ya lebyo**d**ka* – on-board winch) were replaced by more powerful BL-1500 units developing 1,500 kgf (3,306 lbf) each, permitting the loading of trailers and the like weighing up to 8 tons (17,640 lb).

Some sources state that An-12B production in Voronezh began with CCCP-11916 (c/n 2400901); the first Tashkent-built example was a Soviet Air Force aircraft coded '87 Red' (c/n 2340701). Up to and including c/ns 401911 and 3341510 (identity unknown) the

An-12B's dry weight was 34.2 tons (75,400 lb), increasing to 34.45 tons (75,950 lb) on subsequent aircraft.

An-12P Military Transport

Brought out in 1963, the An-12P was basically an An-12 *sans suffixe* with two extra fuel cells under the freight hold floor; the P stood for *[dopol**nitel'nyye** **bah**ki] pod **pol**om* – extra tanks under the floor. The forward cells located between fuselage frames 14 and 24 held 5,500 litres (1,210 Imp gal) and the aft group located between frames 33 and 41 held 4,350 litres (957 Imp gal). Thus the underfloor storage compartments were eliminated and the miscellaneous support equipment had to be stored in the freight hold. The earliest reported example is a quasi-civilian Soviet Air Force aircraft registered CCCP-11864 (c/n 401704); the construction number, however, suggests this is an An-12A or even an An-12B. Most An-12Ps were Voronezh-built, though two Irkutsk-built examples – CCCP-12777 (later CCCP-11322, c/n 0901409) and CCCP-98101 (c/n 1901706) built in 1960 and 1961 respectively – have also been referred to as An-12Ps. (In reality, however, they were more probably An-12APs.)

An-12AP Military Transport

The underfloor fuel tanks soon found their way to the An-12A as well and the resulting combination was designated An-12AP (that is, An-12A *s **bah**kami pod **pol**om*). The total fuel load of this version rose from the original *Cub*'s 10.8 tons (23,810 lb) to 20.3 tons (44,750 lb), increasing maximum range at 9,000 m (29,530 ft) to 5,200 km (3,230 miles). This version was not built as such – all An-12APs were mid-life upgrades; examples include Irkutsk-built CCCP-11322, Voronezh-built UR-PAS (c/n 2401105) and Tashkent-built CCCP-11382 (c/n 2340605).

An-12BP Military Transport

Predictably, the An-12B underwent a similar modification which resulted in the An-12BP (that is, An-12B *s **bah**kami pod **pol**om*). The total number of fuel tanks rose to 29 and the overall capacity to 26,980 litres (5,935.6 Imp gal); some sources state it as 29,350 litres (6,457 Imp gal). The An-12BP's fuel load has been stated as 22,066 kg (48,646 lb) or 22,400 kg (49,382 lb) respectively.

The avionics suite was upgraded and expanded once again. New equipment introduced on the An-12BP included the NAS-1B1-28 self-contained navigation system (*navigatsi**on**naya avto**nom**naya si**ste**ma*) and the RSKM-2 radio coordinate monitoring system (*rah**diolokatsi**on**naya si**ste**ma kont**ro**lya **mes**ta*). Some of the existing avionics items gave place to newer models or ver-

sions, namely the ARK-11 ADF, the RV-5M radio altimeter, the SOD-64 ATC transponder, the improved PDSP-2N system for navigation to the drop zone, and R-863 and R-856MA communications radios replacing the earlier 1RSB-70 and RSB-5 respectively.

Early-production An-12BPs were outwardly identical to the previous versions. In the third quarter of 1965, however, the Tashkent aircraft factory introduced a cargo door widened by 105 mm (4⅛ in) at the bottom to facilitate loading and unloading. The new design was readily identifiable by the prominent bulges near the cargo door threshold. Batch 34 was the first to have the new cargo door design, starting with an Indian Air Force example serialled L2172 (c/n 5343401).

Early/mid-production An-12BPs shared the cabin window placement of the previous versions – that is, ten windows to port (2+emergency exit+1+entry door+3+exit+1) and eight to starboard (1+exit+1+5). The final batches of An-12BPs (built in military and commercial configuration alike – see description of civil version below) had a reduced number of cabin windows – seven to port (2+exit+1+door+1+exit) and five to starboard (1+exit+1+1+1).

An-12BK Military Transport

In 1963 the Antonov OKB and LII undertook a joint flight test programme aimed at increasing the *Cub*'s payload to 30 tons (66,140 lb). To this end a Tashkent-built An-12A coded '05 Blue' (c/n 2340307) was refitted with a new avionics suite including an Initsiativa-2 (Initiative; NATO codename *Short Horn*) panoramic ground mapping radar, an NVU-V navigation computer (*navigatsi**on**noye vychis**litel**'noye oo**stroy**stvo*) and a Trassa-2 (Route, or Trail) Doppler speed/drift indicator. The OPB-1B optical bomb sight and the existing NAI-1 navigation computer were deleted. In May 1963 the aircraft was turned over to GK NII VVS for State acceptance trials, which were performed by project test pilots Platonov and Tkal'.

Tests revealed that the Initsiativa radar had twice the detection range of the RBP-2; at an altitude of 5,000-9,000 m (16,400-29,530 ft) the radar could detect a large city from a distance of 200-260 km (124-161 miles). However, the test protocol said that *'as regards precision paradropping the new avionics suite in its current condition offers no significant advantages over the navigation equipment of production aircraft'*; besides, the new avionics were troublesome.

The results of this programme materialised three years later in the form of a Voronezh-built An-12 with the non-standard registration CCCP-83962 No.2 (c/n 402210). This was the prototype of a new version des-

Above: The An-12BK military transport is readily identifiable by the much-enlarged radome housing an Initsiativa-4-100 radar. This example with an unconventionally placed tactical code was tested by GK NII VVS.

Right: Two of the An-12BKs that participated in the Warsaw Pact exercise *Dvina* in March 1970.

ignated An-12BK which underwent flight tests in August 1966; the K stood for **kompleks** [obo**roo**dovaniya] – equipment suite.

(Note: Under the Soviet civil aircraft registration system in use since 1958 and up to now, the first two digits of the five-digit registration are a sort of code denoting the aircraft type and allowing quick identification by air traffic controllers. An-12s were normally registered in the 11xxx and 12xxx blocks, but quite a few aircraft operated by industrial enterprises (notably MAP enterprises) were registered in several registration blocks which were a mixed bag of aircraft, including 272xx,

'33 Blue' (c/n 9346207), one more An-12BK involved in Exercise *Dvina*.

Above: '15 Red', a Russian Air Force An-12BK, seen a split second before touchdown.
Below: An-12BK '15 Red' (c/n 00347001) passing over Monino on 3rd June 2006 during the celebrations marking the 75th anniversary of the Russian Air Force's military airlift arm (VTA) has the star insignia painted out and the Russian flag applied to the tail instead.

291xx, 48xxx, 693xx, 839xx, 839xx and 981xx. The original CCCP-83962 was a Lisunov Li-2 Meteo weather research aircraft.)

Like the An-12B, the aircraft was powered by 4,250-ehp AI-20M turboprops. The APU, however, was new; the upgraded TG-16M equipped with a GS-24A starter-generator provided in-flight engine starting capability right up to 3,000 m (9,840 ft).

Other changes included the installation of a new GL-1500DP remote-controlled cargo winch (*groozovaya lebyodka s distantsionnym pool'tom*) and a new overhead gantry crane capable of lifting 2,300 kg (5,070 lb) in the freight hold, the provision of vehicle loading ramps which could be converted into troop seats, and a cargo door aperture widened by 105 mm *à la* An-12BP (with associated lateral bulges at the bottom). The An-12BK featured an improved Initsiativa-4-100 radar enclosed by a much larger and deeper radome which was the new version's external identification feature. The new radar required a powerful air cooling system; for want of available space this was installed in the passenger compartment aft of the flight-deck, reducing its seating capacity by almost 50% (to 11). The heavier equipment in the forward fuselage and the augmented load on the nose gear unit necessitated the fitment of heavy-duty K2-92/IV nosewheels – again measuring 900 x 300 mm (35.43 x 11.81 in).

The new model entered production in Tashkent in 1966 and was supplied exclusively to the Soviet Air Force (the earliest known example is '85 Red', c/n 6343901). Interestingly, apart from obvious errors (CCCP-11320 (c/n 4342604) has been reported as an An-12BK but this cannot be true, since the aircraft was built in 1964), some civil aircraft reported in the Western press as An-12BKs had regular-size radomes associated with the RBP-2 radar. However, since they are ex-Air Force aircraft, it is possible they were built as 'BKs but stripped of military equipment before sale to civilian owners, which included a change of radar.

An-12TA, An-12TB, An-12TBP, An-12TBK Transports

Some Soviet/Russian Air Force An-12s from the Voronezh and Tashkent production lines have been reported with the designation An-12TA. The meaning of the T suffix is not clear; deciphering it as *trahnsportnyy [samolyot]* (transport aircraft) doesn't make much sense, since the basic An-12 is a transport anyway, and using it to denote 'civil transport version' (as is the case with the Il'yushin IL-76T/TD) is incorrect because most An-12TAs were military operated. Some sources say the An-12TA was produced in 1964-66; however, all known examples were built in 1962-63. These include Russian Air

Force '20 Blue' (c/n 2400905), CCCP-11385 (c/n 2401004, an Aeroflot/North Caucasian Civil Aviation Directorate example), Soviet Air Force CCCP-11040 (c/n 2340502) and CCCP-11276 (c/n 2340810) and Russian Air Force RA-11037 (c/n 3341103).

Similarly, a number of An-12s with a tail gunner's station and a small radome (military and civil-operated examples alike) have been reported both in official documents and in the press as An-12TBs. Unlike the An-12TAs, these aircraft were mostly civilian – for example, CCCP-11353 (c/n 401811) of Aeroflot's East Siberian CAD, RA-11813 (c/n 3340908) of Amuraviatrans and RA-11025 (c/n 6344103) of Kosmos Air Company. Air Force examples include CCCP-11863 (c/n 401905) and CCCP-11972 (c/n 3341109). RA-11100 (c/n 01347702) of Noril'sk Avia has also been reported as an An-12TB – though other sources report it as an An-12BP with no tail gunner's station, which seems far more likely!

Another mysterious version with a similar designation is the An-12TBP based on the An-12BP. Two Soviet Air Force examples are known – CCCP-12116 (c/n 402108) and CCCP-12119 (c/n 402109).

Similarly, ex-Russian Air Force An-12BK RA-11868 (c/n 9346310) was referred to as an An-12TBK after sale to Aviatrans Cargo Airlines. So was RA-12108 (c/n 9346308) after it had been sold to Gromov Air and refitted with a commercial ROZ-1 Lotsiya (Navigational directions) radar. Surprisingly, this designation has also been quoted for a Russian Air Force example coded '26 Red' (c/n 9346305) which is apparently a standard An-12BK.

An-12AD Transport

A Tashkent-built *Cub* registered CCCP-11528 No.2 (c/n 3341005) has been reported as an An-12AD. No information is available on this version; one can only surmise that the D stood for *dahl'niy* – long-range. (CCCP-11528 No.1 was Irkutsk-built An-12A c/n 8900608.)

An-12A/B/BP/BK Demilitarised Version

Starting in 1959, considerable numbers of An-12As, An-12Bs, An-12BPs and An-12BKs were transferred from the VTA to the Soviet airline Aeroflot and various industry organisations to fill the need for carrying civil cargoes with speed and efficiency. Of course, such aircraft had to be adapted to their new civilian career. Obviously this involved removal of the cannons. As often as not the DB-65U tail turret itself was removed and replaced by a dished fairing (for instance, on An-12B CCCP-11991, c/n 402006); some aircraft (including An-12BP RA-11962, c/n 5343007) simply had the aperture faired over with sheet metal in a similar manner to industry-operated An-8s. Sometimes even the tail gunner's station glazing was overpainted in order to dispel any doubts about the aircraft's civil status. Aircraft with this rear end treatment are hereinafter described as demilitarised.

The paradropping equipment was also removed as unnecessary. Finally, some sensitive avionics items had to be replaced; for instance, the military communications radios were replaced with civilian ones using a different frequency grid. The RBP-2 radar gave way to the civil ROZ-1 *Lotsiya* weather/navigation radar fitting nicely into the existing radome (and bearing the same NATO codename, *Toad Stool*); ROZ denoted *rahdiolokahtor obzora zemlee* – ground mapping radar. Curiously, as mentioned above, some ex-VVS An-12BKs had the ROZ-1 fitted as well, becoming outwardly identical to An-12BPs, while other retained the bulbous radome of the Initsiativa-4-100 radar.

An-12B/BP Commercial Transport Version ('An-12V', 'An-12MGA')

From approximately March 1964 onwards the Voronezh aircraft factory started building a dedicated civil version of the An-12B lacking armament. The tail gunner's station was

Seen here taxying at Kiev-Gostomel', Volare Aircompany An-12BK UR-LMI (c/n 6344605), formerly '73 Blue' with the Ukrainian Air Force, wears appropriate nose titles – a rather uncommon occurrence.

Above: Civil-configured An-12BP CCCP-12962 (c/n 9346406) of the Krasnoyarsk CAD/Noril'sk UAD offloads fuel cisterns at the SP-26 (North Pole-26) drifting research station in April 1974.

This view of Tyumen' CAD/2nd Tyumen' UAD An-12BP CCCP-11031 (c/n 7345003) being unloaded at an ill-equipped airport somewhere in Siberia shows to advantage the shape of the 'commercial' tailcone.

replaced by a neat narrow slab-sided fairing which was semi-circular in side elevation; the ventral doors of the flare bomb compartment were still there but now they provided access to a bay housing 16 additional DC batteries.

The civil version was formally unveiled in 1965 when an Aeroflot aircraft registered CCCP-11359 (c/n 402804) took part in the 25th Paris Air Show. From then on the civil version was often erroneously referred to in the West as the 'An-12V' or 'An-12MGA' (for *Ministerstvo grazhdahnskoy aviahtsii* – Ministry of Civil Aviation) but neither of these designations is found in Soviet/Russian documents. Also, some authors have used the designation An-12BK for the unarmed commercial version in the mistaken belief that the K stood for *kommehrcheskiy*, while others erroneously called CCCP-11359 'An-12D' (see below).

The Tashkent aircraft factory joined in about January 1966 with a similar unarmed version of the An-12BP, the earliest known example being LZ-BAC (ex-CCCP-1100..., c/n 6343708). Production continued until the type was finally phased out of production in 1972; no separate batches were set aside for the civil version – the aircraft were completed with or without tail gunner's station as per customer demand.

Ironically, not all *Cubs* lacking the tail gunner's station were civil! At least two An-12BPs, CCCP-12135 and CCCP-12990 (c/ns 00347002 and 00347304), belonged to the Soviet Air Force (the latter machine was later transferred to MAP), and the communications relay version described below also had no tail gunner's station. Likewise, the two Yugoslav Air Force examples – 73311/YU-AIC (c/n 01348007) and 73312/YU-AID (c/n 01348010) – were built in commercial configuration.

An-12UD/An-12UD-3 Military Transport

The inadequate range of the early versions was one of the *Cub's* chief shortcomings, and increasing it became a top priority for the Antonov OKB (as the reader will have guessed from the descriptions of the An-12A/B/AP/BP). One of the early attempts to crack the problem resulted in the development of the An-12UD (*oovelichennoy dahl'nosti* – with increased range). The prototype was converted from a production Irkutsk-built An-12 (c/n 9901007) by installing two extra tanks holding a total of 7,600 litres (1,672 Imp gal) in the freight hold between frames 16 and 26; the tanks were taken straight from the Myasishchev 3M *Bison-B* strategic bomber. As a result, the fuel capacity rose to a more agreeable 21,870 litres (4,811.4 Imp gal). The engines' oil tankage and the oxygen supply had to be increased accordingly in view of the aircraft's greater endurance.

Flight tests of the An-12UD held jointly by the OKB and the Air Force took place on 20th-27th October 1960, with Yuriy V. Koorlin (Antonov OKB) as project test pilot. The results were encouraging: with a maximum take-off weight and a 3-ton (6,613-lb) payload the range increased by 1,900-2,000 km (1,180-1,240 miles) over the An-12 *sans suffixe*, reaching 4,900 km (3,040 miles). A Tashkent-built example with no registration or

Above: Close-up of the starboard main ski of An-12PL CCCP-11381, showing the V-shaped bottom and the rocking dampers at both ends.

Above right: The uncoded first prototype An-12PL seen during tests.

Right: A heavily retouched photo of the same aircraft in phoney Aeroflot markings; the contours of the vertical tail have become distorted.

Below right: Another view of the starboard main skid of CCCP-11381, showing the oleo strut fairing and the sway braces connecting the skis to the fuselage.

Bottom right: An-12PL CCCP-11381 taxies out for take-off.

tactical code (c/n 3341007) was also reported as an An-12UD.

Some sources state that the aircraft could be fitted with two or three auxiliary tanks holding 4,000 litres (880 Imp gal) each and the two configurations were known as the An-12UD and An-12UD-3 respectively.

An-12BP Polar Version

A special version based on the An-12BP was developed in 1961 for operating in the Polar regions of the USSR and for supporting Soviet Polar research stations in the Arctic. Three bladder tanks with a total capacity of 9,800 litres (2,156 Imp gal) were installed in the underfloor baggage compartments to obtain the required range of 6,000 km (3,725 miles).

An-12PL Polar Transport/Support Aircraft

Also in 1961 another customised version of the *Cub* designed for off-base operation in Arctic and Antarctic regions was developed for Aeroflot's Polar division. Apart from the obligatory extra fuel tanks, the aircraft featured non-retractable streamlined skis equipped with brakes, hence the designation An-12PL (*polyarnyy, lyzhnyy* – Polar, ski-equipped). The V-shaped planing bottoms of the skis were skinned in abrasion-resistant

An-12T Fuel Carrier Aircraft

Specialised versions of the *Cub* began appearing almost immediately. The first of these was probably the An-12T (***top**livo**voz*** – fuel carrier) developed in 1961. The aircraft was designed to transport automotive, aviation and rocket fuels and oxidisers in special tanks installed in the freight hold.

An-12BKT Refuelling Tanker

Whereas the version described above was strictly a fuel carrier, a refuelling tanker version did not appear until much later – and then it was not an IFR tanker but a 'flying petrol station' designed to refuel tactical aircraft on the ground. In 1972 the Antonov OKB brought out the An-12BKT (that is, An-12BK/***top**livoza-prahv**shchik*, refueller). The aircraft could top up two fighters at a time; total transferable fuel was 19,500 litres (4,290 Imp gal).

An-12A Ballistic Missile Transporter Version

In mid-1962 a single Irkutsk-built An-12 ('92 Red', c/n 1901507) was converted for carrying ballistic missiles to their launch sites; no separate designation is known for this version. The freight hold featured a more efficient heating system, additional lighting and a heat insulation curtain installed at fuselage frame No.43 (that is, at the cargo door threshold). In the autumn of 1962 the aircraft was turned over to GK NII VVS for State acceptance trials; project test pilots A. Ya. Bryksin (captain) and A. S. Borzov (co-pilot) flew the machine at this stage, with V. I. Kozlov as project engineer.

The trials revealed that the missile transporter did meet the requirements of the mili-

Above: CCCP-11381 is prepared for a flight, with an air heater based on a GAZ-51A lorry heating the cabin via the starboard emergency exit. The star tracker on the flightdeck roof is a non-standard feature.

OT4-1 titanium alloy and heated by hot air before taxying to stop them from sticking to ice and snow surfaces. The front and rear ends of the main skis were connected to the fuselage by telescopic links/rocking dampers; two more rods connecting the rear ends with a fitting on the fuselage centreline functioned as torque links. All three oleo struts were carefully faired to minimise drag.

The pressure cabin featured heavy-duty heat insulation for operating in extreme cold climates and a powerful self-contained heater for heating the cabin and warming up the engines prior to start-up. Despite the drag created by the fixed landing gear, the range was an impressive 7,500 km (4,650 miles).

Two aircraft were converted to An-12PLs in 1961. One was an Aeroflot aircraft registered CCCP-11381 (c/n 402807); the other was unpainted and wore Soviet Air Force markings (identity unknown – the tactical code has been retouched away by military censors on the only available photo). A photograph exists of a ski-equipped An-12 in a basically natural metal finish with Aeroflot titles and a 'lightning bolt' cheatline but apparently no registration; however, this could be a fake.

CCCP-11398, the prototype of the An-12PS maritime SAR version. Note the external stores pylons fore and aft of the main gear fairings, the photo calibration markings and the cine camera under the wingtip.

Above: An operational Russian Navy An-12PS, '16 Yellow' (c/n 7344702), seen visiting Novofyodorovka AB in Saki, the Ukraine. The external stores pylons have been removed. Production An-12PSs had a distinctive 'lightning bolt' side flash whose colour varied on individual aircraft; '16 Yellow' has a red flash.

Another An-12PS, '17 Yellow' (c/n 7344703), at its home base in Severomorsk, northern Russia; this one has a blue side flash and polar bear nose art signifying the North Fleet. This view shows the SAR version's distinctive rear end housing a PSN-6A life raft and the 'towel rail' aerial on the forward fuselage.

Above: An-12PP '68 Red' (c/n 9346303) based at Chkalovskaya AB is unusual in lacking the active jammers, featuring only the chaff dispensers in the tailcone.

tary in full as far as safety issues were concerned; in particular, it lacked a system for neutralising possible leaks of the missiles' potentially corrosive and toxic oxidiser. In as-was condition the An-12 could carry only *izdeliye* 3R9 and 3R11 intermediate-range ballistic missiles (IRBMs) with solid-fuel rocket motors and unrefuelled R-11M and R-17 IRBMs (the latter type, aka *izdeliye* 9K72, is known to the West as the SS-1 *Scud*). Hence the idea was not pursued further.

An-12BM SATCOM Relay Aircraft

In 1962 a production An-12 (identity unknown) was converted experimentally to evaluate the possibility of long-range satellite communications (SATCOM). Radio signals were relayed via the Molniya-1 (Lightning-1) communications satellite; hence the aircraft was known as the An-12BM (M for **molniya**). The four operator's workstations of the SAT-COM suite were located in the passenger cabin.

An-12 Communications Relay Aircraft (?)

At least seven Voronezh-built examples having no tail gunner's station – An-12A CCCP-11131 (c/n 2400702) and An-12Bs CCCP-11652 (c/n 402702), CCCP-11653 (c/n 402703), CCCP-11654 (c/n 402602), CCCP-11791 (c/n 402611), CCCP-11792 (c/n 402701) and CCCP-11992 (c/n 402604) – were converted into (or possibly purpose-built as) a special mission version of unknown purpose. Despite their unarmed configuration, they were operated by the Soviet, and later Russian, Air Force. The only external recognition feature was an additional TA-6 APU buried in the rear fuselage immediately ahead of the tail unit, with a prominent aft-angled exhaust on the port side. The main air intake, also to port, was closed by an aft-hinged door when not in use, with a small auxiliary intake closed by wire mesh on the starboard side.

The second APU was obviously installed because the aircraft's mission equipment

required so much power that the engine-driven generators could not meet the demand. The question is, *what* mission equipment? Since the aircraft do not have any prominent aerials associated with the intelligence gathering or ECM roles, the most likely explanation is that they are communications relay aircraft.

An-12BK SAR Derivative

A search and rescue (SAR) version based on the An-12BK was developed in the 1960s. Little is known about this version except that it was equipped with an *Istok-Goloob'* (Source [of a river]/Dove) system for homing in on the signals sent by the emergency UHF radio of a downed aircraft.

An-12PS Maritime SAR Aircraft

The An-12PS airborne maritime search and rescue system (PS = *poiskovo-spasahtel'nyy* – SAR, used attributively) was derived from the An-12B in 1969. The aircraft's intended mission was to support the Soviet manned space programme, locating and rescuing space crews in the unlikely event of a splashdown somewhere in the world's oceans, and to operate in the interests of the Soviet Navy, rescuing the occupants of ships in distress or downed aircraft. (Note: Normally the re-entry modules of Soviet/Russian manned spacecraft touch down on the plains of Kazakhstan; thus a splashdown in the ocean is only possible if an emergency necessitates a premature return from the orbit.)

The An-12PS carried a Yorsh (Ruff, aka Type 03447) lifeboat with a displacement of 5.2 tons (11,460 lb) or its improved derivative,

This poor but interesting shot shows an An-12BK-PPS in an unusual configuration with only two of the four strap-on Siren' active jammer pods in place

the 7.4-ton (16,314-lb) *Gagara* (Loon, aka Type 03473); the lifeboat could be paradropped with a crew of three on sighting people in distress. The Gagara had a 500-km (270-nm) range and a top speed of 7 kts; maximum seating capacity was 20 rescuees. A PSN-25/30 inflatable life raft (*plot spasahtel'nyy nadoovnoy*) seating another 25 or 30 persons; this raft could be jettisoned by the crew and subsequently towed by the lifeboat. Additionally, the tail gunner's station of the An-12PS was converted into a bay for PSN-6A life rafts.

Outwardly the SAR version was readily identifiable by the rear-end treatment reminiscent of the on demilitarised An-8s and some demilitarised An-12s (with no tail turret and no side windows in the former tail gunner's station) with Cyrillic 'PSN-6A' stencils on the sides. Also, the aircraft wore distinctive red, blue or yellow 'lightning bolt' side flashes livening up the standard overall grey colour scheme. Since the An-12PS was expected to operate in the northern regions of the Soviet Union, the tops of the outer wings and of the horizontal tail tips were painted red for high definition against ice and snow to assist in locating the aircraft in the event of a forced landing.

The An-12PS prototype, CCCP-11398, lacked the high-viz markings described above but wore photo calibration markings on the rear fuselage. It featured small pylons fore and aft of the main gear fairings for carrying KAS-150 pods (*konteyner avareeynospasahtel'nyy*) filled with small life rafts or other rescue equipment; for some reason these pylons have been removed from in-service aircraft. A handful of An-12PSs were delivered to the Soviet Naval Air Arm (AVMF – *Aviahtshiya Voyenno-morskovo flota*). Known examples are coded '14 Yellow' through '17 Yellow' (c/ns 6344602, 6344608, 7344702 and 7344703); one more example is c/n 7344704 but its tactical code is unknown.

An-12B-I ECM Aircraft

The electronic countermeasures (ECM) role is of special importance among the An-12's many applications. The first version adapted for ECM duties was the An-12B-I active ECM aircraft evolved from the An-12B in 1964. It was equipped with the *Fasol'* (String bean) individual protection active jammer; hence the I suffix (for *individooahl'naya zashchita* – individual protection). Only seven aircraft were built.

An-12PP (An-12BK-PP) ECM Aircraft

The second ECM version was the An-12PP (*postanovshchik pomekh* – ECM aircraft) developed in 1970; it was designed for group protection, operating as part of large formations of regular *Cubs*. The An-12PP had an

Above: An apparently retouched photo of the An-12BK-IS version equipped with four strap-on Siren' ECM pods for self-protection.

A typical An-12BK-IS comes in to land. Note the ECM pod attachment struts, the small pylons under the outer wings and the rear receiver aerials of the ECM suite under the stabiliser tips.

automatic active jammer system which detected enemy air defence radars, determined their location and emitted well-aimed noise signals in their direction. The tail gunner's station was replaced by a slab-sided ogival fairing housing ASO-24 chaff dispensers (*avtomaht sbrosa otrazhateley* – in this case, automatic chaff dispenser) with ventral outlets. The length of the chaff depended on the type of radar to be jammed, being half the radar's wavelength.

Three sets of the *Booket* (Bouquet) automated system for detecting and jamming AD radars were also installed. Their antenna arrays were located on the forward fuselage underside, looking like wide, shallow flat-bottomed bulges with semi-cylindrical fairings side by side; two of these arrays were mounted in tandem ahead of the mainwheel wells and the third set aft of them. Some sources say these bulges also housed a biological protection package to shield the crew from the radiation generated by the mission avionics.

Three pairs of 'elephant's ear' air intakes for the mission equipment heat exchangers were located above one another on the forward fuselage sides, with air outlets aft of them; this required the forward pair of emergency exits to be deleted (that is, there were three windows to port and two to starboard ahead of the wings instead of the usual four and three respectively). A fourth pair of heat exchanger intakes was located above the main gear fairings, with the air outlets in the rearmost cabin windows.

A total of 27 An-12BKs were converted to An-12PP standard; hence this version is sometimes referred to as the An-12BK-PP. Like the other ECM versions, the An-12PP was not exported, even though at least one aircraft operated in phoney Egyptian Air Force markings during a temporary deployment to the Middle East.

Strangely enough, the An-12PP designation was also quoted for several An-12BKs having no active jammers (that is, featuring only the tailcone housing chaff dispensers). Such aircraft include '68 Red' (c/n 9346303) which features two tandem pairs of dorsal rod aerials on the forward fuselage – a non-standard fit.

In the 1980s and 1990s at least two An-12PPs were stripped of mission equipment and sold to civil owners as CCCP-48978 (c/n 9346410) and RA-11301 (c/n 00347107); the ogival tailcone remained, indicating the original role of these aircraft all too clearly.

An-12BK-IS ECM Aircraft

Another ECM variant which entered production in 1970 was the An-12BK-IS based on the standard An-12BK. The mission equipment comprised Fasol' and Siren' (Lilac; pronounced 'seeren') individual protection active jammers (hence the S – that is, *individooahl'naya zashchita s sistemoy Seeren'*). The jammers were housed in four large cigar-shaped pods flanking the forward fuselage and the base of the fin. Their operating principle was to give false guidance signals to incoming SAMs, deflecting them away from the target.

'39 Red' (c/n 02348309), a 1974-standard An-12BK-PPS ECM aircraft, on the hardstand at Vladimirovka AB in Akhtoobinsk. The ventral Booket active jammer antenna arrays, the associated heat exchanger air scoops and the receiver aerials of the Siren' jammers on the nose and the stabilisers are clearly visible.

Left and centre: The port forward Siren' jammer pod of '39 Red', with its own cooling air scoop, and the port forward heat exchanger intakes and outlets.
Right: The port rear Siren' jammer pod. The bulged portions of the pods are dielectric; the four pods provide 360° coverage.

Front view of An-12BK-PPS '39 Red', showing the mounting struts of the jammer pods. In keeping with normal Soviet/Russian Air Force practice the last four digits of the c/n are painted on all air intake covers as an anti-theft measure.

The pods were strut-mounted; each pod had a dielectric portion with a lateral bulge over the emitter antenna and a dorsal cooling intake (the antennas of the forward pods were located at the front while those of the aft pods were located at the rear, giving 360° coverage).

The installation of the ECM pods required some local reinforcement of the airframe. Small receiver aerials associated with the Siren' jammers were located under the stabiliser tips and ahead of the radome, also giving 360° coverage. A dielectric blister mounted on the flightdeck roof escape hatch cover housed the antenna of the Stroy (Formation) formation-keeping system.

40 (some sources say 45) An-12BK-IS aircraft were built as such but this was not nearly enough. Therefore, starting in 1974, a further 105 Cubs were converted to this standard; they differed from the new-build aircraft in the equipment complement, being fitted with Bar'yer (Barrier) and Siren' jammers and automatic infrared jammers. The An-12BK-IS could still fulfil ordinary transport tasks. In the first years of the 21st century, however, a number of surplus An-12BK-ISs have been reconverted to transport aircraft.

An-12BK-PPS *Cub-C* ECM Aircraft

The ultimate ECM variant called An-12BK-PPS appeared in 1971 as an evolution of the An-12PP. Like the latter version, the An-12BK-PPS was designed to operate as part of large formations. Its efficiency was maximised by combining the four strap-on Siren' jammer pods with the built-in Booket jammers and the

Above: An-12R '35 Blue' seen from a shadowing NATO fighter over international waters. The two ventral radomes which are the ELINT version's main identification feature are clearly visible.

Above: Another An-12R in company with an investigating Royal Norwegian Air Force Lockheed F-104G Starfighter; note the blade aerials on the forward fuselage. Like '35 Blue', it is based on the An-12B.

chaff dispenser installation. A fourth pair of mission equipment heat exchangers was added on the forward fuselage slightly aft of the existing three; hence the windows immediately aft of the forward emergency exits were deleted as well (there were only two windows to port and one to starboard ahead of the wings).

The initial version retained the An-12PP's ogival tailcone housing the chaff dispenser

Curiously, some An-12Rs sported civil registrations, as illustrated by CCCP-11038 (c/n 2340709), though the cannons indicated the aircraft's ownership all too clearly.

Left: An-12RR '21 Red' (c/n 3341404) completes its landing run, showing the port RR8311-100 air sampling pod.

Below right: Close-up of the starboard RR8311-100 pod with the nosecone closed and the pylon-mounted sensor pod on the starboard side.

and the twin forward receiver aerials of the Siren' system below the navigator's station. An updated version of the An-12BK-PPS appeared in 1974; aircraft converted to this standard had the tail gunner's station and the chaff dispenser was housed at the rear of the cargo cabin, expelling the chaff through ports in the cargo doors. Some late An-12BK-PPSs, such as '94 Red' (c/n 01347602?), had twin square-section chaff outlet tubes with retaining braces exiting through the cargo door. The chaff was forced out by the slipstream, for which purpose two more air scoops were added on the centre fuselage sides. Also, some An-12BK-PPSs had the forward receiver aerials of the Siren' system located in a common fairing on top of the navigator's station glazing rather than near the radome.

19 An-12BKs were converted to An-12BK-PPS standard, and most of them remain in service with the Russian Air Force. However, once again at least three have been stripped of mission equipment and reconverted to transports; such aircraft are identifiable by the lack of windows on the forward fuselage where the removed heat exchanger air scoops have been faired over. '16 Red' (ex-An-12BK-PPS '36 Red', c/n 00347502) and RA-12709 remain in Russian Air Force service, while '50 Red' (c/n 02348107) was sold to Kyrghyzstan as EX-124.

The type sometimes saw action during in major Russian Armed Forces exercises; for instance, one such command and staff exercise in March 1999 involved three An-12BK-PPSs.

An-12R (?) ELINT Aircraft

A small number of Soviet Air Force An-12s was adapted for electronic intelligence (ELINT) duties in the early 1970s. Outwardly such aircraft could be identified by two small hemispherical dielectric fairings located in tandem ahead of the mainwheel wells and by four additional blade aerials on the forward fuselage (two located dorsally and two ventrally in cruciform fashion). No separate designation has been reported but the most likely one is An-12R ([samolyot-] razvedchik –

Above left: An-12RR '11 Red' (c/n 4342604) was on display at the Business Aviation-2001 show at Pushkin near St. Petersburg in early August 2001 with the air sampling pods removed.

Right: The starboard shackles for the air sampling pod and the sensor pod of '11 Red'.

The An-12VKP (or An-12B-VKP *Zebra*) airborne command post (c/n 9900902) displays its wingtip- and fin-mounted antenna pods and the 'towel rail' aerials on the centre fuselage as it comes in to land at Zhukovskiy.

reconnaissance aircraft). The ELINT version is sometimes misidentified in Western publications as the An-12PS maritime SAR aircraft (see above).

ELINT *Cubs* flew patrol missions over international waters and over Central Europe on a regular basis, monitoring radio traffic in Western Europe and shadowing NATO warships. One quasi-civil example converted from an An-12A (CCCP-11038, c/n 2340709) wore Aeroflot titles but retained the overall grey Soviet Air Force finish. Two other examples coded '07 Red' and '35 Blue' (c/ns unknown) had overt military markings.

A later version featured smaller teardrop-shaped ventral radomes and lacked the additional blade aerials. Two aircraft in this configuration – An-12B '84 Red' (c/n 4341905) and An-12BP CCCP-11875 in full 1973-standard blue/white Aeroflot livery (c/n unknown) – have been identified to date; both were stationed outside the USSR. The NATO codename was *Cub-B*.

An-12BL Experimental Transport/ SEAD Aircraft

Suppression of enemy air defences (SEAD) was recognised as a separate role for combat aircraft during the Vietnam War when surface-to-air missile (SAM) systems became a major threat. Specialised SEAD aircraft (known in US Air Force slang as 'Wild Weasels') were developed from fighter-bombers or attack aircraft. But have you ever heard of a 'Wild Weasel' transport? In 1970 the Antonov OKB decided to give the *Cub* an offensive capabil-

ity, adapting it to a secondary SEAD role in order to ensure mission success; simply jamming the enemy radars was not enough.

The result was the An-12BL – a version of the An-12B armed with four Kh-28 anti-radar missiles for destroying air defence radars. Two of these bulky weapons were carried on pylons flanking the forward fuselage and the other two on pylons under the outer wings. A guidance antenna in a thimble radome was installed in the extreme nose ahead of the navigator's glazing. The An-12BL was tested but the modification did not find its way into service.

An-12RR NBC Reconnaissance Aircraft

Since it was generally assumed that future wars would be fought in a nuclear/biological/ chemical contamination (NBC) environment, in 1968-69 the Soviet Air Force converted a handful of An-12Bs for use on radiation reconnaissance duties. Designated An-12RR (*rahdiatsionnyy razvedchik* – radiation reconnaissance aircraft; sometimes misspelled as 'An-12RKR' or 'An-12RCh' in Western publications), these aircraft had special cradles on the forward fuselage sides for carrying two RR8311-100 standardised air sampling pods. These looked like rather large cylinders with a movable nosecone and a door like a car throttle at the rear to adjust the airflow; a paper filter inside trapped radioactive dust particles for later analysis. Originally developed in 1964 for the Yakovlev Yak-28RR *Brewer-E* radiation reconnaissance aircraft, the pods could be carried by various types, including

the Antonov An-24RR, Tupolev Tu-16R *Badger-K*, Tu-95KM *Bear-C*/Tu-95K-22 *Bear-G* and Yak-25RRV *Mandrake*. A small cigar-shaped pod with air intakes was installed on two tandem horizontal pylons on the starboard side of the nose; this housed air sampling sensors for detecting toxic agents.

Only two aircraft coded '11 Red' (c/n 4342604) and '21 Red' (c/n 3341404) have been identified so far. Additionally, an An-12BK coded '07 Red' (c/n 8345709) was fitted out with RR8311-100 pods; however, this aircraft lacked the sensor pod.

An-12BKV Bomber/Minelayer Aircraft

In 1969 GK NII VVS investigated the possibility of using the *Cub* as an auxiliary bomber. This was because the Soviet Air Force's General Operational Requirements (OTTT VVS – *Obshchiye taktiko-tekhnicheskiye trebovaniya Voyenno-vozdooshnykh sil*) said that a military transport aircraft absolutely had to be capable of dropping bombs – just in case there would be no other aircraft left to drop them, as some observers caustically commented! The An-12's large payload made it all the more attractive for this role.

Designated An-12BKV (the meaning of the V suffix remains unknown), the 'bomber' featured a permanently installed TG-12MB conveyor belt in the freight hold for propelling bombs towards the cargo doors. Several aircraft were converted in this fashion and delivered to the VVS; however, tests revealed that bombing accuracy was appallingly low and the idea was dropped.

Above: Egyptian Air Force An-12B '1223' served as a testbed for the Brandner E-300 turbojet intended for the locally designed Helwan HA-300 light fighter. The development engine was carried on a special pylon replacing the No.2 turboprop.

An-12BSh Navigator Trainer

A special version of the An-12B designated An-12BSh (**shtoormanskiy** – for navigators) was developed for training navigators for the VTA. Little is known about this version, except that it had ten trainee workstations in the freight hold.

An-12BKSh Navigator Trainer

A similar navigator trainer version designated An-12BKSh was evolved from the An-12BK in 1970. As was the case with the An-12BSh, this version was obtained by converting standard An-12BKs at the Tashkent aircraft factory.

An-12BKK *Kapsoola* VIP Aircraft

A single An-12BK transport was converted into a VIP/executive aircraft for the Commander of the Soviet Air Force's transport arm (VTA) in 1975. The aircraft was known as the An-12BKK *Kapsoola* because a pressurised passenger module (or 'capsule') with all appropriate furnishings was installed in the normally unpressurised freight hold. Unfortu-

nately the identity of the An-12BKK is unknown.

An-12VKP (An-12B-VKP) *Zebra* Airborne Command Post

A single Irkutsk-built An-12A ('19 Red', c/n 9900902) was converted into an airborne command post (ABCP) version designated An-12VKP *Zebra* (*vozdooshnyy komahndnyy poonkt* – ABCP). The aircraft sported three cigar-shaped fairings at the wingtips and atop the fin which housed antennas associated with the secure HF communications suite. Additionally, long 'towel rail' aerials ran along the upper and lower fuselage sides from the wing trailing edge to a point in line with the front end of the fin fillet. Obviously a pressurised compartment used as a 'war room' by Army commanders was provided in the freight hold, as was a communications and encoding/decoding equipment bay.

No longer wearing a tactical code or a civil registration, the An-12VKP was tested at LII in Zhukovskiy. The aircraft remained a one-off

because the IL-18D airliner with its fully pressurised fuselage was far better suited for the ABCP role; presently Ilyushin brought out the IL-22 *Coot-B* which entered production and service with the Soviet Air Force in substantial numbers. Interestingly, the initial version of the IL-22 (aka IL-18D-36) bore the same Soviet codename, *Zebra*; the later IL-22M, however, was coded *Bizon* (Bison)

Later the An-12VKP was deployed in East Germany, operating for the 16th Air Army – the Air Force component of the Group of Soviet Forces in Germany. According to press reports, in the winter of 1991-92 the aircraft was damaged beyond repair in a hard landing at Mahlwinkel AB, one of the East German airfields used by the GSFG. The outwardly intact aircraft was to languish at Mahlwinkel until finally scrapped in the spring of 1995.

An-12M Development Aircraft

In 1972 a standard production *Cub* (identity unknown) was re-engined with 5,180-ehp AI-20DM turboprops driving AV-68DM propellers of 4.7 m (15 ft 0²⁷⁄₆₄ in) diameter. Despite its higher performance, the aircraft, designated An-12BM (*modifitseerovannyy* – modified), remained a one-off because the AI-20DM did not enter quantity production.

An-12BSM Commercial Transport

In 1973 the Antonov OKB developed an improved commercial transport version called An-12BSM (the meaning of the suffix is unknown). Unlike the basic *Cub*, the An-12BSM was designed with containerised and palletised goods in mind. The freight hold was equipped with two gantry cranes each

An-12B CCCP-11417, one of the avionics testbeds operated by LNPO Leninets, in its revised form. The aircraft was used for testing ASW systems.

Top and above: An-12B '08256' (c/n 402207) on the hardstand at Zhukovskiy. These views show the SLAR antenna arrays, the ventral sensor and the tail radome. The combination of a civil registration and Air Force insignia is unusual. Note the An-12BK prototype (CCCP-83962) in the background.
Below left: The same aircraft on short finals to runway 30 in Zhukovskiy.
Below right: The rear end of An-12B c/n 402207 (the callsign 08256, which became the aircraft's registration, has yet to be applied). This view shows well the rear radome and the unidentified boxy equipment housings extended aft through the open cargo door.

capable of lifting 2,500 kg (5,510 lb), guide rails and roller conveyors for container/pallet handling; special panels were installed between fuselage frames 34 and 43 to provide a smooth freight hold floor, eliminating the step at frame 34.

The aircraft could carry eight UAK-2,5 air freight containers, each of them measuring 1,456 x 2,438 x 1,900 mm (4 ft 9⁹⁄₁₆ in x 8 ft 0 in x 6 ft 2¹³⁄₁₆ in); or PA-2,5 rigid pallets measuring 1,456 x 2,438 mm (4 ft 9⁹⁄₁₆ in x 8 ft 0 in), each weighing 2,500 kg (5,510 lb) fully loaded.

An alternative payload was four 5,000-kg (11,023-lb) UAK-5A containers measuring 2,991 x 2,438 x 1,900 mm (9 ft 9¾ in x 8 ft 0 in x 6 ft 2¹³⁄₁₆ in) or four PA-5,6 pallets measuring 2,991 x 2,438 mm (9 ft 9¾ in x 8 ft 0 in), each weighing 5,670 kg (12,500 lb).

Above: An-12A CCCP-11790, an ECM or ELINT testbed operated by the Yermolino Flight Test Centre. The antenna arrays replacing the tail turret and obstructing the cargo door are clearly visible.

Above: An-12AP CCCP-11916 was another testbed operated by the same test centre and featured a similar tail radome, plus a 'thimble' with a dielectric insert supplanting the nose glazing.

The rear end of An-12A '15 Red' (c/n 1340105) with radiometric and spectrometric equipment supplanting the DB-65U tail turret.

An-12BP IFR Tanker Conversion

One of the An-12BP transports delivered to the Iraqi Air Force was reportedly converted in situ into a single-point hose-and-drogue IFR tanker. Unfortunately no details are known, except that the aircraft was used operationally during the Iran-Iraq war of 1980-88. Later the aircraft was replaced in IrAF service by a similar one-off conversion of an IL-76M.

An-12B Instrumentation Calibration Laboratory

In 1972 a single An-12 (identity unknown) was equipped as 'a flying laboratory for running metrological checks on a range of measuring instruments used by Soviet Air Force regiments' (*sic*). The aircraft was known as *izdeliye* 93T. The nature of the equipment to be checked is unclear but one might suppose that the aircraft was a mobile lab for calibrating the flight instruments of tactical aircraft.

An-12B (LIAT) Air Accident Investigation Laboratory

Again in 1972, another Soviet Air Force *Cub* (identity unknown) was converted into a mobile air accident investigation laboratory designated An-12B (LIAT) which could travel to the airbase where a crash had taken place. The LIAT suffix stood for *laboratoriya issledovaniya aviatsionnoy tekhniki* – aviation hardware examination laboratory. The freight hold housed specialised equipment for analysing the flight data recorder and cockpit voice recorder readouts of the crashed aircraft; it also featured a crew rest area, a galley and toilet facilities.

An-12 Engine Testbed (Soviet)

From the outset the An-12 was extensively used for test and research purposes, since its large payload and capacious freight hold accommodating a lot of test equipment made it eminently suitable for this role. Thus, as early as 1959 an An-12 (identity unknown) was used as a testbed for the Ivchenko AI-24 turboprop (initially rated at 2,500 ehp). The engine and the associated AV-72 four-bladed reversible-pitch propeller of 3.9 m (12 ft 9½ in) diameter developed by the Stoopino Machinery Design Bureau had been created for the An-24 twin-turboprop regional airliner, which entered flight test on 20th October 1959. The An-24 turned out to be highly successful and became the progenitor of a whole family of twin-turboprop aircraft (see Red Star Vol. 12); most of them were powered by the same engine which, in its ultimate form (AI-24VT) was uprated to 2,820 ehp.

An-12B Engine Testbed (Egyptian)

In 1962 the Egyptian Air Force converted one of its An-12Bs serialled 1223 (c/n 402309) for testing the 4,800-kgp (10,580-lbst) E-300

Above: The An-12B *Koobrik* avionics testbed has few competitors for the title of the Most Bizarre *Cub* Ever! Note the tail gunner's station moved aft by inserting a plug; the PRS-4 Krypton gun ranging radar was developed for the IL-76.

afterburning turbojet, which had been developed by the German engineer Dr. Ferdinand Brandner for the Egyptian Helwan HA-300 light fighter. The development engine was housed in a compact nacelle with a short pylon replacing the port inboard AI-20 turboprop. However, the flight-cleared engine was never installed in the real thing; the two HA-300 prototypes, the first of which made its maiden flight on 7th March 1964, were both powered by 2,200-kgp (4,850-lbst) Bristol Orpheus BOr 12 turbojets.

Eventually Egypt's attempt to create an indigenous combat aircraft was cut short by financial problems; the programme was closed down in 1968 and the HA-300 did not progress beyond the prototype stage. As for the An-12, it was reconverted to standard configuration, serving on with the EAF as 1223/SU-AOS until finally retired and scrapped.

An-12B BLC Testbed (?)

An overall grey 'military' An-12B with the non-standard registration CCCP-29110 (c/n 402502) was apparently used for boundary layer control (BLC) experiments. This aircraft had four cigar-shaped fairings installed on the wing upper surface in line with the engine nacelles; this and the fact that the machine was used for soggy runway tests gives reasons to believe that CCCP-29110 was fitted experimentally with blown flaps. Later the system was removed from this aircraft.

An-12B ELINT Equipment Testbed

The majority of An-12 testbeds were used to test new avionics and equipment. One of them was An-12B c/n 402207, which was used for testing ELINT and optoelectronic reconnaissance systems from 1964 to 1998.

Wearing standard overall grey camouflage and VVS star insignia but sporting the non-standard registration 08256 (*sic*; originally the aircraft's ATC callsign) in lieu of a tactical code, this *Cub* sported numerous tell-tale 'bumps and bulges'. Long slab-sided fairings with streamlined front and rear ends and dielectric panels were mounted high on the rear fuselage sides, housing a side-looking airborne radar (SLAR); the panels were flat,

except for an elliptical bulge at the front, and canted slightly outward.

The tail turret was supplanted by a long ogival dielectric fairing looking like a supersonic fighter's radome; the tail gunner's station probably accommodated one of the test engineers. Additional boxy fairings were located low on the starboard side of the forward fuselage and beneath the starboard SLAR fairing; the rear 'box' was much larger

Top and above: The An-12VKP was converted into a VLF communications equipment testbed with a cobweb-like mesh of wire aerials above the fuselage. Note the stabilising drogue of the trailing wire aerial.

Top and above: An-12B CCCP-11819 was fitted out as an avionics testbed with a 'proboscis', a conical tail fairing and a ventral canoe fairing. Note the non-standard livery with a blue/white tail.

and incorporated what appears to be two rows of eight four-round flare launchers. Two oblong square-section boxes with unidentified equipment could be extended aft through the open cargo doors. Finally, a bulged observation blister was built into the forward starboard emergency exit. The aircraft was based at the LII airfield in Zhukovskiy.

An-12A/B ASW Equipment Testbed

A quasi-civil grey-painted An-12A or B registered CCCP-11417 (c/n unknown) was used for testing anti-submarine warfare (ASW) equipment – most probably by the All-Union Electronics Research Institute (VNIIRA – *Vsesoyooznyy naoochno-issledovatel'skiy institoot rahdioelektroniki*), aka LNPO Leninets (Leninist), in Leningrad. This establishment, a division of the Ministry of Electronic Industry (MRP – *Ministerstvo rahdio-elektronnoy promyshlennosti*), was one of the Soviet Union's leading avionics houses. (Note: LNPO = *Leningrahdskoye naoochno-proizvodstvennoye obyedineniye* – Leningrad Scientific & Production Association. LNPO Leninets is now known as the Leninets Holding Company.)

Originally large cylindrical pods with cropped conical ends were mounted on the forward fuselage sides beneath the cabin windows; these housed a *Sablya* (Sabre) monobloc SLAR, aka *izdeliye* 122, of the type fitted to the Mikoyan MiG-25RBS reconnaissance/strike aircraft. A smaller rectangular box located ventrally on the centreline in line with their aft ends accommodated a Bulat (Damask steel, pronounced *boolaht*) radar. A fairly large rounded radome mounted on a hinged frame was installed at the rear of the freight hold, protruding through a cutout in the starboard cargo door segment; it was semi-recessed in the fuselage for take-off and landing and fully extended in flight. A small angular fairing – probably a camera housing – projected downwards from the rear cargo door segment.

Top and above: CCCP-11531, one of the two An-12BP Tsiklon (An-12BPTs) weather research aircraft, with cloud seeding agent dispensers carried on pylons. Note the nose logo worn by all of the Tsiklon weather research fleet. The outlines around the emergency exits make them look 'larger than life'.

The first test flights performed by NII VVS crews gave disappointing results. The lateral pods generated powerful vortices and the turbulent airflow from the port pod was caught by the propeller of the No.2 engine, striking the entry door. As a result, the door would vibrate, producing a deafening roar that was absolutely unbearable. Besides, the frame of the rear radome was not rigid enough and the radome started swaying dangerously. To remedy the situation the SLAR antennas were attached directly to the fuselage sides slightly lower than before and enclosed by huge teardrop fairings, and the said frame was stiffened.

Later the aircraft had an *Oospekh* (Success) search radar in a large quasi-spherical radome installed beneath the tail gunner's station; this radar had been developed for the Kamov Ka-25Ts Hormone-B shipboard over-the-horizon (OTH) targeting helicopter. The test missions flown by CCCP-11417 took it over the Barents Sea where it was intercepted by Royal Norwegian Air Force Lockheed F-104G Starfighters in the summer of 1984.

An-12A ECM/ELINT Equipment Testbed

Another quasi-civil overall grey An-12A, CCCP-11790 (c/n 1400302), served as an ECM or ELINT testbed with the Yermolino flight test centre south-east of Moscow in the early 1980s. It featured a large boxy structure incorporating five dielectric panels of different size attached to the aft fuselage underside, supplanting the rear cargo door segment, and a fairly long square-section 'stinger' fairing protruding from the tail gunner's station in lieu of a turret. The aircraft was later stripped of all non-standard appendages, serving as a transport with the Yermolino Flight Test & Research Enterprise (YeLIIP – *Yermolinskoye lyotno-ispytahtel'noye issledovatel'skoye predpriyahtiye*) as RA-11790; the DB-65U turret was reinstated.

An-12AP ECM/ELINT Equipment Testbed

One more avionics testbed operated by the Yermolino flight test centre was An-12AP CCCP-11916 (c/n 2400901). It also wore grey Air Force colours, featuring an identical 'stinger' fairing replacing the tail turret and a large cylindrical 'proboscis' extending forward from the navigator's station, which required most of the glazing to be removed. Again, the aircraft was reconverted to standard configuration by 1993 and was operated by YeLIIP as RA-11916 in Aeroflot colours.

An-12BP ECM/ELINT Equipment Testbed

An-12BP CCCP-11819 (c/n 6344009) wearing an experimental version of Aeroflot's 1973-

Above: CCCP-11530, the other An-12BP Tsiklon, in flight, showing the Groza-26 radar replacing the tail turret.

Above: One of the An-12BP Tsiklons at rest on the GosNII GA apron at Moscow/Sheremet'yevo-1. The fairing at the base of the striped air data boom housed a BMR-1 weather research radar.

The cargo cabin of the An-12BP Tsiklon where part of the experimental and data recording equipment was installed. The roller conveyor on the left probably served for dumping rainmaking chemicals overboard.

Above: A fine landing study of An-12BPTs CCCP-11530 at Moscow-Sheremet'yevo.

Above: Two views of LII's An-12M LL multi-purpose testbed (An-12BK '43 Red', c/n 8345902) outfitted for ejection seat trials. In this case the ejection seat module is set for an ejection in simulated inverted flight.

Here, the aircraft has the ejection seat module fitted with 60° right bank. Note the test equipment heat exchangers aft of the wings and the LII badge on the nose.

standard livery with a blue/white tail served as a testbed for unidentified ECM or ELINT equipment. The greater part of the navigator's station glazing was replaced by a long conical fairing with a rounded tip and a ventral excrescence near the tip; a smaller upturned conical fairing replaced the tail turret, and a small ventral canoe fairing was located immediately ahead of the wings. This aircraft, too, was reconverted to standard configuration and transferred to the transport department of the Khar'kov aircraft factory.

An-12A/B SATCOM Equipment Testbed

An unidentified An-12A or B in Air Force colours was fitted out for testing what appears to be satellite communications (SATCOM) equipment. The aircraft sported a large teardrop fairing housing antennas on top of the forward fuselage.

An-12A SLAR Testbed

A grey-painted An-12A with the non-standard registration CCCP-13321 (c/n 2340301) had been used by NPO Vzlyot (Take-off) as a SLAR testbed at one time. When first noted at Zhukovskiy in August 1992 the aircraft appeared perfectly standard at first glance, but careful inspection of the rear fuselage sides showed traces of antenna fairings similar to those of An-12B 08256.

An-12BP Radar Testbed

'Military' An-12BP CCCP-13402 (c/n unknown) in 1973-standard blue/white Aeroflot colours was probably another LNPO Leninets testbed. This aircraft had a huge quasi-spherical radome housing an Oospekh radar instead of the normal chin-mounted RBP-2; the thing looked like the vocal sac of a tree frog! As in the case of CCCP-11417, the rear cargo door segment carried a camera fairing.

An-12BK Radar Testbed

A Russian Air Force An-12BK (identity unknown) was seen at one of the Russian airbases with a curious truss-type structure on top of the fuselage; it was made of thin metal tubes and looked almost like a construction scaffolding. This aircraft was reportedly used to test the mock-up installation of some radar antenna, although it appears highly unlikely that it could have flown in this guise.

An-12A Spectrometric Equipment Testbed

Soviet Air Force An-12A '15 Red' (c/n 1340105) was used by LII to test spectrometric and radiometric equipment. The test equipment

sensors were installed in lieu of the DB-65U tail turret and gun ranging radar.

An-12B *Koobrik* Avionics Testbed

In 1969 a Soviet Air Force An-12B coded '77 Red' (c/n unknown) was extensively modified to become the An-12 *Koobrik* (crew quarters on a ship) – a testbed for thermal imaging systems and IR sensors designed for detecting targets on water, land and in the air. The aircraft looked positively hair-raising. The navigator's station glazing was almost entirely supplanted by a cylindrical metal adapter mounting a conical radome at the front and a small teardrop radome underneath; the adapter also incorporated two small air scoops. A large boxy dorsal canoe fairing ran nearly the full length of the forward fuselage from just aft of the flightdeck to the wing leading edge, carrying a large cylindrical 'smokestack' near its aft end. A small bullet-shaped pod was car-

Top: The An-12M LL fires a Zvezda K-36D-3,5 ejection seat in an inverted position during the MosAeroShow '92. Note the video cameras under the wingtips.
Above: The same aircraft comes in to land

Above, left and right: Tests of the Zvezda K-37 lightweight ejection seat created for the Kamov Ka-50 Black Shark attack helicopter. The seat is extracted by a squib attached to a telescopic boom. Note that the An-12M LL still has the hinged booms under the rear fuselage dating back to an aerial recovery programme.

Above: The ejection seat module of the An-12M LL (with a K-36D seat and a dummy inside) was displayed alongside the aircraft at the MAKS-95 airshow. Note the photo calibration markings and the LII badge.

The rear end of the An-12M LL at the MAKS-95 airshow; an IL-114 tailcone has been fitted for the purpose of testing the airliner's VD-100M APU. Note the video camera above the tail gunner's station window.

ried on a short forward-swept pylon installed under the port forward emergency exit.

The rear end was non-standard as well. The tail gunner's station was moved aft appreciably by inserting a 'plug' between it and the rest of the airframe. It carried a PRS-4 Krypton gun ranging radar with a distinctive boxy radome (hence the NATO codename *Box Tail*; PRS = *pritsel rahdiolokatsionnyy strelkovyy* – gunner's radar sight), aka *izdeliye* 4DK; the cannons were replaced by some kind of sensor. Finally, a camera fairing protruded from the rear cargo door segment.

An-12BK Navigation System Testbed
The An-12BK prototype (CCCP-83962 No.2) was used in 1966-69 to test the *Polyot-1* (Flight-1) navigation system and the *Koopol* (cupola – or rather, in this context, parachute canopy) precision paradropping system developed for the An-22 *Antey* (Antheus; NATO *Cock*) heavy military transport.

An-12B/BP Navigation System Testbed
One more *Cub* served for long-range radio navigation (LORAN) systems development in 1977-82; the research culminated in the Alpha LORAN system fitted to some Soviet combat aircraft. The aircraft was referred to as 'An-12 No.3108' – that is, either An-12B c/n 403108 or An-12BP '15 Red' (c/n 5343108); if the latter machine was involved, it was later transferred to the airlift regiment at Kubinka AB.

An-12 Thermal Imager Testbed
Another An-12 served as a testbed for the Prostor (wide expanse, or ample space) thermal imager in 1968-70. The unit was designed for infrared mapping and locating fires.

An-12A Trailing Wire Aerial Testbed
In 1975 the former An-12VKP ABCP (c/n 9900902) operated by LII served as a testbed for the mighty BLT-5 winch driven by a ram air

Above: CCCP 04366, the custom-made An-12TP-2 geophysical research aircraft. The 'commercial' tailcone housed a telescopic magnetic anomaly detector (MAD) boom.

turbine; the winch was used to deploy a 2,500-m (8,200-ft) trailing wire aerial (TWA) with a stabilising drogue at the end. The unit had been specially developed for the Tu-142MR *Bear-J* communications relay aircraft whose mission was to maintain very low frequency (VLF) communications between submerged nuclear missile submarines and land-based or airborne command posts in the event of a nuclear attack (in this case R stands for *retranslyator* – communications relay installation). The aircraft also featured a whole network of wire aerials stretched from the tail unit to the wings, looking almost like a spider's web. The tests were filmed from a Tu-124 airliner acting as a chase plane.

An-12BPTs Tsiklon Weather Research Aircraft

By the mid-1970s radar technologies of weather and atmospheric research had gained wide

Above: Close-up of the An-12TP-2's nose, showing the non-standard large radome. This aircraft and IL-18V CCCP-75743 visible beyond made a trip to Antarctica in December 1961/February 1962.

CCCP 04366 taxies at Ice Station Molodyozhnaya, one of the Soviet research stations in Antarctica. During the Antarctic operations the An-12TP-2 was temporarily fitted with skis.

An excellent view of the An-12TP-2 during one of the refuelling stops en route to Antarctica. The red-tailed IL-18V CCCP-75743 is just visible beyond.

use. The use of radar made it possible to study the distribution of clouds and precipitation over wide areas, follow the development of storm nuclei. Therefore a special equipment suite called *Tsiklon* (Cyclone) was developed to meet an order placed by the Soviet Union's State Committee for Hydrometeorology and Environmental Control (**Gos**komghidro**met**).

In 1976-79 two Tashkent-built An-12BPs, CCCP-11530 and CCCP-11531 (c/ns 6344503 and 6344506), were converted into An-12BPTs Tsiklon weather research aircraft. This version is often referred to as An-12BP Tsiklon or simply An-12 Tsiklon – and sometimes called An-12BKTs in error.

The technologies employed by the Tsiklon system allowed stand-off research of clouds – that is, without actually entering them, which could change their shape and structure (and could be dangerous for the aircraft itself, since severe turbulence is often encountered in clouds, not to mention lightning!). Apart from studying the principal thermodynamic and electric parameters of the atmosphere and cloud formations, the aircraft were designed to perform cloud-seeding missions for the purpose of making rain – for example, in order to prevent an impending hailstorm which could destroy crops (or to scatter rain clouds which could ruin a public holiday).

Outwardly the An-12BPTs Tsiklon bore a strong resemblance to the unique Lockheed C-130K-140-LM Hercules W.2 (XV208) operated by the Royal Air Force's Weather Research Flight and nicknamed 'Snoopy'. The nose terminated in a long pointed boom tipped with sensors, leaving the navigator's station with just one small window on each side; the boom was painted in black and white zebra stripes to avoid damage by ground vehicles. A small rounded radome at the base of the boom housed a specialised BMR-1 weather research radar (the standard ROZ-1 chin-mounted radar was retained). More sensors were located dorsally and ventrally on the forward fuselage centreline.

The tail turret gave place to a fairly large rounded radome enclosing an RPSN-3S *Groza-26* (Thunderstorm) weather radar borrowed from the An-26 transport (RPSN = **rah**diolokatsi**on**nyy pri**bor** sle**poy** navi**gah**tsii – blind navigation radar device). The nose-mounted instrumentation boom and rear radome increased the overall length from 33.1 m (108 ft 7⁵⁄₃₂ in) to 38 m (124 ft 8 in).

Two large pylons were installed on each side fore and aft of the main gear fairings, An-12PS style, for carrying cloud-seeding chemical pods. Finally, three observation blisters were provided on each side for filming purposes. The aircraft wore full blue/white Aeroflot colours but the cheatline was broken

beneath the flightdeck by the eye-catching Tsiklon emblem.

Two research equipment consoles were located in the pressurised forward cabin, with two more in the freight hold. The mission equipment comprised a measurement suite, data recording/processing equipment and cloud-seeding equipment. The **measurement suite** included, firstly, a *thermodynamic measurement system* comprising a TsSV-3M-1KM central air data system, an EM TsAO electric meteorograph developed by the Central Aerological Observatory, a PK G-load measuring kit, an SAMB-70 airborne automatic weather research module, an ASTA-74 airborne automatic thermo-anemometer, an RV-18Zh radio altimeter and an SG-1 airborne humidity meter. It recorded the outside air temperature and its fluctuations, the aircraft's speed and heading, the wind speed and direction, airflow pulsations, static and dynamic air pressure, barometric and true altitude, vertical gusts and G loads acting on the aircraft. The second major component was the *cloud and precipitation microstructure measurement system* comprising an IRCh water/ice particle size meter and an SEIV-3 airborne electric cloud water content meter. The third component was the *meteorological radar system* – the aforementioned BMR-1 in the nose for vertical scanning of the atmosphere and the Groza-26 radar in the tail.

Finally, there was a PNP meter for measuring electric fields and the aircraft's electric charge.

The **data recording/processing equipment** consisted of a K60-42 magnetic recorder, an AKS-2 cine camera and an SYeO common time indication system. The K60-42 automatically recorded signals generated by the thermodynamic and cloud measurement systems for future computer analysis. The cine and photo cameras were used to film the outside conditions, using the observation blisters.

The **cloud-seeding equipment** designed to generate rain from cumulus and stratus clouds included seven KDS-155 dispensers and four ASO-2I dispensers mounted on the cargo doors, an ITU solid carbon dioxide atomiser and, as an option, four external pods for dispensing powdered rainmaking agents, primarily silver iodide. The KDS-155 and ASO-2I were adapted from stock chaff/flare dispensers used on Soviet military aircraft for passive ECM and infrared countermeasures (IRCM). Instead of bundles of chaff, aluminium-coated glass needles or PPI-26 IRCM magnesium flares (**peeropatron infrakrahsnyy** – infra-red [countermeasures] cartridge) they fired special PV-26 cartridges loaded with chemicals triggering the formation of ice crystals. The latter became too heavy to be supported by the air currents inside the cloud and started falling as hailstones; however, these melted and turned into rain before reaching the ground.

Since the An-12BPTs was to operate over vast stretches of water if necessary when chasing storms, it was provided with appropriate long-range radio navigation (LORAN) equipment.

The aircraft had a flight crew of five plus a 14-man team of researchers. In fully equipped configuration with four external pods the TOW amounted to 61 tons (134,480 lb); top speed was 550-600 km/h (340-372 mph) and the service ceiling was 8,700 m (28,540 ft). The An-12BPTs could stay airborne for up to eight hours, with a maximum range of 5,000 km (3,105 miles).

The two weather research *Cubs* were operated by the State Civil Aviation Research Institute (GosNII GA – *Gosoodarstvennyy naoochno-issledovatel'skiy institoot grazhdahnskoy aviahtsii*) and home-based at Moscow-Sheremet'yevo but were seldom seen there, travelling far and wide in pursuit of their mission. Among other things, they deployed to Cuba from time to time because the Caribbean, with its frequent typhoons, offered plenty of material for research. The aircraft were quite efficient economically in their designated role due to the high accuracy of measurements, the ability to track changes in the meteorological processes in real time,

influence them quickly and check the results immediately. Incidentally, CCCP-11530 and CCCP-11531 were but two of a range of assorted weather research aircraft bearing the Tsiklon name; these included an IL-18D four-turboprop airliner (CCCP-75442), a Tu-104A twinjet airliner (CCCP-42454), a pair of demilitarised Tu-16K-26 *Badger-G Mod* naval missile strike aircraft (CCCP-42355 No.1 and CCCP-42484) and an as-yet unidentified An-26.

Regrettably, in the general chaos that followed the demise of the Soviet Union these aircraft found themselves unwanted. The Tupolev jets were withdrawn from use as time-expired while the turboprops, including both An-12s, were stripped of their special equipment and used as cargo aircraft. Interestingly, the navigator's station glazing was never fully reinstated (there was a solid panel replacing the two upper windows in the second row) and the tail radomes on both aircraft remained, though they were empty now. The two aircraft served on with GosNII GA as RA-11530 and RA-11531 for a while; the latter aircraft was then sold to Angola as D2-FVG No.1.

An-12BK Ejection Seat/APU/Recovery Systems Testbed (An-12M LL)

In 1989 An-12BK '43 Red' (c/n 8345902) was converted into a multi-purpose testbed to be used by LII and the Parachute Systems Design Institute. In some sources this aircraft has been called An-12M LL (*letayuschchaya*

Top and centre: An-12AP CCCP-12186 was converted into a geophysical survey aircraft in 1982, being used by the Earth Magnetism Institute in the *Magnitometr* and *Relikt* research programmes.
Above: Close-up of the MAD boom fitted to CCCP-12186.

laboratoriya – lit. 'flying laboratory'). This Russian term is used indiscriminately for any kind of testbed (avionics, engine, equipment, weapons, whatever), an aerodynamics research aircraft or control configured vehicle (CCV), a weather research aircraft, a geophysical survey aircraft and so on.

One of its functions was to test an aerial recovery system intended for picking up film capsules ejected by surveillance satellites. The system was patterned on the Fulton STAR recovery gear fitted to the US Air Force version of the Lockheed HC-130H SAR aircraft. Two long booms were hinged to the aft fuselage underside, swinging down to snag the capsule's parachute as the capsule floated earthwards. A similar system had been used in the USA where a specially modified JC-130 picked up film capsules ejected by Lockheed GTD-21 high-speed reconnaissance drones.

The second mission fulfilled by '43 Red' at this stage was the testing of new models of ejection seats. To this end the tail turret was replaced by a detachable elongated pod emulating the cockpit of a combat aircraft. The 'cockpit' was attached by multiple bolts and could be installed at any angle from upright to inverted (0° to 180°) at 30° increments to emulate different attitudes of the stricken aircraft at the moment of ejection. This was because state-of-the-art ejection seats, such as the famous Zvezda K-36, were designed to ensure safe ejection even in inverted flight at low altitude – the worst possible combination. Two video cameras in orange egg-shaped pods were mounted under the wingtips to capture the ejection sequence; test equipment heat exchangers in characteristic white-painted teardrop fairings were installed high on the fuselage sides immediately aft of the wings.

The existence of An-12BK '43 Red' was revealed in photo form at the *Konversiya '91* trade fair held at the VDNKh fairground in Moscow in December 1991. (The word *konversiya* [conversion] means the adaptation of military technologies and defence industry enterprises to civilian needs.) At that time the aircraft still had the 'grabbing booms' left over from the previous programme but these were later removed as unnecessary. The testbed made demonstration flights involving live ejections of a seat with a dummy at the MosAeroShow '92 (11th-16th August 1992) and MAKS-97 (19th-24th August 1997) airshows in Zhukovskiy; on the former occasion (15th August) a standard K-36DM was fired from an inverted position, while at the MAKS-97 the latest K-36D-3.5 (featuring a reduced 3.5-G load limit to prevent pilot injuries) was fired with the cockpit set at 60° right bank.

As an alternative to the ejection cockpit a module with an auxiliary power unit could be installed. Thus by May 1994 An-12BK '43 Red' was fitted with the tailcone of the IL-114 twin-turboprop regional airliner housing a VD-100M APU. In this guise the aircraft was displayed statically at the MAKS-95 airshow (22nd-27th August 1995).

An-12TP-2 Geophysical Survey Aircraft

A single An-12B with the non-standard Polar Aviation registration CCCP 04366 (unusually, the registration was painted on with no dash; c/n unknown) was custom-built for long-range transport and geophysical survey duties in the Antarctic. The aircraft had a non-standard radar in a much longer and deeper radome extending all the way aft to the nose-wheel well (the ventral flightdeck escape hatch was thus blocked). There was no tail gunner's station, but a long slender magnetic anomaly detector (MAD) boom protruded from the 'civil' tailcone. The pre-1973 red/white colour scheme worn by Aeroflot *Cubs* (patterned on that of the An-10) was modified: the lower fuselage was white instead of grey, the vertical tail and propeller spinners were painted orange and the tops of the outer wings and stabilisers were red for high definition against white backgrounds. To make its mission patently clear the aircraft wore additional '*Polyarnaya aviatsiya*' titles and penguin tail art.

Designated An-12TP-2, the aircraft took part in an expedition to the Antarctic in December 1961. On arrival in the Antarctic CCCP 04366 was re-equipped with a non-retractable ski undercarriage as fitted to the An-12PL. Interestingly, the *Cub* was referred to as an An-10 in Soviet press reports of the expedition because the designation An-12 was still classified at the time; this misinformation found its way into Western publications as well.

An-12AP 'Magnitometr'/'Relikt' Geophysical Survey Aircraft

An-12AP CCCP-12186 (c/n 1901807) was another geophysical survey aircraft developed in 1982 for the Leningrad branch of the Earth Magnetism Institute (a division of the Soviet Academy of Sciences). The design and conversion work was performed by the Soviet Navy's 20th Aircraft Overhaul Plant in Pushkin near Leningrad.

The aircraft, which wore full 1973-standard Aeroflot blue/white livery, was fitted with an 8 m (26 ft 2⁶¹⁄₆₄ in) tapered MAD boom supplanting the tail turret. A small 'superstructure' housing an L-14MA astro-inertial navigation system was mounted on top of the boom near the front, making it look like a submarine en miniature. As with CCCP-11417, a camera fairing protruded from the rear cargo door segment. There were three researchers' workstations in the pressure cabin, with most of the equipment being installed in the freight hold.

Originally the aircraft bore the codename *Magnitometr* (magnetometer). In 1990 CCCP-12186 was upgraded by installing new scientific instrumentation and the codename was changed to *Relikt* (relic). The aircraft was used for studying the structure of the Earth's magnetic field and for making gravimetric measurements as requested by various government agencies and ministries.

An-12 'Tanker' De-icing Systems Test Aircraft

LII's large fleet of test and research aircraft included an An-12BK in ex-VVS grey colours which initially wore the non-standard civil registration CCCP-48974 No.2 (c/n 6344510) inherited from one of MAP's Li-2s. At first this machine was used as a 'spray tanker' for testing the de-icing systems of other aircraft. Developed in 1981, the modification involved the fitment of an 8,000-litre (1,760 Imp gal) water tank and a drum from which a 47-m (154-ft) hose terminating in a circular sprinkler grid was deployed through the cargo door, the grid acting as a stabilising drogue. The whole thing looked so much like a single-point hose-and-drogue IFR tanker that the aircraft was immediately dubbed 'Tanker'. This fairly complex arrangement was needed to keep the grid and the aircraft being tested out of the tanker's wake vortex.

The water was presumably fed by gravity; the delivery rate could vary up to 4 litres (0.88 Imp gal) per second. The aircraft created a cloud of water mist measuring 3-5 m (10-16 ft) in diameter. Depending on the flight speed and delivery rate, the mission time could be anything between 30 minutes and six hours.

CCCP-48974 No.2 is known to have been used in the trials of the An-72 short take-off and landing (STOL) transport. Using the 'tanker' allowed the time required for verifying a new aircraft's de-icing system to be reduced by a factor of four; it also enhanced flight safety and allowed icing tests to be performed at realistic speeds (that is, the ones at which the aircraft was likely to operate). Curiously, the An-12/An-72 combination was displayed in model form at the 1983 Paris Air Show; the *Cub* featured its actual registration but was painted in 1973-standard blue/white Aeroflot colours. This puzzled Western observers completely, leading to the misconception that the model represented an IFR tanker akin to the RAF's C-130K Hercules C.1K *and that the new tanker was perhaps intended to have some kind of civilian role* (!).

Later the An-12 was extensively modified. A section of a wing with a symmetrical airfoil and a leading-edge de-icer was installed vertically aft of the wing centre section, requiring the fin fillet to be cropped slightly. A large circular sprinkler grid with bracing struts was mounted ahead of the wing centre section. The freight hold accommodated test equipment consoles and a water tank; a big 'elephant's ear' air intake was provided on each side in line with the wing trailing edge for pressurising this tank and feeding water to the nozzles. The first cabin window to port was blanked off with sheet metal; cameras were installed in special fairings on the wing upper surface near the inboard engines, allowing the icing process to be filmed. Later, a large observation blister was added high on each side of the forward fuselage, providing a view of the grid and the test article.

By 1987 the aircraft had lost its civil identity for some reason, gaining Air Force insignia and the tactical code '10 Red'; the registration CCCP-48974 passed to a brand-new An-32A transport (c/n 1407) in late 1987.

In early 1992 the An-12 testbed was stripped of all non-standard features except the blisters and the abbreviated fin fillet, receiving the non-standard registration RA-13331. Later it was sold to a Russian airline called Start and repainted in basic Aeroflot colours, receiving an ROZ-1 radar in a small radome at the same time.

Miscellaneous Testbeds

An-12BP '85 Red' (c/n 6344204) was used by LII in 1972-74 to investigate IFR system parameters. Little is known, except that the results were used to develop the hose-and-drogue IFR system fitted as standard to some Soviet types.

A quasi-civil An-12BP (registration unknown, c/n 6344701) with grid-type photo calibration markings on the rear fuselage was used by the MKPK Ooniversahl company for

testing new paradropping equipment. Later the enterprise used another An-12BP, '42 Red' (c/n 5343403), with identical markings for this purpose.

One of the Soviet-built An-12BPs supplied to China (B-201, later B-3151, c/n 6344402) – misidentified by some Western observers as 'an early Shaanxi Y8 with a short nose glazing' (see next chapter) – was converted into a testbed of some sort with a simple conical fairing supplanting the tail turret. There have been speculations this might be an MAD fairing or even a 'cable guide for an in-flight refuelling hose'.

An-12 c/n 9900902 was used for performing test drops of the spherical re-entry capsule of the first Soviet manned spacecraft, *Vostok* (East), in 1960 and the re-entry capsule of the *Voskhod* (Sunrise) and *Soyooz* (Union) manned spacecraft in 1967-72.

Above: The An-12BK 'Tanker' water sprayer used for testing the de-icing systems of other aircraft ('10 Red', c/n 9344510). Here the sprinkler grid is partially stowed; note the observation blister on the forward fuselage.

Right: The grid and hose are deployed. Note the dorsal test equipment heat exchanger and the lateral air scoops for water tank pressurisation.

Below: ...and the water flows.

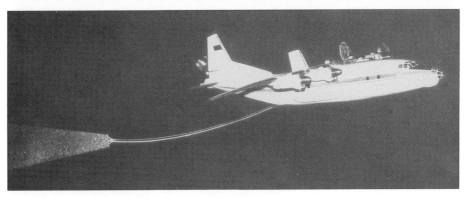

Left: The An-12BK 'Tanker' trails a pall of exhaust smoke from the engines and a pall of water mist from the sprinkler grid.
Right: A drawing depicting the aircraft with its own dorsally mounted test article and associated fixed sprinkler grid.

The An-12BK 'Tanker' in its original guise as CCCP-48974. The observation blisters high on the forward fuselage for monitoring a dorsally mounted test article are not yet fitted, but the cine cameras on top of the wings used for the same purpose are already there. The grid seems bound to scrape the runway on rotation.

Other test and research missions performed by the *Cub* in the Soviet Union included tests of optical and optoelectronic airborne surveillance/reconnaissance systems (1963-65); investigating the integral and spectral properties of the heat signature of various aircraft types; and tests of the UPAZ-1A *Sakhalin* (an island in the Soviet Far East) refuelling pod. The latter was developed by NPP *Zvezda* ('Star'; formerly OKB-918) under Guy Il'yich Severin – the same house that created the K-36 ejection seat. (Note: NPP = *naoochno-proizvodstvennoye predpriyahtiye* – Research & Production Enterprise; UPAZ = *oonifitseerovannyy podvesnoy agregaht zaprahvki* – standardised suspended (= external) refuelling unit. The 'standardised' part of the name means it can also be used as a 'buddy' refuelling pack by tactical aircraft – for example, the Sukhoi Su-24M tactical bomber, Su-30 interceptor and Su-33 shipboard fighter.)

***

'Paper' Projects
Regrettably, some versions of the An-12 never reached the hardware stage. True, some of the projects involved an extensive redesign (sometimes to the point where the aircraft was no longer an An-12), which the industry would rather avoid. On the other hand, they would have expanded the *Cub*'s capabilities considerably, making it more on a par with its American counterpart, the Hercules.

An-12U Military Transport
This project developed in 1962 envisaged the use of boundary layer control (BLC) on the wings and tail unit, hence the designation An-12U (for *oopravleniye [pogranichnym*

sloyem] – BLC). Simple flaps equipped with boundary layer control ducting were to be fitted instead of double-slotted Fowler flaps, the air for the BLC system being supplied by two DK1-26 compressors in underwing pods. The use of BLC, coupled with jet-assisted take-off (JATO) solid-fuel rocket boosters, was expected to give dramatically improved field performance.

An-12 Military Transport with Underwing Tanks and IFR Capability
One more projected version, also developed in 1962, featured two 6,000-litre (1,320 Imp gal) external tanks carried on pylons between the inner and outer engines, as on the C-130E and later versions. It was also to be fitted with an IFR probe in the manner of the RAF's C-130K Hercules C.1P.

An-12RU Military Transport
Yet another project of 1962, the An-12RU (*s raketnymi ooskoritelyami* – with rocket boosters), envisaged the installation of two PRD-63 solid-propellant rocket boosters on the aft fuselage sides to improve take-off performance, in a manner similar to the wheel/ski-equipped LC-130. The boosters were to be jettisoned after burnout.

An-12B-30 Military Transport
In 1963 the Antonov OKB proposed increasing the An-12B's load-carrying capacity over a 1,500-km (930-mile) range to 30 tons (66,140 lb). Designated An-12B-30 to reflect the increased payload, the aircraft was to be powered by 5,180-ehp AI-20DK engines driving new propellers of increased diameter (5.1 m; 16 ft 8²⁵⁄₃₂ in). The specified maximum take-off weight and cruising speed were

75,650 kg (166,780 lb) and 600 km/h (372 mph) respectively. Some flight test work under the An-12B-30 programme was reportedly undertaken jointly with LII in 1964, but eventually the aircraft was never built.

An-12D Military Transport
On 23rd May 1964 the Council of Ministers issued a directive ordering the development and production of a radically redesigned aircraft designated An-12D. Actually the development work had begun in 1963; the objective was to increase the payload to 20 tons (44,090 lb) and the range to 1,600-1,800 km (993-1,118 miles).

Like the An-12B-30 described above, the aircraft had AI-20DK engines driving propellers of 5.1 m diameter. The wing span was increased to 44.2 m (145 ft 0⁵⁄₃₂ in) and the wing area to 170 m² (1,828 sq ft); the aircraft was 35.5 m (116 ft 5⅝ in) long and stood 12.5 m (41 ft) tall when parked. The new tail unit was superficially similar to that of the An-24 airliner, featuring slight sweepback on all surfaces, except that the stabilisers had no dihedral and the fin fillet was much deeper.

The main landing gear was completely new, comprising four separate levered-suspension units with large single wheels which retracted inwards into reshaped fairings; this arrangement later found use on the An-72/An-74 STOL transport. The fat low-pressure tyres were to permit operations from airfields with a bearing capacity of no more than 4-5 kg/cm² (57-71 lb/sq in).

The An-12D featured a fully pressurised freight hold of increased length (13.9 m; 45 ft 7¹⁵⁄₆₄ in) and width (3.45 m; 11 ft⁵³⁄₆₄ in); the pressure differential was 0.25 kg/cm² (3.57 psi). The rear fuselage was more sharply

Above: An-12BK '10 Red' (c/n 6344510) in its final test configuration with a dorsally mounted test article and sprinkler grid and associated observation blisters. Note the additional sensors (possibly temperature probes) below the said blister.

Right: Close-up of the test article, an airfoil section. Note the black stripes applied to the leading edge for icing visualisation.

Below right and bottom right: The same aircraft as CCCP-48974, shortly before being repainted in military markings.

upswept and incorporated a larger cargo door facilitating the loading and unloading of any bulky items. Cargo handling equipment included a new gantry crane which could move out beyond the cargo door threshold for straight-in loading from a truck bed. Remarkably, the An-12D had no defensive armament.

With an MTOW of 75 tons (165,340 lb), the An-12D was expected to have a cruising speed of 500-600 km/h (310-372 mph), a service ceiling of 10,000 m (32,810 ft) and a ferry range of 7,500 km (4,658 miles). The project was not proceeded with as such but served as a stepping-stone towards the projected An-40 (see below).

An-12D-UPS Military Transport

A version of the An-12D developed in parallel featured a boundary layer control system, hence the designation An-12D-UPS (*oopravleniye pogranichnym sloyem* – BLC). The BLC system comprised three turbine-driven compressors, two of which were housed in fairings atop the wing centre section close to the trailing edge, serving the flaps, and the third was buried in the fin fillet, serving the tail surfaces. The system was to reduce the take-off run to 550-600 m (1,800-1,970 ft) and the landing run to 650-700 m (2,130-2,300 ft).

Above: An-12BP '42 Red' (c/n 5343403) withdrawn from use at Kirzhach. This machine, which made its last flight in 1996, was used by the MKPK Ooniversahl enterprise for testing new paradropping systems, hence the grid-like photo calibration markings on the rear fuselage.

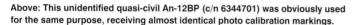

Above: This unidentified quasi-civil An-12BP (c/n 6344701) was obviously used for the same purpose, receiving almost identical photo calibration markings.

Right and above right: At an early stage of its test career, An-12A c/n 9900902 was used for paradropping a mock-up version of the Vostok spacecraft's spherical re-entry capsule and testing its parachute recovery system.

An-12DK Military Transport

This was a projected version re-engined with 5,500-ehp Ivchenko AI-30 turboprops in order to improve performance. Unfortunately little else is known.

An-12SN Military Transport

In 1965 the Antonov OKB started work on a derivative of the An-12B designated An-12SN (*[samolyot] spetsiahl'novo naznacheniya* – special-mission aircraft). This version was optimised for transporting the T-54 main battle tank weighing 37.2 tons (82,010 lb) –

the principal tank type operated by the Soviet Army and the Warsaw Pact nations. The fuselage diameter was increased, thereby increasing the freight hold width from 3.0 m (9 ft 10⁷⁄₆₄ in) to 3.45 m (11 ft⁵⁵⁄₆₄ in), and the cargo doors were redesigned accordingly. The powerplant consisted of 5,180-ehp AI-20DK engines augmented by a 3,800-kgp (8,380-lbst) Mikulin RD-9 turbojet of the type fitted to the Mikoyan/Gurevich MiG-19 fighter. The jet booster was installed at the base of the fin, supplanting the tail gunner's station. A brake parachute was provided for shorten-

ing the landing run. Part of the standard *Cub's* equipment was deleted to save weight. The project was not proceeded with because the larger An-22 could cope better with this task.

An-12R Military Transport

This was a redesign so radical that the resulting aircraft was not an An-12 any more. Designated An-12R (*reaktivnyy* – jet-powered), this project, completed in 1969, envisaged a transport powered by four 6,500-kgp (14,330-lbst) Lotarev D-36 high-bypass turbofans; the aircraft had swept wings and a swept T-tail. The freight hold was fully pressurised, being 15 m (49 ft 2³⁵⁄₆₄ in) long, 3.45 m (11 ft⁵⁵⁄₆₄ in) wide and 2.5 m (8 ft 2²⁷⁄₆₄ in) high. The tail gunner's station was replaced by a remote-controlled cannon barbette.

With a 90-ton (198,410-lb) MTOW the An-12R was to carry a 25-ton (55,115-lb) payload over a distance of 2,500 km (1,550 miles). The design maximum speed was 850 km/h (528 mph). The An-12R was not built but the project evolved into the An-112 transport (the designation speaks for itself) which lies outside the scope of this book – and which, too, remains a 'paper aeroplane' as of the time of writing.

An-12BZ-1 Military Transport and An-12BZ-2 IFR Tanker

Also in 1969 the Antonov OKB proposed giving the *Cub* IFR capability. Two versions were envisaged which would work together. One, called An-12BZ-1, was a single-point hose-and-drogue tanker similar to the C-130K Hercules C.1K, except that the hose drum unit was podded, not built-in. The receiver aircraft designated An-12BZ-2 was similar to the C-130K Hercules C.1P, featuring a fixed IFR probe atop the nose (the Z stood for *zaprahvka* – refuelling). The upgrade, which was to be performed in situ, was expected to boost the *Cub*'s range to 3,800 km (2,360 miles) with a 20-ton (44,090-lb) payload and 6,900 km (4,285 miles) with a 7-ton (1,540-lb) payload.

An-40 Military STOL Transport

Of all the upgrade projects described in this section, this one came closest to materialising. The redesign was extensive enough to warrant a new designation, An-40. Design work started in 1964 as a further development of the An-12D project. Looking at first glance like a 'stretched' An-12BK, the aircraft was powered by four 5,500-ehp AI-30 turboprops driving four-bladed propellers of 5 m (16 ft 4⁵⁵⁄₆₄ in) diameter. These were augmented by four 2,550-kgp (5,620-lbst) Kolesov RD36-35 booster/brake turbojets fitted with thrust reversers installed in paired nacelles between the inner and outer engines.

The nose gear unit was similar to that of the An-12 while the main gear consisted of four independent inward-retracting levered-suspension struts with single large wheels; all five landing gear struts were equipped with small skids to permit operations from dirt or snow strips with a bearing strength of 4-6 kg/cm² (57-85 lb/sq in).

Instead of a tail gunner's station, the An-40 featured a DB-75 remote-controlled tail turret mounting two 23-mm (.90 calibre) Gryazev/Shipoonov GSh-23 (aka AO-9) double-barrelled cannons. A PRS-4 Krypton gun

Above: This Russian Air Force An-12BK carries a curious-looking contraption atop the fuselage that is said to be the mock-up of some radar antenna array. The thing looks a bit too flimsy, though

ranging radar and a VB-257A-5 computer were mounted at the base of the rudder above the turret. The gunner now sat in the pressure cabin aft of the flightdeck under a large observation/sighting blister.

The cargo door design was completely new. The upward-opening rear segment was still there but the two inward-opening doors were supplanted by a cargo ramp of unique design invented and patented by the Antonov OKB. First used on the An-26 transport (and later on the An-32, An-72/An-74 and An-38), the ramp could be either lowered conventionally for loading/unloading troops and vehicles or slid forward under the aft fuselage for straight-in loading from a truck bed – or paradropping. The cargo door was flanked by large ventral strakes similar to those of the An-32; these were meant to optimise the airflow around the aft fuselage, reducing vibrations and ensuring acceptable paradropping conditions.

The forward pressure cabin accommodated 17 persons. In troopship configuration the An-40 could carry 125 troops with full kit;

alternatively, 82 stretchers could be installed for casualty evacuation duties.

The OKB built a full-scale mock-up, which was approved by the mock-up review commission in 1965; still, all further work on the project was halted because the Soviet military did not believe in turboprops anymore. Jet aircraft appeared more promising, and eventually the VVS selected the larger and faster Ilyushin IL-76 *Candid* as the successor of the *Cub*. (Well, 'successor' is not exactly true; the two types were destined to serve side by side for quite some time yet.)

An-42 Military STOL Transport

This was a version of the An-40 featuring a BLC system similar to that of the An-12D-UPS, with three turbocompressors based on the Kolesov RD36-35 turbojet atop the wing centre section and in the fin root. Structurally the An-42 was almost identical to the An-40, except for the airframe changes associated with the turbocompressor installation and the use of simple hinged flaps instead of double-slotted flaps.

The huge teardrop fairing on top of this An-12's forward fuselage suggests that the aircraft was a testbed for satellite communications or satellite navigation equipment.

Above: The highly unusual rear end of this An-12 indicates this is a former An-12PP ECM aircraft converted into an avionics testbed. Note the lack of the port forward emergency exit. The combination of a military tactical code ('07 Yellow') and a Russian flag is also noteworthy, as are the 'ANTONOV 12' nose titles.

An-40PLO ASW Aircraft

The Antonov OKB also envisioned an ASW version designated An-40PLO (*protivolod-ochnaya oborona* – ASW). An unusual feature of this aircraft was its powerplant, which was to run on both kerosene and hydrogen; to this end the freight hold was to accommodate high-pressure tanks holding 134.5 m³ (4,750 cu ft) of compressed hydrogen. The 10-ton (22,045-lb) weapons load comprising ASW torpedoes and depth charges was to be housed in the suitably lengthened forward portions of the main gear fairings.

According to preliminary design documents the An-40PLO was to have a 90-ton

A model of the proposed Sever air cushion vehicle based on the An-12's airframe.

(198,410-lb) maximum TOW. In maximum-range mode the aircraft would cruise at 550 km/h (341 mph); the maximum range was 15,500 km (9,627 miles). Maximum on-station loiter time when patrolling at 500 m (1,640 ft) and 350 km/h (217 mph) was 22 hours at a distance of up to 7,750 km (4,813 miles) from the base; maximum endurance in cruise at 9,000 m (29,530 ft) was 27 hours.

Sever ACV

Though not an aircraft, this project deserves mention because it was based on the An-12. In 1983 Professor V. Ignat'yev, a department head at the Kuibyshev Aviation Institute (KuAI,

now the Samara State Aviation University), proposed converting time-expired turboprop transports, including the An-12, into air cushion vehicles (ACVs) for use in the northern regions of the USSR; hence the family bore the generic name Sever (North). The conversion included cropping the wings so that only the inboard engines were left, fitting a large platform with flexible 'skirts' to the centre fuselage underside and installing ducts on the existing propellers to maximise their thrust. The latter was an absolute necessity because the ducts incorporated air scoops diverting part of the prop wash under the platform to create the air cushion. The standard landing gear was retained but the radar was removed and a hemispherical fairing was fitted instead of the navigator's glazing.

The idea won support from the rector of KuAI and several scientists, including Academician A. Trofimook who headed the Sibir' (Siberia) multi-aspect regional development programme. Ignat'yev started development work in 1983 with a small group of fellow enthusiasts. In 1987 a model of the Sever ACV based on the An-12 with a tail gunner's station was displayed at the International Trade Fair in Leipzig in former East Germany. (Apart from the An-12, Ignat'yev proposed similar conversions of the An-22 and An-26.) However, by 1987 the team still hadn't succeeded in obtaining a surplus airframe for conversion purposes and the project came to naught.

Chapter 3

An-12 Anatomy

The following structural description applies to the basic An-12BP. Details of other versions are indicated as appropriate.

Type: Four-engined medium military and commercial transport. The military transport version was originally intended to transport and paradrop personnel, as well as vehicles, such as the BTR-152 and BTR-40 armoured personnel carriers, ASU-57 paradroppable self-propelled guns and ZiL-157 6x6 lorries. The airframe is of all-metal construction.

Fuselage: Semi-monocoque stressed-skin structure of beam-and-stringer construction with 68 frames and 110 stringers; the skin thickness is 1-2 mm (0.039-0.078 in). Chemical milling is used on some panels. The riveted fuselage structure is made mainly of D16 duralumin; some structural components are made of MD8 and ML5-T4 magnesium alloy. Attachment bolts and fittings are made of 30KhGSA and 40KhNMA grade steel.

Structurally the fuselage is made up of four sections: the forward fuselage (frames 1-13), the centre fuselage (frames 13-41), the rear fuselage (frames 41-65) and the aft fuselage or tail section (frames 65-68). The latter is a flattened fairing on the commercial version (with a semi-circular contour in side view) or the tail gunner's station on the military version. All four sections are joined by flanges. On production aircraft the latter two sections effectively form a single whole. The fuselage cross-section is basically circular up to frame 41; further aft it is progressively flattened from below. Maximum fuselage diameter is 4.1 m (13 ft 5½ in).

The pressurised *forward fuselage (Section F1)* includes the crew section (the flightdeck plus the navigator's station) and a compartment for persons accompanying the cargo or vehicle crews). The flightdeck accommodates the pilots, flight engineer and radio operator; the navigator sits slightly below them in the extreme nose. The volume of the pressure cabin is 18.5 m³ (653.32 cu ft). Section F1 terminates in a flat rear pressure bulkhead.

The navigator's station features extensive glazing (frames 0-2) with curved Plexiglas panels and an optically flat elliptical lower forward panel. The flightdeck glazing frame is located between frames 4-8, with optically flat bird-proof triplex panes at the front; the side panes and eyebrow windows are made of Plexiglas. The flightdeck features two triangular sliding direct vision windows which can be used as emergency exits on the ground. An inward-opening dorsal escape hatch is located in the same area between frames 7 and 8 to be used in the event of ditching; there is also a ventral entry/escape hatch between frames 6-8 (the hatch cover is hinged at the front, acting as a slipstream deflector when the crew bails out).

An unpressurised bay for the radar antenna is located beneath the navigator's compartment between frames 2-4; the nose-wheel well is located behind it between frames 9-13. Sheets of APBL-1 armour 8 mm (0⁵⁄₁₆ in) thick are installed beneath the pilots' seats and along the flightdeck sides; the seats themselves have 16-mm (0⅝ in) armoured backs made of AB-548 steel.

The *centre fuselage (Section F2)* accommodates the unpressurised freight hold, which is 13.5 m (44 ft 3³¹⁄₆₄ in) long, 3.0-3.5 m (9 ft 10⅞₄ in to 11 ft 5⁵⁄₆₄ in) wide and 2.4-2.9 m (7 ft 10³⁄₆₄ in to 9 ft 6¹¹⁄₆₄ in) high; the height and width vary. The freight hold volume is 123.3 m³ (4,354 cu ft).

Fuselage mainframes 25 and 30 serve as attachment points for the wing centre section's front and rear spars respectively. The wing/fuselage joint is enclosed by a fairing.

The freight hold floor is an important structural component of the fuselage. It consists of a load-bearing framework and a skin

This side view of a Russian Air Force An-12B ('17 Red', c/n 5342810) shows well the tapered forward fuselage and the upswept rear fuselage with a flattened underside.

Above, right and above right: The forward fuselage. Note the faired window of the optical sight between the navigator's station glazing and the radome on some military An-12; it is absent on civil examples.

Below and bottom: The cargo hatch in the rear fuselage underside is closed by three door segments; the rear segment incorporates a camera port.

with stiffening ribs. Parts of the fuselage frames act as transverse members of the framework, which is also formed by beams, stamped profiles and channels (U-section profiles) supporting the skin.

Two luggage compartments used for storing engine covers, wheel chocks and the like (except on the An-12P/AP/BP/BK, where they house underfloor fuel cells) are located under the freight hold floor between frames 13-25 and 33-41. They are accessed from outside via downward-opening ventral doors offset to starboard (between frames 16-19 and 35-37 respectively) and from within via hatches in the freight hold floor. The volume of the forward and aft luggage compartments is 11.4 m³ (402.58 cu ft) and 5.3 m³ (187.16 cu ft) respectively. The space between the compartments (frames 27-30) is occupied by the mainwheel wells separated by the fuselage keel beam.

A quasi-oval rearward-hinged entry door with a window opening inwards is located on the port side between frames 22-24. Three square-shaped emergency exits with windows are provided in the hold (on both sides between frames 14-16 and on the port side between frames 37-39). The cabin features 15 circular windows of 384 mm (1 ft 3⁷⁄₆₄ in) diameter: 2+exit+1+door+3+exit+1 to port and 1+exit+1+5 to starboard.

Two elongated fairings of semi-circular cross-section are located on the centre fuse-

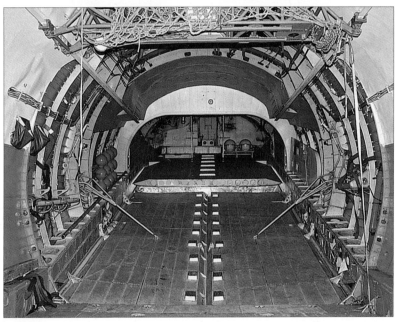

Above: The open cargo doors of An-12AP UR-21510. The forward segments lie flat against the walls; the black areas are abrasion-resistant liners protecting the skin where parachute static lines scuff against the doors.

Above right: A look inside the cargo cabin with the vehicle loading ramps in place.

Right: The closed cargo doors seen from within, looking aft. The steps on the inside lead to the doorway leading into the pressurised tail gunner's compartment. Note the oxygen bottles near the said doorway, the cargo door actuators and the overhead gantry crane running on tracks.

Below: The starboard wing of a Russian Air Force An-12BK-PPS. The two slits just inboard of the aileron show the position of the roll control spoilers used at high speeds. Note the leading edge kink caused by the outer wing anhedral.

Below right: The starboard wing of an An-12B with the flaps fully deployed. Note the heat-resistant liners on the flaps.

RA-11991

Top left: The aft fuselage (tail section) and tail unit of an early 'military' An-12. The door underneath the tail gunner's station is the gunner's escape hatch used for baling out. Note that the rudder trim tab stops short of the top.

Top right: The tail unit of Russian Air Force An-12B '95 Red' (c/n 4342410) featuring a full-span rudder trim tab. Normally the c/n is stencilled on the 'superstructure' forming the transition from the dorsal fin to the tail section, as here, though some An-12s carry the c/n on the detachable fin.

Above left: The rear fuselage, aft fuselage and dorsal fin of Soviet Air Force An-12BP '30 Red' (c/n 5343508). On this machine the fin de-icer and the flush aerials of the SHORAN system and ATC transponder in the detachable fin section are clearly visible.

Above: The tail gunner's station glazing and the DB-65U tail turret with twin AM-23 cannons.

Left: The horizontal tail, showing the de-icers, the access covers near the elevator hinge brackets and the faired dipole aerials of the radio altimeter.

Top left and above left: Two versions of the fairing replacing the tail turret on demilitarised An-12s.
The dished version (top) is much more common. Note the exposed radio altimeter aerials.
Top right: The tail section of a 'civil' An-12.
Above right: The tailcone of a demilitarised An-12PP ECM aircraft that used to house ASO-24 chaff dispensers.

lage sides between frames 22-38, enclosing the main gear fulcrums and actuators. These fairings accommodate the APU (in the rear section of the port fairing), as well as components of the pressurisation, hydraulic, electric and fuel systems.

The unpressurised *rear fuselage (Section F3)* incorporates attachment points for the vertical tail (at mainframes 59 and 62) and horizontal tail (at mainframes 62 and 65). A cargo floor of similar design to the one in Section F2 is fitted between frames 41 and 43. A dorsal escape hatch for troopers (used in the event of ditching) is provided between frames 42 and 44 immediately to the right of the fuselage centreline.

Section F3 features a large cargo hatch between frames 43-59 which is closed by three cargo door segments; the two forward segments (frames 43-51) open inwards and upwards to lie flat against the sides of the freight hold and the rear segment upwards. The hatch is flanked by beams serving as attachment points for the doors. The doors incorporate steps used for access to the tail gunner's station on armed military versions; the outer skin of the doors (and the rear fuselage between frames 59-61) is protected by titanium sheets to prevent damage by parachute static lines during paradropping.

As already mentioned, the *aft fuselage or tail section (Section F4)* is just an unpressurised fairing on the commercial version or a tail gunner's station on the basic military transport. The An-12PP ECM version and the initial version of the An-12BK-PPS have an elongated ogival fairing housing chaff dispensers and ESM equipment; on the An-12PS SAR version the tail gunner's station is converted into a bay housing a rescue raft.

On military versions the tail gunner's station is a pressure compartment accessed from the freight hold by walking up the inside of the cargo doors and through a pressure door in the front wall (frame 65). A ventral escape hatch is provided, the cover opening forwards hydraulically to act as a slipstream deflector for baling out. The gunner's station features three rear windows made of bulletproof glass 110-135 mm ($4^{35}/_{64}$ to $5^5/_{16}$ in) thick and two side windows made of 14-mm ($0^{35}/_{64}$ in) Plexiglas. The gunner is also protected by a removable 20-mm ($0^{25}/_{32}$ in) armour shield.

Above: The main landing gear fulcrums and actuators are enclosed by neat semi-cylindrical fairings which also house various equipment.

Left: The starboard main gear unit of an An-12BP.

Below left: Occasionally one may see early-model KT-77M mainwheels with lightening holes and the heavy-duty KT-77U wheels on the same bogie. Note the drag strut and the torque link.

Below: The nose gear unit. The axle is hollow, allowing the forked towbar to be attached.

Wings: Cantilever shoulder-mounted monoplane wings of basically trapezoidal planform, mounted above the fuselage to leave the interior unobstructed. The wings are all-metal, stressed-skin two-spar structures made of V95T aluminium alloy. They are built in five sections: the centre section (which is integral with the fuselage), inner wings (which carry the engine nacelles) and outer wings. Sweepback at quarter-chord 9°56', 1° dihedral on inner wing panels and 3° anhedral on outer wing panels, incidence 4°, no camber, aspect ratio 11.85, taper 2.8. The wings utilise TsAGI S-5-18, S-3-16 and S-3-14 airfoils. Wingspan is 38.0146 m (124 ft 8⅜ in); the wing area is 121.73 m² (1,308.9 sq ft) overall or 119.5 m² (1,284.9 sq ft) less the wing centre section.

The wing panels are joined by attachment fittings and splice plates; the wing skins incorporate numerous removable panels for access to the control runs, hydraulic and electric system components, fuel tank filler caps

and fuel meters. The wing/fuselage joint is covered by a fairing (see above).

The inner wings are equipped with three-section double-slotted flaps; there are two-section ailerons on the outer wings and twin spoilers on the inner wings (see Control system). Flap settings are 5° for take-off and 25° for landing.

Tail Unit: Conventional tail unit of all-metal stressed-skin construction. The *vertical tail* consists of a fin with a prominent fillet and a one-piece rudder (see Control system). The fin is a two-spar structure built in two sections (the upper portion is detachable); the lower portion built integrally with the aft fuselage features a large root fillet and incorporates a passage to the tail gunner's station. The fin spars are attached to aft fuselage mainframes 59 and 62. There are three rudder mounting brackets. Vertical tail area, including fin fillet, is 21.534 m² (231.5 sq ft).

The cantilever *horizontal tail* of similar two-spar construction consists of two stabilisers and one-piece elevators (see Control system); it utilises a NACA-0012M symmetrical airfoil and has no dihedral. Horizontal tail span 12.196 m (40 ft 0%₂ in), horizontal tail area 26.95 m² (289.78 sq ft). There are three elevator mounting brackets on each stabiliser.

Landing Gear: Hydraulically retractable tricycle type, with free-fall extension in emergency. The twin-wheel nose unit retracts aft; the main units with four-wheel bogies retract inwards. Early versions have 900 x 300 mm (35.43 x 11.81 in) K2-92/I non-braking wheels on the nose gear unit; on the An-12BP/An-12BK they were replaced by K2-92/IV wheels of the same size. The mainwheel bogies have 1,050 x 300 mm (41.33 x 11.81 in) KT-77M brake-equipped wheels (*koleso tormoznoye*) replaced by reinforced KT-77U

Left: The Nos. 3 and 4 AI-20M engines and AV-68I propellers of an An-12BP. Note the open cowlings on the inboard engine. The dorsal air intakes are for cooling the generators.
Right: This view shows the chin-mounted oil cooler.

wheels of the same size on the An-12BP and An-12BK.

The nosewheel well is closed by two lateral doors and a small forward door segment hinged to the oleo strut. Each main unit has a large main door attached to the fuselage keel beam and a curved door segment hinged to the oleo which closes the cutout in the main gear fairing. All doors open only when the gear is in transit; this prevents mud, water and slush from entering the wheel wells.

All landing gear struts have oleo-pneumatic shock absorbers; the steerable nose unit can turn ±35° for taxying and is equipped with a shimmy damper. Tyre pressure is 6-6.5 bars (86-93 psi) for the mainwheels and 5 bars (71 psi) for the nosewheels. Landing gear wheelbase is 9.576 m (31 ft 5 in), landing gear track 4.92 m (16 ft 1⁴⁵⁄₆₄ in) if measured by the oleos or 5.412 m (17 ft 9⁵⁄₆₄ in) if measured by the outer mainwheels.

Powerplant: The An-12 *sans suffixe* is powered by four Ivchenko AI-20A turboprop engines rated at 4,000 ehp for take-off and 2,300 ehp for cruise; these are substituted by AI-20K engines with a take-off rating of 4,250 ehp and a cruise rating of 2,700 ehp on the An-12A or identically rated AI-20Ms (alias AI-20 Srs VI) on the An-12B/BP/BK. The engine was manufactured by the Zaporozhye Engine Factory (ZMZ) from 1958 to 1963; in 1966 production switched to the Perm' Engine Production Association (PPOM).

The AI-20 is a single-shaft turboprop with an annular air intake, a 10-stage axial compressor, an annular combustion chamber, a three-stage uncooled turbine and a fixed-area jetpipe with a conical centrebody; power is transmitted via a planetary gearbox with a reduction ratio of 0.087. Engine pressure ratio 8.5 (AI-20A) or 9.2 (AI-20M); mass flow at take-off rating 20.9 kg/sec (46 lb/sec) for the

AI-20A or 20.7 kg/sec (45.6 lb/sec) for the AI-20M. Turbine temperature is 1,080° K for the AI-20A and 1,173° K for the AI-20M. Engine speed is 10,400 rpm at ground idle and 12,300 rpm at full throttle.

Specific fuel consumption (SFC) at take-off rating 0.259 kg/hp·hr (0.57 lb/hp·hr) for the AI-20A and 0.243 kg/hp·hr (0.53 lb/hp·hr) for the AI-20M; cruise SFC 0.21 kg/hp·hr (0.46 lb/hp·hr) for the AI-20A and 0.197 kg/hp·hr (0.43 lb/hp·hr) for the AI-20M.

Length overall 3,097 mm (10 ft 1¹⁵⁄₁₆ in), width 842 mm (2 ft 9⁵⁄₃₂ in), height 1,180 mm (3 ft 10²⁹⁄₆₄ in); dry weight 1,080 kg (2,380 lb) for the AI-20A and 1,040 kg (2,290 lb) for the AI-20M. The AI-20M has a 24,000-hour service life and a 7,000-hour time between overhauls.

Construction is of steel and magnesium alloy. The spool rotates in three bearings: a roller bearing in the air intake assembly (with

A cutaway AI-20M engine used as a teaching aid, showing the reduction gear, the compressor stages, the combustion chamber, the turbine and the conical centrebody in the jetpipe.

an extension shaft to the reduction gear), a ball thrust bearing and a roller bearing in the combustion chamber casing. The air intake assembly has inner and outer cones connected by six radial struts; it is de-iced by engine bleed air. The combustion chamber has ten burner cones, with igniters and pilot burners at the top. The outer casing is split horizontally for access to the burner cones.

Two accessory gearboxes (dorsal and ventral) are provided, the accessories proper being mounted on the forward casing. The pressure-feed lubrication system uses a 75/25% mixture of MK-8 oil and MS-20 or MK-22 oil. The AI-20 is started by twin STG-12TMO-1000 starter-generators using DC power from the APU or a ground power source; the engine starting sequence is 1-4-3-2. Operational ambient temperature limits are –60°/+50°C (–76°/+122°F).

The engines are mounted in individual nacelles attached to the underside of the inner wings and carried in truss-type bearers; the engine attachment lugs are mounted on the forward and centre casings. Each nacelle consists of a one-piece annular forward fairing incorporating a chin-mounted oil cooler (with a rear airflow adjustment flap), four upward-hinged cowling panels, a fixed portion and a detachable rear fairing fitting around the extension jetpipe.

The engines drive AV-68I four-blade reversible-pitch automatically feathering propellers with spinners turning clockwise when seen from the front; diameter 4.5 m (14 ft 9⁵⁄₃₂ in), weight 370 kg (815 lb). Blade pitch is adjusted hydraulically. The propeller features electric de-icer cuffs. The AV-68 is developed and manufactured by the Stoopino Machinery Design Bureau (now NPP Aerosila).

A Kazan' Machinery Design Bureau TG-16M auxiliary power unit is installed in the rear portion of the port main gear fairing for self-contained engine starting and ground power supply (except on the An-12 *sans suffixe* and An-12A/AP). Maximum continuous power is 81.6 hp and rotor speed is 24,000 rpm. The APU has an upward-opening rear-hinged dorsal intake door, a one-piece upward-hinged cowling and a lateral exhaust.

Control System: Conventional mechanical dual control system with push-pull rods, control cranks and levers. An AP-28D1 autopilot is fitted.

Roll control is provided by two-section ailerons on the outer wings assisted by two-section spoilers/lift dumpers on the inner wings. The ailerons have geared trim tabs on the inner sections; each section is hinged on two brackets.

Pitch control is provided by one-piece elevators. Each elevator is hinged on one root support and three brackets and incorporates a trim tab. The elevators are mass-balanced; the balancing may be changed on the ground by means of movable counterweights.

Directional control is provided by a one-piece rudder of single-spar construction with an auxiliary spar. The rudder is likewise mass-balanced and features a spring-loaded servo tab at the root, with a trim tab above it. On early-production aircraft the trim tab terminated some way short of the top but was later extended all the way to the top. The rudder is hinged on three brackets plus upper and lower supports.

Fuel System: On all versions the fuel system is divided into port and starboard subsystems, each of which is split into two groups, one for each engine. The two subsystems are connected by means of a cross-feed valve, enabling each engine to draw fuel from any group of tanks.

The An-12 *sans suffixe* has 22 bag-type fuel tanks (fuel cells) in the inner wing and centre section torsion box; the inner wing fuel cells are self-sealing for better protection against battle damage, while those in the wing centre section are not. On the An-12A the number of fuel cells was increased to 26 by adding four self-sealing tanks in the portions of the inner wings adjacent to the engine nacelles; the An-12B introduced two integral fuel tanks in the outer wings.

The An-12P has 24 fuel cells (22 in the wings and two in the former underfloor baggage compartments); similarly, the An-12AP features underfloor fuel cells in addition to the 26 wing tanks, while the An-12BP/An-12BK has 26 flexible tanks in the wings, two more under the floor and two outer wing integral tanks. Total fuel capacity is 15,440 litres (3,396 or 3,652 Imp gal) for the An-12A; 18,240 litres (4,012.8 Imp gal) for the An-12B; 25,290 litres (5,536.8 Imp gal) for the An-12AP and 28,090 litres (6,179.8 Imp gal) for the An-12BP/BK. (Note: Some sources give different figures – 16,600 litres (3,652 Imp gal) for the An-12A, 19,500 litres (4,290 Imp gal) for the An-12B, 26,450 litres (5,819 Imp gal) for the An-12AP and 29,350 litres (6,457 Imp gal) for the An-12BP/BK.)

The An-12 has single-point pressure refuelling. Fuel grades used are Russian T-1, TS-1 or T-2 jet fuel, Western Jet A-1, DERD.2494 and DERD.2498 (NATO F35 and F43) or equivalent.

An inert gas pressurisation system is provided on military versions to pressurise the fuel tanks and reduce the hazard of explosion if hit by enemy fire.

Hydraulics: Two separate hydraulic systems (port and starboard) powering the landing gear, wheel brakes, spoilers, cargo doors and windshield wipers. Nominal hydraulic pressure is 150 kg/cm² (2,140 psi).

Electrics: The electric system serves for engine starting and operates part of the de-icing system, fuel system components (pumps and cocks), avionics, cargo handling equipment, defensive and offensive armament and reconnaissance cameras. There are three subsystems: 28.5 V DC, 115 V/400 Hz single-phase AC and 36 V/400 Hz three-phase AC.

Main DC power is supplied by eight engine-driven STG-12TM or STG-12TMO-1000 starter-generators, four SGO-12 generators and the APU. The electric system includes two PT-500Ts three-phase AC con-

The flightdeck of an An-12. The control panel above the main instrument panel is for the Koors-MP compass system. Note the rubber-bladed cooling fans characteristic of Soviet aircraft designed in the 1950s and 1960s.

Above: The flightdeck of Bright Aviation Services An-12BP LZ-BRC shows a slightly differing instrument fit. The centre portion of the instrument panel holds engine gauges; the twin handles to the left of it are for emergency braking.

Right: The passage leading to the navigator's station; normally the navigator sits facing left on his swivelling seat.

Below: The overhead circuit breaker panel.

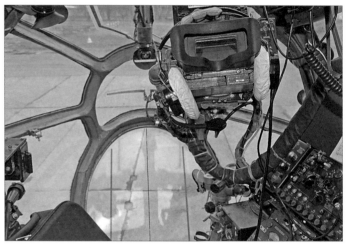

Left and top: The navigator's instrument panel and map table.

Above: The extensive nose glazing provides the navigator with a superb field of view. Note the display of the navigation/weather radar equipped with a rubber sunblind.

Below: Part of the switches is located on the starboard side of the navigator's station. Note the GPS receiver on this upgraded Russian An-12.

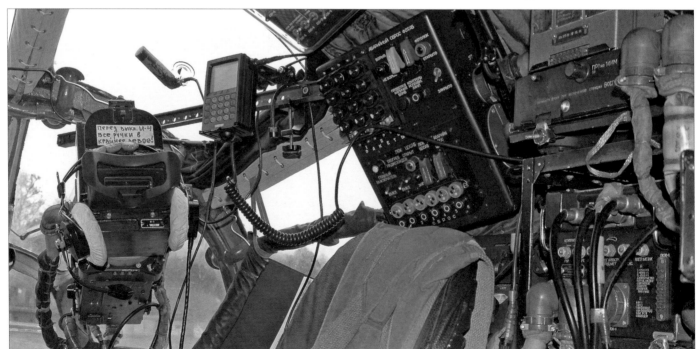

verters (*preobrazovahtel' tryokhfahznyy*), one PAG-1FP AC converter and one PO-750A backup single-phase AC converter (*preobrazovahtel' odnofahznyy*). Back-up DC power is provided by seven 12SAM-28 batteries on the An-12 *sans suffixe* (17 on subsequent versions). A ground power receptacle is provided.

Oxygen System: Liquid oxygen (LOX) bottles and a KPZh-30 LOX converter (*kislorodnyy pribor zhidkosnyy*) are installed in one of the main gear fairings to provide breathing oxygen for the crew and troops in the freight hold. Six KP-23 breathing apparatus are provided for the crew to ensure survival in the event of baling out at high altitude.

De-icing System: The wing leading edge, engine air intakes, oil coolers and flight-deck/navigator's station side windows are de-iced by engine bleed air. Electric de-icing on the fin and stabiliser leading edges, propeller blades and spinners, pitot heads, static ports, windscreens and navigator's station forward glazing panel.

Fire Suppression System: Three groups of fire extinguisher bottles charged with carbon dioxide for each engine. The first shot is triggered automatically by flame sensors in the engine nacelles; the second and third shots are fired manually. A separate fire extinguisher is provided for the APU bay.

Air Conditioning & Pressurisation System: The crew section, 'passenger cabin' immediately aft of it and, on armed versions, the tail gunner's station are pressurised by engine bleed air. Pressurisation air is cooled by a heat exchanger located in the forward portion of the port main gear fairing, with a small air intake at the front and efflux gills on the underside. A mobile air conditioning unit may be connected to the aircraft on the ground, using a connector in the nosewheel well; alternatively, hot air supply trunks may be passed directly into the freight hold through the emergency exits.

Accommodation/Cargo Handling Equipment: The standard An-12 is equipped for transporting personnel, combat vehicles (complete with crews and a supply of ordnance), engineering troops vehicles and other loads and delivering them by landing or paradropping. seats along the freight hold walls. In troopship/paradrop configuration tip-up seats along the freight hold walls and quickly removable seats along the centreline permit the carriage of up to 96 troops with full kit or 58 paratroopers. Vehicles and other loads are paradropped, using PDMM-47 sacks, PDUR-47 energy-absorbing straps and PDTZh-120 rigid containers.

Static line attachments can be configured in different ways, depending on what is to be dropped (cargo or troops). A siren and illuminated signs are provided for initiating the drop sequence.

Self-propelled wheeled and tracked vehicles are driven onto/off the aircraft, using two detachable vehicle loading ramps stowed in the freight hold when not in use. In this case an adjustable circular telescopic support is installed immediately ahead of the cargo door lip to stop the aircraft from falling over on its tail; the An-12BP (An-12BK) has two such supports side by side. Two BL-52 winches (An-12 *sans suffixe*/An-12A/P/AP), BL-1500 winches (An-12B/BP) or GL-1500DP winches (An-12BK) are installed in the freight hold for loading unpowered vehicles weighing up to 8 tons (17,640 lb). A gantry crane with a lifting capacity of 2,100 kg (4,630 lb) on most versions or 2,300 kg (5,070 lb) on the An-12BK is used for handling other heavy cargoes.

The freight hold floor features numerous threaded holes into which cargo tie-down lugs can be screwed; these are otherwise stored in special canvas bags attached to the walls and the holes are closed by screw-in plugs. The cargo is secured by nets, chains

The flight engineer's workstation on An-12BP LZ-BRC.

The cannons are belt-fed; the ammunition supply is 350 rounds per gun. The ammunition boxes are located in the unpressurised rear fuselage between frames 60-61 and accessed from the freight hold.

Ranging and aiming is by means of a Gamma-547 gun ranging radar installed at the base of the rudder above the gunner's station, a KPS-53N or KPS-53A collimator gunsight (*kollimahtornaya pritsel'naya stahntsiya*) and a VB-155 ballistic computer (*vychislitel' ballisticheskiy*; replaced by a VB-257-1 unit from An-12A c/n 9900902 onwards).

Two bomb cradles can be fitted under the forward portions of the main gear fairings at fuselage frames 24-25 for carrying 100-kg (220-lb) FotAB-100-80 flare bombs, NOSAB-100 night marker bombs or DOSAB-100 day marker bombs. Additionally, six 10-kg (22-lb) TsOSAB-10 coloured marker bombs, OMAB-5-8N maritime marker bombs or paradroppable radio beacons can be carried vertically on a DYa-SS-AT rack enclosed by clamshell doors between frames 62-64 to designate the drop zone for oncoming aircraft in a large formation.

The An-12 has an offensive capability as well, operating as an auxiliary bomber. Up to seventy 100-kg HE or incendiary bombs, or up to thirty-two 250-kg (551-lb) HE/fragmentation, incendiary, armour-piercing or cluster bombs, or up to twenty-two 500-kg (1,102-lb) HE, incendiary, HE/incendiary or cluster bombs, or up to 18 UDM-500 anti-shipping mines can be carried in the freight hold; these are propelled towards the cargo doors by a TG-12MB conveyor belt. An NKPB-7 night-capable collimator bombsight and an AIP-32 optical bombsight (an OPB-1R with an infra-red imaging adapter) are installed at the navigator's station for bomb-aiming and precision paradropping.

Avionics and Equipment: The An-12 is fully equipped for all-weather day/night operation, including automatic flight assisted by an autopilot.

Navigation and piloting equipment: Military An-12s *sans suffixe*, An-12As, An-12Bs, An-12Ps, An-12APs and An-12BPs are equipped with an RBP-2 panoramic navigation/ground mapping radar in a chin radome. Alternatively, civil examples have an ROZ-1 Lotsiya panoramic navigation/weather radar in an identical radome, while the An-12BK has an Initsiativa-4-100 panoramic navigation/ground mapping radar in a much larger radome.

The navigation suite also includes an RSBN-2S Svod (Dome) short-range radio navigation (SHORAN) system with flush antennas built into the fin, an SP-50 Materik instrument landing system and a KS-6G compass system. The aircraft is equipped with an

A circuit breaker panel for the powerplant, fuel, oil, air conditioning, firefighting and other systems installed on the rear wall of the flightdeck at the flight engineer's workstation.

and turnbuckles. If the mission requires paradropping heavy equipment on PGS-500 pallets, a hydraulically-powered TG-12 conveyor (*transportyor groozov* – cargo transporter) can be installed on the freight hold floor to propel the pallets towards the cargo hatch where they are whisked away by drogue parachutes.

The floor also incorporates fittings for installing stretcher supports allowing the aircraft to be configured for the casualty evacuation (CASEVAC) role. In this case the An-12

can carry up to 60 patients on standardised army stretchers plus a medical attendant.

Armament: Most military versions feature a PV-23U or PV-23US defensive armament system (*pushechnoye vo'oroozheniye* – cannon armament) comprising a DB-65U powered tail turret with two 23-mm (.90 calibre) Afanas'yev/Makarov AM-23 cannons, an electric remote control system and a ballistic computer. The AM-23's rate of fire is 1,250-1,350 rounds per minute.

An-12 Family Specifications

	An-12 sans suffixe	An-12A	An-12B	An-12BP
Crew	7	7	7	7
Powerplant	4 x AI-20A	4 x AI-20K	4 x AI-20M	4 x AI-20M
Power, ehp	4 x 4,000	4 x 4,250	4 x 4,250	4 x 4,250
Length overall	33.1095 m	33.1095 m	33.1095 m	33.1095 m
	(108 ft 7³³⁄₆₄ in)	(108 ft 7³³⁄₆₄ in)	(108 ft 7³³⁄₆₄ in)	(108 ft 7³³⁄₆₄ in)
Height on ground*	11.44 m	11.44 m	11.44 m	11.44 m
	(37 ft 6²⁵⁄₆₄ in)	(37 ft 6²⁵⁄₆₄ in)	(37 ft 6²⁵⁄₆₄ in)	(37 ft 6²⁵⁄₆₄ in)
Wing span	38.015 m	38.015 m	38.015 m	38.015 m
	(124 ft 8²¹⁄₃₂ in)	(124 ft 8²¹⁄₃₂ in)	(124 ft 8²¹⁄₃₂ in)	(124 ft 8²¹⁄₃₂ in)
Wing area, m² (sq ft)	121.73 (1,308.9)	121.73 (1,308.9)	121.73 (1,308.9)	121.73 (1,308.9)
Empty weight, kg (lb)	36,000 (79,365)	36,500 (80,467)	37,000 (81,570)	37,000 (81,570)
Take-off weight, kg (lb):				
normal	56,000 (123,456)	56,000 (123,456)	56,000 (123,456)	56,000 (123,456)
maximum	61,000 (134,480)	61,000 (134,480)	61,000 (134,480)	61,000 (134,480)
Maximum fuel load, kg (lb)	11,000 (24,250)	12,500 (27,557)	14,500 (31,966)	23,200 (51,146)
Paradroppable load, kg (lb):				
normal	10,000 (22,045)	10,000 (22,045)	10,000 (22,045)	10,000 (22,045)
maximum	20,000 (44,090)	20,000 (44,090)	20,000 (44,090)	20,000 (44,090)
Personnel capacity:				
troops	91	91	96	96
paratroopers	60	60	58	58
casualties	85	85	85	85
Maximum speed, km/h (mph)	n.a.	650 (403)	656 (407)	656 (407)
Service ceiling (at normal TOW), m (ft)	10,500 (34,450)	10,500 (34,450)	9,600 (31,500)	9,600 (31,500)
Range, km (miles):				
at 1,000 m (3,280 ft)	1,300 (807)	1,580 (981)	1,940 (1,205)	3,290 (2,043)
at 9,000 m (29,530 ft)	2,120 (1,316)	2,690 (1,670)	3,290 (2,043)	5,910 (3,670)

* Some documents quote the height on ground as 10.53 m (34 ft 6⁹⁄₁₆ in).

Weights of Some An-12 Versions

	An-12 sans suffixe	An-12A	An-12B	An-12P	An-12AP	An-12BP
TOW, kg (lb)	61,000 (134,480)	61,000 (134,480)	61,000 (134,480)	61,000 (134,480)	61,000 (134,480)	61,000 (134,480)
Dry weight, kg (lb)	33,500 (73,853)	35,000 (73,853)	35,000 (73,853)	35,000 (73,853)	35,000 (73,853)	35,000 (73,853)
Fuel load, kg (lb)	11,000 (24,250)	12,500 (27,557)	14,500 (31,966)	18,700 (41,225)	20,300 (44,753)	22,400 (49,382)
Payload, kg (lb)*	15,000 (33,068)	11,500 (25,352)	9,500 (20,943)	5,800 (12,786)	3,700 (8,157)	1,600 (3,527)

* Not the maximum payload!

RV-2 Kristall radio altimeter with dipole aerials under the stabiliser tips, an ARK-5 Amur automatic direction finder (replaced by the ARK-11 from the An-12A onwards) with a dorsal strake aerial on the forward or aft fuselage, an MRP-56P Dyatel marker beacon receiver, SOD-57M distance measuring equipment (**stahn**tsiya opredel**en**iya **dahl'**nosti – DME), an SPI-1M receiver/indicator unit and an NI-50BM-1 navigation display.

Military An-12s also have a long-range radio navigation (LORAN) system with an additional dorsal strake aerial offset to starboard aft of the wings and a PDSP-2S Proton-M receiver for homing in on the drop zone. Some aircraft feature an SP-1M astrosextant in the flightdeck roof escape hatch.

Communications equipment: 1-RSB-70 HF communications radio with an RPS receiver; Gheliy or Neon or RSB HF comms radio; RSIU-4V UHF command radio (replaced by the RSIU-5V from the An-12A onwards), served by dorsal and ventral blade aerials on the forward fuselage. An AVRA-45 emergency radio (*ava**reey**naya **rah**diostahntsiya*) is fitted for sending distress signals. An SPU-6 or SPU-7 intercom (*samo**lyot**noye perego**vor**noye oostroystvo*) provides communication between crew members.

IFF system: SRO-2 Khrom (Chromium; NATO *Odd Rods*) IFF transponder (*samolyotnyy rahdiolokatsionnyy otvetchik* – lit. aircraft-mounted radar responder), replaced by the SRO-2M from the An-12A onwards. The characteristic triple IFF aerials are located ahead of the flightdeck glazing and under fuselage section F4.

Electronic support measures (ESM) equipment: S-3M Sirena-2P radar homing and warning system (RHAWS) with aerials on the forward/aft fuselage sides and wingtips, replaced by the Sirena-3 from the An-12A

Range of Some An-12 Versions

	Fuel load, kg (lb)	Payload, kg (lb)*	Range, km (miles): at 500 m (1,640 ft)	at 1,000 m (3,280 ft)	at 5,000 m (16,400 ft)	at 9,000 m (29,530 ft)
An-12 *sans suffixe*	5,000 (11,020)	20,000 (44,090)	300 (186)	320 (198)	400 (248)	n.a.
An-12 *sans suffixe*	11,000 (24,250)	14,000 (30,864)	1,210 (751)	1,300 (807)	1,780 (1,105)	2,120 (1,316)
An-12A	12,500 (27,557)	11,500 (25,352)	1,470 (913)	1,580 (981)	2,160 (1,341)	2,590 (1,608)
An-12B	14,500 (31,966)	9,500 (20,943)	1,810 (1,124)	1,940 (1,205)	2,680 (1,664)	3,290 (2,043)
An-12UD	16,800 (37,037)	7,700 (16,975)	2,160 (1,341)	2,310 (1,434)	3,240 (2,012)	4,030 (2,503)
An-12P	18,700 (41,225)	5,800 (12,786)	2,460 (1,528)	2,640 (1,639)	3,710 (2,304)	4,640 (2,882)
An-12AP	20,300 (44,753)	3,700 (8,157)	2,730 (1,695)	2,920 (1,813)	4,090 (2,540)	5,200 (3,230)
An-12BP	22,400 (49,382)	1,600 (3,527)	3,700 (2,298)	3,290 (2,043)	4,630 (2,875)	5,910 (3,670)

* Not the maximum payload!

Take-off Performance

Take-off weight, kg (lb)	Take-off run, m (ft)	Take-off distance, m (ft)	Unstick speed, km/h (mph)
61,000 (134,480)	1,230 (4,035)	2,520 (8,270)	230-240 (143-149)
58,000 (127,865)	1,160 (3,805)	2,420 (7,940)	228 (141)
56,000 (123,460)	900 (2,950)	2,100 (6,890)	221 (137)
54,000 (119,050)	835 (2,740)	2,050 (6,725)	219 (136)
52,000 (114,640)	750 (2,460)	1,800 (5,900)	215 (133)
50,000 (110,230)	675 (2,215)	1,650 (5,410)	211 (131)
48,000 (105,820)	625 (2,050)	1,580 (5,180)	207 (128)
46,000 (101,410)	560 (1,840)	1,490 (4,890)	203 (126)
41,000 (403,880)	460 (1,510)	1,100 (3,610)	190 (118)

Landing Performance

Landing weight, kg (lb)	Landing run, m (ft)	Landing distance, m (ft)	Touchdown speed, km/h (mph)
38,000 (83,770)	620 (2,030)	1,370 (4,490)	186 (115)
40,000 (88,180)	650 (2,130)	1,430 (4,690)	191 (118)
43,000 (94,800)	700 (2,300)	1,500 (4,920)	198 (123)
46,000 (101,410)	760 (2,490)	1,610 (5,280)	205 (127)
48,000 (105,820)	810 (2,660)	1,740 (5,710)	208 (129)
50,000 (110,230)	860 (2,820)	1,880 (6,170)	218 (135)
51,000 (112,430)	890 (2,920)	1,990 (6,530)	220 (136)
52,000 (114,640)	960 (3,150)	2,080 (6,820)	223 (138)
53,000 (116,840)	965 (3,165)	2,200 (7,220)	225 (139)
58,000 (127,865)	1,125 (3,690)	2,260 (7,415)	230-240 (143-149)

onwards. Some Soviet/CIS aircraft have four 30-round ASO-2 dispensers mounted in tandem pairs low on the forward fuselage sides, firing 26-mm (1.02-in) PPI-26 magnesium flares or bundles of chaff to provide a passive ECM/IRCM capability. Alternatively, two streamlined fairings housing twelve 32-round chaff/flare dispenser modules can be permanently installed on the centre fuselage sides as an upgrade.

Specialised ECM versions feature additional active/passive ECM equipment mounted internally and in removable pods. For example, the An-12PP has a triple Booket active jammer system buried in the lower fuselage and ASO-24-E7R chaff dispensers in an ogival tail fairing supplanting the tail gunner's station; the An-12BK-IS is equipped with strap-on Fasol' active jammers, and the An-12BK-PPS has both of these systems.

Photo equipment: An AFA-42/20, AFA-42/75 or AFA-42/50 vertical camera for day photography or an NAFA-MK/25 camera for night photography can be installed in the aft portion of the starboard main gear fairing or in the aft fuselage between frames 57-58, shooting through a hatch offset to starboard in the rear cargo door segment.

Data recording equipment: Standard Soviet MSRP-12-96 primary flight data recorder (FDR), K-3-63 backup FDR and MS-61B cockpit voice recorder (CVR).

Exterior lighting: Port (red) and starboard (green) navigation lights at the wingtips; white tail navigation light on the tailcone (commercial version) or under the tail gunner's station. Three retractable landing/taxi lights on the flightdeck ventral entry/escape hatch and under the front ends of the main gear fairings. Red SIM-1VM rotating anti-collision beacons in teardrop-shaped Perspex fairings ahead of the cargo door lip and at the top of the fin (replaced by SMI-2KM red strobe lights on late-production An-12Bs, 'BPs and 'BKs). Three EKSR-46 electric signal flare launchers (*elektricheskaya kasseta signahl'nykh raket*) on the starboard side of the aft fuselage between frames 43-46; each launcher fires four 26-mm (1.02-in) flares (red, green, yellow and white).

Chapter 4

Beyond the Great Wall

Apart from the Soviet Union, the An-12 was manufactured in the People's Republic of China to fill a heavy transport aircraft requirement formulated by the People's Liberation Army Air Force (PLAAF). The Chinese aircraft industry had been established with Soviet assistance and had been building mostly Soviet aircraft under licence – or, after the break between Moscow and Beijing on ideological grounds in 1960, without the benefit of a licence. On the other side of the Great Wall the *Cub* – known locally as the Y8 (Yunshuji-8 – transport aircraft, Type 8) took its own line of development, and new versions still keep appearing! The Chinese variants are dealt with in this chapter.

Shaanxi Y8 Military Transport

China started gearing up for An-12 production in 1960 – that is, immediately before the rift in Sino-Soviet relations. The latter (or rather the events that caused it) came at a most unfortunate time. According to Prime Minister Chou En-Lai's plan the Chinese aircraft industry was to proceed from copying Soviet designs to developing and manufacturing indigenous aircraft. However, this plan suffered a serious setback because of Mao Tse-Tung's notorious Cultural Revolution and the equally notorious accelerated industrial development plan known as the Great Leap Forward. On reflection, this plan should be called the Great Leap Backward, as it had an immense negative effect on the national economy, including the aircraft industry. Like everywhere else, quantity was considered the prime target to the detriment of quality and the industry was completely disorganised.

Originally the aircraft factory in Xian (sometimes spelled Xi'an or Sian), the capital

Above: The first Chinese-built Shaanxi Y8s were outwardly identical to the Soviet-built An-12BPs supplied to China, an example of which (B-3152) is seen here preserved at Tianjin.

Above: A lorry with a twin-barrel anti-aircraft gun in tow is driven aboard a PLAAF Y8 serialled '31042 Red'. Note the cannons in the tail turret, a fairly rare occurrence on the Y8.

Stills from a cine film showing, left to right, Chinese paratroopers boarding a Y8, palletised cargo being loaded from a flatbed trailer and crates being paradropped.

Above: This immaculate Y8 serialled '9342 Black' is a Chinese Naval Air Arm (PLANAF) aircraft. The Y8's distinctive extended nose is clearly visible. This 'lightning bolt' cheatline was standard for military Y8s.

of Shaanxi (Shensi) Province, was chosen to build the *Cub* but the Cultural Revolution put these plans on hold, and it was not until 1972 that the work resumed. A year later, however, all the jigs and tooling for Y8 production, together with all components manufactured so far, were transferred to the brand-new Shaanxi Transport Aircraft Factory built in Hanchung, also in Shaanxi Province.

The first prototype Y8 (c/n 000801 – that is, Batch 00, 08 = Y8, 01st aircraft in the batch) assembled from Xian-manufactured and Soviet-supplied components took to the air on 25th December 1974, the first locally-manufactured example following almost exactly a year later on 29th December 1975. Destructive testing of a static test airframe was completed on 29th September 1976 and the Y8 received its type certificate in February 1980.

(Note: On the Y8 the c/n is normally stencilled on the fin and sometimes under the wing leading edge at the roots. On some aircraft the type designator is omitted; thus, Y8F-100 B-3101 has the c/n painted on as 1001, though logically it should be 100801.)

The 4,250-ehp AI-20K engine was also reverse-engineered and put into production by the Zhuzhou factory in Shanghai (now called SMPMC – South Motive Power & Machinery Co.) as the WJ-6 (Wojiang-6 – turboprop engine, Type 6), while the Chinese copy of the AV-68 propeller was designated J17-G13 (J for Jiang – propeller). Chinese efforts to improve the reliability of the engine paralleled those in the USSR, and in due course the TBO of the WJ-6 was increased from 300 to 2,000 hours. The TG-16 APU was likewise copied and put into production at Xian as the WDZ-1.

Initial production aircraft assembled from Soviet-made components and on Soviet-supplied jigs were almost identical to genuine Soviet-built An-12BPs with a tail gunner's station, having the same nose contour. Soon, however, a longer and more pointed nose borrowed from the Tupolev Tu-16 medium bomber was grafted on ahead of the flight-deck glazing, giving the Y8 a distinctive 'Pinocchio look'. It is not known whether this was meant to improve the navigator's working conditions or to provide commonality with the Tu-16, which was manufactured in Xian as the H-6 (Hongzhaji-6 – bomber, Type 6). Also, the DB-65U tail turret was replaced by a DK-7 turret mounting the same two AM-23 cannons with 500 rpg, likewise borrowed from the Tu-16; it is of basically cylindrical shape, not spherical. The aircraft incorporated the wide cargo door characteristic of the An-12BP/BK, with the associated bulges on the lower aft fuselage sides.

The Y8 was 34.02 m (111 ft 7⅜ in) long, with a 38.0-m (124 ft 8¼₆ in) wingspan, and stood 11.16 m (36 ft 7⅜ in) tall on the ground. The empty weight was 35.5 tons (78,260 lb); the aircraft had a maximum take-off weight of 61 tons (134,480 lb) and a maximum landing weight of 58 tons (127,865 lb), hauling a 20-ton (44,090 lb) payload. The maximum speed and the cruising speed were 662 km/h (411 mph) and 550 km/h (341 mph) respectively; the aircraft had a service ceiling of 10,400 m (34,120 ft) and a ferry range of 5,615 km (3,487 miles). Thus, the performance of the Y8 matched that of the An-12B, except for the slightly longer take-off run and the slightly shorter landing run.

Interestingly, the PLAAF sometimes refers to the baseline Y8 as a 'Category I platform' – that is, for various special mission versions, such as airborne warning and control systems (AWACS), electronic warfare and intelligence (EW/ELINT), and maritime patrol. These versions are dealt with later in this chapter.

Y8A Military Transport

In 1985 the Shaanxi Transport Aircraft Factory developed a specialised version of the Y8 optimised for rapid deployment of the PLAAF's Sikorsky S-70C-2 Black Hawk helicopters to remote locations (specifically to Tibet). These military utility helicopters (despite the 'civilian' designation, they were effectively UH-60L Black Hawks with the addition of a chin-mounted search radar as fitted to the MH-60G combat SAR version) were a key asset of the PLAAF.

Designated Y8A, the helicopter transporter featured a C-130 style one-piece downward-hinged cargo ramp replacing the baseline version's inward-opening doors hinged at the sides, obviating the need for

A Chinese Army S-70C-2 serialled 5676 is wheeled into an apparently unmarked Y8A helicopter carrier. The hydraulically powered integral cargo ramp and the faired-over tail gunner's station are of note.

detachable vehicle loading ramps. Since loading and unloading the choppers was basically a roll-on/roll-off operation, the overhead gantry crane was deleted to increase available 'headroom' by 120 mm (4²³⁄₃₂ in). A special hydraulically-powered support under the rear fuselage prevented the aircraft from tipping over on its tail during loading and unloading.

The Y8A prototype first flew on 3rd November 1985; deliveries to the PLAAF began in 1987. The aircraft had the DK-7 tail turret replaced by a fairing similar to that of demilitarised Soviet-built *Cubs* and the gunner's station glazing faired over (except for the side windows); the deletion of the armament was probably a weight-saving measure.

Y8B Commercial Transport

Development of a commercial version for the Civil Aviation Administration of China (CAAC) – one might call it the 'Chinese Aeroflot', since it was the nation's sole air carrier at the time – began in 1986. The unnecessary paradropping equipment and other military equipment items were deleted, giving a weight saving of 1,720 kg (3,790 lb). Surprisingly, the commercial variant retained the tail gunner's station, featuring the 'demilitarised' rear end treatment described above.

The Y8B prototype first flew in 1986. Testing was quite protracted and the type certificate was issued only in 1993, by which time CAAC was no longer extant, having been deregulated into numerous independent airlines back in 1987.

Y8C Military Transport

This upgraded version was developed with assistance from the Lockheed Company in the late 1980s. The Y8C had the same cargo ramp design as fitted to the Y8A. Unlike earlier versions, the freight hold was fully pressurised for personnel carriage, increasing the volume of the pressurised area from 31 m³ (1,095 cu ft) to 212 m³ (7,847 cu ft). Hence the rear fuselage emergency exits were enlarged, and the pressurisation/air conditioning and oxygen systems were improved. Provisions were made for carrying standard air freight containers and pallets; the navigation and communications suites were updated. Aircraft intended for the civil market were to have the tail gunner's station deleted (in reality it was simply faired over).

There were plans to re-engine the aircraft with General Electric CT7 turboprops driving Western propellers (various versions of this engine are rated at 1,600-1,870 ehp). However, the brutal suppression of student unrest in Beijing's Tiananmen Square in 1989 caused a rift in Sino-American relations and the 'westernisation' plan was shelved for the time being.

Above: Although it is operated by the Sri Lankan Air Force, CR-873 is not an export Y8D but a second-hand commercial Y8B, as indicated b y the basic livery of the Chinese carrier ACA Air Changan Airlines.

Above: '182 Black', the prototype of the fully pressurised Y8C, in AVIC demonstrator colours at Zhuhai-Sanzao during Airshow China '96.

Another Y8C in a very similar colour scheme – or possibly the same aircraft at a later date – with the temporary (Class B) Chinese civil registration B-504L.

The Y8C prototype, '182 Black', was converted from the first Shaanxi-built Y8 and the c/n was amended to 001802 (in Y8C c/ns the version designator is changed to 18 to stress the scope of the changes). The first flight took place on 17th December 1990. On 5th-10th November 1996 '182 Black' was displayed at Airshow China '96 in Zhuhai (Sanzao airport), wearing Aviation Industry Corporation (AVIC) demonstrator colours. (Note: AVIC was founded in June 1993 as the successor of the dissolved Ministry of Aerospace Industry. In so doing the Shaanxi Transport Aircraft Factory was rebranded SAC – Shaanxi Aircraft Company or SAIC – Shaanxi Aircraft Industry (Group) Company)

Five Y8Cs had been delivered by January 1994. The fully pressurised Y8C is referred to by the PLAAF as a 'Category II platform'.

Y8D and Y8D II Export Versions

A version of the military transport equipped with Litton and Collins avionics was offered for export as the Y8D. The first flight took

place in 1987 and deliveries started that same year; in 1992 the original version was superseded by the upgraded Y8D II. Only eight examples of both varieties had been delivered by early 1997 (four to the Myanmar Air Force, two to the Sri Lankan Air Force and two to the Sudanese Air Force) and no further orders were placed.

Interestingly, all known examples except Sri Lankan Air Force CP-701 (later reserialled CR-871, c/n 060801) were demilitarised. Even so, the Sri Lankan examples were used as makeshift bombers in a manner similar to the An-12BKV. Y8D CR-871, which had a fully equipped tail turret, was shot down by Tamil Tiger separatists on 18th November 1995.

Y8E Drone Launcher Aircraft

In 1986 the PLAAF placed a requirement for a drone launcher aircraft to replace its ageing Tu-4 *Bull* 'mother ships'. Ten of these long-range bombers – modified locally by substituting the Shvetsov ASh-73TK radials and V3B-A5 propellers with locally made WJ-6

Above: The prototype of the Y8E drone launcher aircraft was converted from a standard long-nosed Y8, '4139 Red'. Here it is seen with a WZ-5 (Chang Hong-1) drone under the starboard wing.

Above left: Another view of the drone and of the lattice-like rack to which it is attached.
Above right: Y8E '4139 Red' climbs away, toting two WZ-5 drones.

Above: Still in zinc chromate primer finish, the Y8F-100 prototype ('182 Black') is seen here at Zhuhai-Sanzao.

Y8F-100 B-3103 is one of several operated by China Postal Airlines in this livery.

turboprops and J17-G13 propellers – had been adapted to carry and launch two Chang Hong-1 (Long Rainbow-1) jet-propelled target drones. The Chang Hong-1, also known as WZ-5 (Wuzhen – unmanned aerial vehicle), was derived from the Ryan AQM-34N Firebee reconnaissance drone which had been reverse-engineered by the Beijing University of Aeronautics and Astronautics (BUAA), using the examples shot down over China during the Vietnam War. By the end of the 1980s the 'Turbo *Bulls*' had run out of service life and a replacement was urgently required.

The design work began in 1988. Designated Y8E, the new version of the *Cub* was the Chinese counterpart of the Lockheed DC-130E, except that it had no underwing tanks and no guidance antenna in an under-nose radome. Two lattice-like racks were fitted between the inner and outer engines for carrying the drones. The pylons were similar to those of the Tu-4 drone launchers but rather longer because of the Y8's high-wing layout.

The Y8E prototype was converted in March 1990 from a standard PLAAF Y8 serialled '4139 Red'. Interestingly, the tail turret had been faired over prior to the conversion. The first test launch of a Chang Hong-1 drone was carried out successfully in October 1990. The aircraft entered service with the PLAAF at the end of the year.

There have been suggestions that the standard navigation radar might be replaced with a drone guidance antenna on the Y8E.

Y8F Livestock Carrier

A rather unusual version of the *Cub* created in China was the Y8F dedicated livestock carrier aircraft developed in early 1990. The freight hold featured three tiers of cages on either side accommodating up to 350 sheep or goats. The Y8F's raison d'être was the need to carry livestock to and from pastures in remote areas of the country, which were inaccessible (or required too much time to reach) by other kinds of transport. The first flight took place on 19th November 1988 (some sources say early 1990) and Chinese certification was achieved in 1994.

Y8F-100 Commercial Transport

A further upgraded 'glass-nosed' commercial version was brought out as the Y8F-100. The prototype was converted from the Y8C prototype, '182'. China Postal Airlines was the launch customer for this version, taking delivery of at least five Y8F-100s – B-3101 (c/n 1001), B-3102 (c/n 1002), B-3103 (c/n 1005), B-3109 (c/n 1303) and B-3110. The aircraft listed here were delivered as 'freighters with a 16-ton (35,270-lb) payload'; hence they may be specialised mailplanes. Like the basic Y8, the aircraft had an unpressurised freight hold.

Y8F200 (Y8F-201) Commercial Transport

A further version similar to the Y8F-100 but featuring a fully pressurised freight hold was designated Y8F-200. The demilitarised prototype bearing no civil registration wore Y8F-201 nose titles. Another demonstrator was registered B-576L.

Y8F-300 Commercial Transport

This is an upgraded civil version equipped with Western avionics, including a conventionally mounted Rockwell Collins TWR-850 weather radar in a new, shorter but more streamlined 'solid' nose, a Universal Avionics UNS-1K flight management system, Rockwell Collins VHF-42B and HF-9000 communications radios and so on, plus an advanced cargo handling system. The 'nose job' reduced the aircraft's overall length to 32.93 m (108 ft 0½ in). The flightdeck is reconfigured for a crew of three (two pilots and a flight engineer) but the freight hold is still unpressurised. The tail gunner's station is deleted and replaced by a fairing with a sloping trailing edge. The new version was announced by the China Aircraft Technology & Industry Corporation (CATIC) at Airshow China 2000, which took place at Zhuhai-Sanzao on 6th-12th November 2000.

Y8F-400 Commercial Transport

The Y8F-400 was outwardly identical to the Y8F-300 but featured a pressurised freight hold. A desktop model displayed at Airshow China 2000 where the aircraft was announced created the impression of a new and much fatter fuselage, but such models have a way of being inaccurate. Registered B-575L, the prototype flew in August 2001 – still with WJ-6 engines, although plans were in hand to re-engine it with Pratt & Whitney Canada PW150A turboprops driving six-bladed propellers. China Postal Airlines was reportedly the launch customer for this version, placing an order for a single example with the AVIC II concern for delivery in 2002.

(Note: AVIC was reorganised in 1998, with two competing but co-operating industrial groups – AVIC I and AVIC II – being formed with effect from July 1999; the Shaanxi aircraft factory belonged to the latter group.)

Y8F-600 Transport/Special Mission Platform

Ten years after the Tiananmen massacre the sanctions imposed against China had been lifted, and the idea of 'westernising' the *Cub* was dusted off. In 1999 CATIC began development of a much-modernised version designated Y8F-600 in cooperation with the Antonov ASTC acting as a risk-sharing partner. Pratt & Whitney Canada joined the programme in 2000; that year the project was

Above: B-576L, the smartly painted Y8F-200 demonstrator. This aircraft was later converted into the first prototype of the KJ-200 'Balance Beam' AWACS.

Above: B-575L, the prototype of the 'radar-nosed' Y8F-400, wore a rather gaudy colour scheme. Apart from the shorter and more rounded 'solid' nose, it was outwardly identical to the Y8F-200.

Above: This desktop model of the Y8F-600 displayed at one of the Zhuhai airshows features no other differences from the Y8F-400 than the powerplant and the forward position of the entry door; the nose and the rear fuselage with a faired-over tail gunner's station have remained unchanged.

In contrast, the actual Y8F-600 prototype (seen here during the rollout) has a redesigned nose with twin radomes (front and chin-mounted), revised flightdeck glazing and a simple tailcone.

Above: This Y8 in CAAC livery registered 980 is the obscure Y8H survey aircraft identifiable by the flat-bottomed bulge aft of the radome – presumably housing some kind of sensor array.

unveiled at Airshow China 2000 together with the two versions described above.

The Y8F-600 had a fully pressurised fuselage featuring a recontoured flightdeck section with curved windshield panels; the 'solid' nose was tipped with a thimble radome, while a second radome was mounted in the chin position, as on the standard Y8. The two-man flightdeck was equipped with an electronic flight instrumentation system (EFIS). The crew entry door was located in line with the nose gear unit instead of amidships and the tailcone was rather smaller and neater. The Y8F-600 became the first version to feature the intended Western powerplant – 5,070-ehp PW150B turboprops driving Dowty R-408 six-bladed low-noise propellers of 4.115 m (13 ft 6 in) diameter with scimitar-shaped composite blades. The maximum take-off weight was increased to 65 tons (143,300 lb).

Construction of two prototypes commenced in 2000, with the intention of flying the first aircraft in late 2001. However, the pro-

gramme ran into development problems, and the maiden flight did not take place until 14th January 2005. Apart from the basic transport role, the Y8F-600 was regarded by the PLAAF as a potential platform for special mission aircraft known as the 'Category III platform'.

Y8F-800 Commercial Transport (project)

A further commercial version designated Y8F-800 was announced in 2000. This is to be a radically redesigned aircraft having a stretched fuselage, new wings and a redesigned landing gear. The aircraft is to be capable of transporting a 30-ton (66,140-lb) payload over a range of 7,780 km (4,833 miles).

Y8G ELINT Aircraft (project – first use of designation)

Turboprop conversions of Tu-4s were used for various purposes by the Chinese; a few were operated by the People's Liberation

Army Naval Air Force (PLANAF) until the early 1990s as maritime ELINT aircraft. As the need to replace the ageing *Bulls* grew increasingly acute, the Chinese aircraft industry started work on an ELINT version of the *Cub* provisionally designated Y8G. The aircraft was to feature a powerful radar and a mix of Western and indigenous mission avionics. GEC Marconi assisted with the development of the Y8G but pulled out after Tiananmen and the project was shelved before a prototype could be built. (That was not the end of it, though – see next entry.)

Y8G IFR Tanker (project – second use of designation)

According to some sources, it was decided to convert the Y8G airframe, which never received its mission avionics and was sitting idle, into an in-flight refuelling (IFR) tanker prototype with the same designation. Other sources, though, claim the Y8G ELINT airframe never existed and the designation was merely reallocated after the demise of the former programme.

Work on a tanker version had been under way in China since the mid-1980s. The first evidence came in 1986 when a model of a tanker-configured Y8 was displayed at an aviation trade fair in Beijing. The British company Flight Refuelling Ltd. must have rendered assistance with the project because the aircraft was equipped with two compact refuelling pods under the outer wings similar to the FR Mk 32 hose drum units (HDUs) fitted to the Vickers VC.10 C.1K tanker/transport. The Y8 tanker was to work primarily with Nanchang Q-5 (A-5) *Fantan* fighter-bombers retrofitted with fixed IFR probes ahead of the cockpit, as was illustrated by the accompanying models of two such aircraft.

Once again, however, the project was shelved. As a result, the PLAAF and the People's Liberation Army Naval Air Force (PLANAF) have to rely on HU-6 (or H-6U) and H-6DU tanker versions of the H-6 bomber for IFR capability for their tactical aircraft.

Y8H Survey Aircraft

The designation Y8H has been reported for an obscure survey version for which no official details are yet known. The aircraft in question may be a 'glass-nosed' example wearing full CAAC colours but sporting the military-style serial '980 Black'; outwardly it differed from the standard Y8 in having a flat-bottomed bulge between the radome and the nose-wheel well.

Y8 Geophysical Survey Aircraft

Another survey version of the Y8 was converted from a Y8 registered B-4071 (c/n unknown), with a strut-braced MAD boom protruding aft from the tail gunner's station

Above and below: Y8 B-4071 operated by OK Air is a geophysical survey aircraft with an MAD boom.

Above and below: '9301 Black', one of the two known examples of the Y8J naval AWACS aircraft with a Racal Skymaster radar in a grossly bulged nose radome.

instead of the tail turret. This aircraft wore the smart livery of the Chinese airline OKAir.

Y8J AWACS Aircraft

In the early 1990s China purchased six to eight sets of the Skymaster I-band pulse Doppler search radar developed by the British company Racal (now called Thales) for about US$66 million – allegedly for use in coastal anti-smuggling missions; this deal was revealed in August 1996. The true purpose came to light in May 2000 when the Air Forces Monthly magazine reported that an AEW version of the Y8 had been developed for the PLANAF. No separate designation was stated at the time, but the aircraft is now known to be designated Y8J.

The aircraft has a rather bizarre appearance, featuring a bulbous drooped nose instead of the usual glazed navigator's station. The nose incorporates a large radome for the Skymaster radar; the shape of the nose is optimised to give the radar full 360° coverage. A similar 'droopsnoot' radome had been used earlier on the Britten-Norman Searchmaster – an experimental airborne early warning (AEW) version of the Britten-Norman BN-2T Defender twin-turboprop utility aircraft equipped with a Racal Searchwater radar from which the Skymaster is derived. The cargo door/ramp is eliminated and the former cargo cabin houses workstations for the mission crew, as well as an 8-kW generator powering the mission equipment. The tail gunner's station glazing is faired over. Available sources say the Y8J is based on the fully pressurised Y8C, which makes sense, as the cargo cabin has to house the mission operator workstations; however, there is photoproof that the machine lacks the Y8C's one-piece cargo ramp, retaining the old-style laterally hinged doors.

As compared to the Searchwater model (which is also fitted to the Royal Navy's BAe Nimrod MR.2 maritime patrol aircraft and the

Westland Sea King AEW.2 helicopter), the Skymaster has enhanced capabilities against surface targets. With a detection range of 85 km (52.79 miles) in look-down mode and 110 km (68.32 miles) in look-up mode, the radar can be used against aircraft and ships alike and is capable of detecting objects as small as a submarine periscope within its range. The radar system has two crew workstations, one for target detection/identification (IFF) and one for interceptor guidance. The workstations are equipped with digital data processing, 40-mm (1.57-in) colour displays and touch-screen controls. The system utilises Thorn EMI 32-bit microprocessors and a distributed processing structure. The radar, inertial navigation system (INS) and other avionics communicate via a MIL-STD-1553B databus.

Apart from vectoring offensive and defensive aircraft towards their targets, the Y8J can provide over-the-horizon (OTH) targeting for the PLA Navy's surface ships, including Luda and Luhu class destroyers. Reports on the system's detection range vary, but the provisional figure of more than 200 km (124 miles) at high altitude cited by AFM renders the Y8J suitable for monitoring the Strait of Taiwan.

The Y8J has a length of 34.02 m (111 ft 7⅜ in) and stands 11.6 m (38 ft 0⁴⁵⁄₆₄ in) tall when parked. Empty weight is 35,488 kg (78,236 lb), the normal and maximum take-off weight

being 54,000 kg (119,050 lb) and 61,000 kg (134,480 lb) respectively. The internal fuel load of 22,910 kg (50,510 lb) gives the aircraft an endurance of 10.5 hours and a ferry range of 5,620 km (3,490 miles); there is no provision for external fuel tanks. The cruising speed is 550 km/h (341 mph) and the maximum speed 662 km/h (411 mph); the service ceiling is 10,400 m (34,120 ft) and maximum rate of climb at sea level 10 m/sec (1,970 ft/min). The take-off run is 1,270 m (4,170 ft) and the landing run 1,050 m (3,440 ft).

At least two Y8Js serialled '9281 Black' and '9301 Black' are in service with the PLANAF, operating from Dachang naval air base near Shanghai. The first evidence of their operational use came in 2001 when they participated in naval exercises. They were also reported to have been chasing US Navy aircraft carrier combat groups in the East China Sea.

Y8MPA Maritime Patrol/ASW Aircraft (Y8X – second use of designation)

In October 1983 the Shaanxi Aircraft Co. was tasked with developing a long-range multi-mission version of the Y-8 transport for the PLANAF. The aircraft was to perform maritime patrol, reconnaissance, anti-submarine warfare (ASW) and search and rescue (SAR) missions. The government directive set the first delivery date for 1984.

Top and above: Y8MPA (Y8X) '9271 Red' flies over the sea, showing off the grey/blue/white colour scheme worn by most examples. Note the open camera port aft of the main gear fairing in the top photo.

Above: A fine landing study of a Y8MPA (serialled '9291 Red'?), showing to advantage the deeper chin radome, the dished tail fairing and the mission equipment mounted on the rear cargo door segment.

This Y8MPA serialled '9261 Black' sports an overall gloss grey colour scheme.

SAC quickly drafted a design proposal which was approved by the customer in November 1983. The design effort was completed in less than a year, involving more than 20 tests. Initially the aircraft bore the Western-style designation Y8MPA (Maritime Patrol Aircraft). The all-Western mission equipment included a Litton Canada AN/APS-504(V)3 search radar in a deeper, flat-bottomed chin radome to give 360° coverage (which gave the Y8MPA a certain degree of similarity to the An-12BK), optical and infrared cameras, sonobuoys and a mission computer for processing data generated by the buoys. The rear cargo door was locked closed, incorporating a large mission equipment window for sonobuoys and cameras. The tail turret was removed and the tail gunner's station reconfigured as the sonar operator's workstation. The equipment also included defensive ECM and infrared countermeasures kits, a dual Litton LTN-72 INS and a Litton LTN-211 Omega navigation aid. Apart from the larger radome, the Y8MPA was identifiable by the sensor array on the rear segment of the cargo door and the lack of the port rear emergency exit. The last-but-one window on each side was eliminated and replaced by an oblique camera port, which was closed by a door when not in use.

The Y8MPA prototype was reportedly quasi-civil and registered B-4101; a photo of the aircraft, however, shows full PLANAF markings and the serial appears to be '9211 Red'. The first Y8MPA was delivered to the PLANAF on schedule in late 1984, and the aircraft achieved type certification in 1985.

Between March and June 1986 a Y8MPA flew five reconnaissance missions to the Xisha (Paracel), Zhongsha, and Nansha (Spratly) Islands in the South China Sea, covering a total distance of 17,000 km (10,560 miles). The flights furnished a large amount of photo intelligence on these islands, which were regarded as highly valuable to support of the PLA's operation in the region in a war scenario. Since the late 1990s the Y-8MPAs have been frequently spotted operating in the East China Sea region, shadowing foreign warships and flying near foreign airspace. Some of these aircraft are believed to be fitted with ELINT/signals intelligence (SIGINT) equipment. In 1993 the Y8MPA was reportedly redesignated Y8X.

KJ-200 (Y8 'Balance Beam') AWACS Aircraft

In the late 1990s China started work on a tactical AWACS aircraft codenamed 'Project No.5'. The Shaanxi Y8 transport was selected as the platform. The aircraft was fitted with a linear-shape electronically steered phased-array radar similar to the Swedish Ericsson PS-890 Erieye fitted to the SAAB 340AEW (alias S 100B Argus) and the Embraer EMB 145AEW&C (R-99A). As on these aircraft, the radar antenna arrays were housed in a slab-sided pod mounted above the centre fuselage by struts; this design is particularly suitable for smaller aircraft with limited space and payload. The radar is capable of 360° detection and tracking of air (and possibly surface) targets over the horizon. Unlike the S 100B and the R-99A, the inverted-V supporting struts were very tall and the aft-mounted drag strut was attached to the rear pair. Because of the pod's distinctive appearance the AWACS-configured Y8 was nicknamed 'Balance Beam' by military specialists.

The first prototype (or rather technology demonstrator) was converted from the Y8F-200 demonstrator (B-576L), making its first flight on 8th November 2001; it retained the blue/white AVIC demonstrator colours and. The second prototype representing the definitive configuration was based on the much-improved Y8F-600 (also known as the 'Category III platform'); in addition to the radar array, the machine had a dielectric tailcone, dielectric wingtip pods of cylindrical shape and a small fin-tip pod with a dielectric rear portion (probably associated with ECM).

The still unpainted aircraft bearing the test serial 'T0673 Red' made its maiden flight on 14th January 2005. This aircraft received the service designation KJ-200. Flight tests of the KJ-200 began at the China Flight Test Establishment (CFTE) in Yanliang, Shaanxi Province. However, the programme suffered a major setback on 4th June 2006 when one of the prototypes crashed, killing all on board.

Y8 AWACS Aircraft with Rotodome

In parallel with the KJ-200 (Y8 'Balance Beam'), the Chinese aircraft industry developed and built a further AWACS version of the *Cub* for which no separate designation is yet known. The aircraft has a conventional 'saucer' rotodome mounted aft of the wings on twin inward-canted pylons; the greater part of the rotodome is dielectric.

The existence of the 'conventional' AWACS derivative became known in 2005. An early desktop model of reasonably high quality suggested that the aircraft was based on one of the 'glass-nosed' versions – presumably the fully pressurised Y8C or Y8F-200. However, the actual prototype wearing a civilian-style blue/white colour scheme and the test serial 'T0518 Red' is based on the radar-nosed Y8F-400 ('Category II Platform'). Contrary to some sources, the base aircraft is not the Y8F-600 – the WJ-6A engines with four-bladed propellers, the shape of the nose and tailcone and the amidships position of the entry door prove otherwise. Directional stability is augmented by hexagonal endplate fins on the horizontal tail similar to those of the

Above: Y8F-200 B-576L after conversion as the first prototype KJ-200 'Balance Beam' AWACS. The odd-looking structure atop the fuselage is the strut-mounted antenna pod under wraps.

Top and above: The second prototype KJ-200 was based on the Y8F-600. It is seen here parked at Yanliang AB and completing a test flight; the Y8F-600's new rear fuselage and vertical tail are noteworthy.

A poor but interesting image of the second prototype ('T0673 Red') painted in a two-tone grey camouflage.

Above, left and right: Two views of the AWACS with a conventional rotodome based on the Y8F-400 ('T0518 Red'). Note the ventral dielectric fairing and the lateral dielectric panels ahead of the wings. Interestingly, the aircraft has had PLAAF insignia added in the right-hand photo.

Another view of 'T0518 Red', showing to advantage the (apparently dielectric) tailcone replacing the usual tail gunner's station, the An-10 style rear fuselage lacking a cargo door and the soot-stained An-10 style endplate fins. Note the sentry with rifle in hand standing beside the aircraft.

Above: The airborne command post version of the Y8 has the same rear fuselage/tailcone design as the above AWACS, plus a teardrop-shaped dielectric blister aft of the wings over SATCOM gear. Note also the additional blade aerials on the forward fuselage.

Left: A rather crude model of a proposed AWACS version with large nose and tail radomes.
Right: Still in primer finish, the prototype of the battlefield surveillance version comes in to land after a test flight.

pre-upgrade An-10/An-10A. The cargo ramp is eliminated, further adding similarity with the An-10. The aircraft has a ventral dielectric 'bathtub' fairing aft of the nose gear and four blade aerials mounted in tandem on top of the forward fuselage.

Y8 AWACS Aircraft with Nose/Tail Arrays (project)

There is evidence that yet another AWACS version was under development. It featured huge radomes in the nose and aft of the tail unit in a manner similar to the Royal Air Force's BAe AEW Nimrod. This is hardly a matter of chance, as the radar was almost certainly the same. The project was apparently scrapped in favour of more promising designs.

Y8 Airborne Command Post

An airborne command post (ABCP) version based on the Y8F-200 was undergoing flight test at the CFTE in 2006. The unpainted and unserialled aircraft has the cargo ramp faired over and a tail fairing (apparently dielectric) replacing the tail gunner's station. A fairly large teardrop-shaped dielectric blister (apparently associated with satellite communications) is located dorsally aft of the wing trailing edge, and a series of blade aerials is mounted dorsally and ventrally on the forward fuselage. A small circular outlet – possibly the exhaust of a turbine-powered generator catering for the mission equipment – is visible on the starboard side of the rear fuselage. No further details regarding the status of this aircraft are available at this stage.

Y8 Battlefield Surveillance Aircraft

The Y8F-400 (not Y8F-600 as sometimes reported) has served as the basis for a mysterious special mission aircraft reported to be a battlefield surveillance aircraft similar in function to the USAF's Boeing E-8 JSTARS (Joint Surveillance/Target Attack Radar System).

The aircraft has two huge dielectric cheek fairings looking like sections of vertically positioned cylinders on the forward fuselage sides just ahead of the wings (these fairings blend into the main gear actuator fairings). These fairings may accommodate a side-looking airborne radar (SLAR) for ground surveillance. Smaller fairings also housing electronic equipment are located laterally ahead of the cheek fairings, on the centreline between the cheek fairings and at the top of the fin. The aircraft has a rear fuselage design identical to that of the Y8 ABCP (that is, minus cargo ramp but featuring a turbo generator outlet to starboard). Large blade aerials are located dorsally aft of the wings and ventrally just aft of the nose radome.

The aircraft wears a grey camouflage scheme with lighter grey undersurfaces and

Top and above: These views of the battlefield surveillance version show the huge SLAR cheek fairings, the centreline radome and the fintop fairing housing more antennas.

This Y8 with a ventral canoe fairing and a plethora of blade aerials on the rear fuselage underside is apparently an ELINT aircraft.

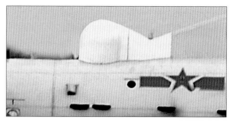

Left and lower left: '9351 Black', one of the PLANAF's bizarre Y8DZ electronic warfare aircraft, shows off its huge dorsal and ventral radomes and assorted aerials on the fuselage and wings.

Above: The dorsal antenna fairing of the Y8DZ blends into the fin fillet. Note the open air intake scoop and exhaust of the additional turbo generator powering the mission equipment.

Left: One of the three known configurations of the CFTE's Y8CB radar testbed. A technician has opened an access cover in the adapter carrying the experimental radar and is checking the radar set.

Above and below: Another configuration of the same aircraft with a hemispherical nose radome. The placement of the serial aft of the flightdeck is unusual.

PLAAF insignia; the serial may be '9104 Red'. Its exact status is unknown.

Y8DZ Electronic Warfare Version

One of the most bizarre versions of the *Cub* developed in China is an electronic warfare (EW) variant whose exact function remains unknown; it may be electronic intelligence (ELINT) or offensive electronic countermeasures (ECM), or both.

The most obvious external identification features of the Y8DZ are the huge chin radome (surpassing in size the radome of the An-12BK) and a dielectric fairing of similar shape and size located dorsally immediately ahead of the fin fillet – actually blending into it. A small thimble fairing housing antennas is mounted at the forward extremity of the navigator's station glazing frame. A huge trapezoidal aerial is located dorsally aft of the flightdeck, while the forward/centre fuselage underside mounts, consecutively, an oval fairing with two cylindrical protuberances; a small trapezoidal aerial; a flat-bottomed elliptical fairing carrying five rod aerials, and a large blade aerial. More aerials are mounted on the rear fuselage sides, on the wing leading edge near the wingtips and under the tail gunner's station.

There have been rumours that some of the mission equipment may come from the US Navy Lockheed EP-3 Orion ELINT aircraft that made an emergency landing on Hainan Island in April 2001 after colliding with a Chinese fighter. However, the equipment could just as easily be totally indigenous.

The existence of the Y8DZ came to light in the summer of 2004. At least two grey-painted examples serialled '9351 Black' and '9361 Black' are operational with the PLANAF.

Y8 ELINT Version

A different ELINT version of the Y8 has a rather more conventional appearance; with nothing more than a ventral canoe fairing halfway between the nose gear unit and the main gear fairings, plus an extensive farm of blade aerials on the underside of the cargo doors. The serial appears to be '31011 Red'.

Y8CB Avionics Testbed

At least one Y8 wearing an airline-style blue/white livery and the serial '079 Black' is operated by CFTE as an avionics testbed used in various programmes. Some sources refer to this aircraft as the Y8CB. Among other things, it has played an important role in the development of fire control radar systems for China's new-generation combat aircraft, including the Chengdu J-10 tactical fighter, the Shenyang J-11 multi-role fighter (licence-built Sukhoi Su-27SK) and the Xian JH-7 strike aircraft (aka FBC-1 Flying Leopard). The radar is installed on a special adapter supplanting the nose glazing; the standard chin radome is retained. Other non-standard features are a test equipment heat exchanger mounted low on the starboard side of the nose and a wide flat-bottomed fairing located on the centreline just ahead of the cargo door. The aircraft carries 'CFTE' and 'RETA' titles (the meaning of the latter acronym is unknown).

Three configurations are known. In one of them '079 Black' had a downward-angled ogival radome painted dark grey (apparently the radar in question was intended for the JH-7). The second version had a simple conical radome painted black. A third variant had a hemispherical nose radome; the application of this radar is unknown. This 'thimble-nosed' version figured in an advertising leaflet of AVIC I, one of whose divisions was probably responsible for the radar.

Y8 Gunship (project)

An artist's impression exists showing a projected 'gunship' version of the Y8C clearly inspired by the USAF's Lockheed AC-130H Spectre and AC-130U Spooky. Two ports for heavy cannons are provided immediately aft of the port main gear fairing; additionally, three heavy machine-guns (HMGs) fire through the entry door and two port side windows in the passenger compartment aft of the flightdeck. The weapons are aimed by means of a compact fire control radar immediately ahead of the entry door (in similar manner to the AC-130) and a gyrostabilised optoelectronic surveillance/sighting system in a 'ball turret' under the nose. The optoelectronic system turret takes up the position normally occupied by the chin radome, ousting the latter to a position low on the port side of the nose. A movable floodlight is installed in a fairing on the port wing leading edge to dazzle the enemy and assist the aircraft's gunners. Additionally, fairings associated with ECM/ESM are located on the port side of the rear fuselage and at the top of the fin.

Above: Another view of the Y8CB in its 'dog nose' configuration. All four engines are being worked on.

Above: Two views of the Y8CB as used for testing the radar intended for the Chengdu J-10 fighter. Note the differing placement of the test equipment heat exchanger.

An artist's impression of a 'gunship' version based on the Y8C (note the cargo ramp).

Y9 Military Transport
(project; Y8X – first use of designation)

In 2001 the Shaanxi division of AVIC II began development of a new-generation medium transport aircraft to meet a PLAAF requirement for a capable and advanced successor to the ageing Y-8. The aim of the project was to create a multi-purpose transport aircraft that approaches or in some aspects exceeds the performance of the Lockheed Martin C-130J Super Hercules. Originally known as the Y8X, the project was unveiled under this tentative designation at Airshow China 2002 in Zhuhai. Although this is, strictly speaking, a separate design (at the September 2005 International Aviation Expo in Beijing, SAIC re-unveiled the aircraft as the Y9 to underscore the scope of the redesign), it is nevertheless mentioned here because it is still a descendant of the An-12.

The Y9 features a much-modified fuselage, all-new wings and tail surfaces and a modified landing gear. The fuselage is similar to that of the Y8F-600 as regards the shape of the nose and the forward location of the entry door, but the shape of the rear fuselage is different. The wings have constant anhedral from the roots, lacking the kink at the inner/outer wing joints characteristic of the An-12 (Y8). The tail surfaces have slight sweepback and the vertical tail lacks the large dorsal fin of the preceding versions.

The original intention was to use Western turboprops in the 6,500-ehp class. Now, however, the Y9 is to have improved WJ-6C turboprops driving indigenous JL-4 six-blade propellers made of composite materials. The internal fuel load is 23 tons (50,700 lb).

The aircraft will have a four-man 'glass cockpit' and a more capacious cargo cabin equipped with efficient cargo handling devices for fast loading/unloading. The cargo cabin is 16.2 m (53 ft 1⁵⁄₆₄ in) long, 3.2 m (10 ft 5⁶³⁄₆₄ in) wide and 2.35 m (7 ft 8³³⁄₆₄ in) high. The maximum payload is 20 tons (44,090 lb); payload options include wheeled or tracked vehicles, helicopters, and cargo containers or pallets. The latter comprise thirteen 1-metre (3 ft 3 in) size pallets, or three 4-metre (13 ft 1½ in) size pallets, or one 6-metre (19 ft 8 in) pallet. The Y9 will be able to paradrop single loads grossing at up to 8.2 tons (18,080 lb), or multiple loads totalling up to 13.2 tons (29,100 lb), or 98 paratroopers with full kit. In medevac configuration it will be able to carry 72 stretcher cases or 98 walking wounded, plus three medical attendants.

With a maximum take-off weight of 65 tons (143,300 lb), the aircraft is to have a maximum speed of 650 km/h (403 mph) and a cruising speed of 550 km/h (341 mph); the service ceiling is 10,100 m (33,140 ft) and the cruise altitude 8,000 m (26,250 ft). The required runway length is 1,350 m (4,430 ft).

Top left: An artist's impression, from a Shaanxi ad, of what was then the Y8X. Note the swept fin.
Above left: A rather provisional model of the Y8X at Airshow China 2002.
Left: This model represents the current configuration of the Y9 (formerly Y8X).
Below: Artist's impressions of the Y9 in cruise flight (left) and delivering cargo in low-level flight.

Chapter 5

At War and At Work

In 1959 the An-12 achieved initial operational capability with the Soviet Air Force. Two airlift regiments based at Krechevitsy AB near Novgorod and Seschcha AB near Bryansk (both part of the 12th *Mginskaya* GvVTAD headquartered in Tula) were the first to re-equip; they were tasked with holding service trials and developing operational tactics. The evaluation included flights of large groups of An-12s to areas with widely different climates, landings on semi-prepared tactical airstrips and training in paradropping techniques. About the same time the 3rd GvVTAD headquartered in Vitebsk (Belorussian Defence District) began converting to the An-12, followed by other VTA formations and units.

Soviet Air Force units equipped with the type included the 3rd GvVTAD comprising the 339th VTAP in Vitebsk, 103rd *Krasnosel'skiy* GvVTAP in Smolensk, 196th *Minskiy* GvVTAP at Migalovo AB near the city of Kalinin (May 1966) and 334th *Berlinskiy* VTAP at Kresty AB near Pskov (May 1963); 6th *Zaporozhskaya*

GvVTAD headquartered in Krivoy Rog (1960) including the 37th VTAP, 338th VTAP and 363rd *Cherkasskiy* VTAP; 12th GvVTAD/566th *Solnechnogorskiy* GvVTAP in Rakveri, Lithuanian SSR (1959-1970); 14th *Zaporozhskaya* GvVTAD headquartered in Zavitinsk, Amur Region, comprising the 192nd VTAP in Ukurey and the 930th VTAP (1967); 11th *Taganrogskaya* GvVTAD (Baltic DD) comprising the 128th VTAP in Panevezhis, Lithuania (later moved to Orenburg, Russia) and the 600th VTAP in Kedainiai, Lithuania (1964; later moved to Shadrinsk, Russia), 978th VTAP at Klin-5 AB in Klin near Moscow, 223rd OSAP at Chkalovskaya AB near Moscow, and 517th VTAP of the 610th TsBP i PLS (*Tsentr boyevoy podgotovki i pereoochivanita lyotnovo sostahva* – combat & conversion training centre) at Ivanovo Severnyy AB.

Despite the inevitable teething troubles and the accidents associated therewith, VTA crews quickly took a liking to the An-12 and came to trust the machine. The *Cub* demon-

strated rugged dependability even in the harshest of environments and the ability to make do with an absolute minimum of maintenance. (Everything has a limit, though, and 'an absolute minimum of maintenance' taken too literally (= neglect) is bound to end in trouble sooner or later!)

Gradually, as VTA crews mastered the type, Soviet Air Force An-12s were used on an increasingly wide scale for tackling both military and civil transport tasks. (Using the VTA fleet in the interests of the national economy was, and still is, common practice.) For instance, in the late 1960s a task force of 35 An-12s commanded by M. M. Gamaris flew to the Polar regions of the Soviet Union for several months, redeploying troops. Notable missions of a more peaceful nature included a case when mobile compressor units weighing 8 tons (17,640 lb) apiece had to be urgently delivered from Krasnodar in the south to Noril'sk in the north. As a result of such operations the An-12's payload limit was

These red-coded An-12BPs wearing a non-standard colour scheme with a Dayglo orange cheatline edged in red and white demonstrated a massive landing assault during the grand airshow at Moscow-Domodedovo airport on 9th July 1967.

An ASU-57 self-propelled gun bearing the VDV badge is prepared for loading into an An-12B.

increased from 12 tons (26,455 lb) to 16 tons (35,270 lb).

The introduction of the An-12 turned the Soviet Airborne troops (VDV) into a powerful geopolitical instrument allowing the Soviet Union to project its military might at will (as demonstrated by the invasion of Czechoslovakia in 1968). Being the main transport aircraft of the Warsaw Pact until the late 1970s, the An-12 played a key role during major military exercises. For example, in 1970 a swarm of nearly 200 *Cubs* paradropped 8,000 personnel and a large number of combat vehicles in just 22 minutes during Exercise *Dvina*. The might of the VDV was bolstered considerably when the VTA mastered the technique of paradropping combat vehicles (such as the purpose-built ASU-57 self-propelled gun) on lightweight PGS-500 pallets equipped with a five-canopy parachute system (*para**shoot**naya groozo**va**ya sis**te**ma* – parachute cargo system). To minimise deployment time during an airborne assault, a technique of paradropping vehicles with the crews already inside was devised at the initiative of VDV Commander Gen. Vasiliy F. Marghelov.

In 1974 the VTA began re-equipping with the Ilyushin IL-76. Thus the *Cub* was relegated to second place, and many were transferred to Aeroflot as surplus. Nevertheless, the An-12 was still an important element of the Soviet military airlift force, to say nothing of the various specialised versions which the *Candid* could not replace.

Soviet Air Force An-12s were also permanently deployed in some Warsaw Pact nations, including Czechoslovakia (Central Group of Forces), East Germany (Western Group of Forces) and Poland (Northern Group of Forces). The ones stationed in Czechoslovakia operated from Mladá-Milovice AB near Mladá Boleslav. The 'Polish' *Cubs* served with the 245th OSAP (*otdel'nyy **smesh**annyy avi**apolk*** – independent composite air regiment) at Legnica AB which was part of the 4th VA (*voz**doosh**naya **ar**miya* – air army).

In East Germany the type was operated by the 226th OSAP and 39th ORAO (*otdel'nyy raz**ved**yvatelnyy **avia**otryad* – independent reconnaissance air detachment) at Sperenberg AB near Berlin plus another unit at Oranienburg, which were part of the 16th VA. Most aircraft wore VVS insignia, although two were originally quasi-civil. Most 226th OSAP An-12s were standard transports which flew resupply and troop rotation missions for the Soviet forces stationed in East Germany. A few, however, were fitted out for special missions, including An-12RR '11 Red' (c/n 4342604) and ELINT-configured An-12B '84 Red' (c/n 4341905). VVS An-12s occasionally operated from Köthen AB and the so-called 'Netzeband highway strip', a stretch of motorway 5 km (3.1 miles) northwest of Neuruppin AB. Later, An-12s were used, along with other Russian Air Force transports to carry personnel and materiel during the Russian withdrawal from Germany in 1991-94. One of the 226th OSAP *Cubs*, An-12B '96 Red' (c/n 4341708) was the last Russian Air Force aircraft based in Germany to leave German soil.

Since 1961, when the new airlifter had its public debut at the annual Tushino flypast, military An-12s were regular participants in various airshows. The first of these was probably the grand show held at Moscow-Domodedovo airport on 9th July 1967 when about a dozen An-12BPs staged a simulated landing assault for the spectators. The static display at several 'open houses' at Kubinka AB near Moscow, the Pushkin flight test centre near St. Petersburg and other bases featured An-12s whose interiors were wide open for inspection. Foreign *Cubs* had their share of airshow performances, too.

On 26th October 1988 a group of Czech skydivers used the An-12 for setting two national records. One of the resident Soviet Air Force An-12As (CCCP-11833, c/n 3341008) took the parachutists aloft from Mladá-Milovice AB, the skydivers taking the jump at 10,100 m (33,140 ft) and 10,500 m (34,450 ft).

The *Cub* at War

Like its US counterpart, the An-12 has fully proved its worth in combat, participating in numerous armed conflicts around the world. Initially the *Cub*'s real-life combat operations involved delivering Soviet military aid to numerous 'friendly nations' which were habitually at war. The first major operation of this kind was the military airlift in North Yemen (the Yemen Arab Republic) performed by the 6th GvVTAD/363rd VTAP, assisted by the Egyptian Air Force, in 1963-67 during the Yemeni civil war. Brand-new quasi-civil An-12s were accepted and test flown by the personnel of the 363rd VTAP and put into action straight away. After accumulating about 250 flight hours in Yemen the aircraft were returned to the Soviet Union, yielding their place to fresh ones. The operation continued until 28th November 1967; An-12Bs replaced the Soviet aircraft at the closing stage of the airlift.

In the late summer and autumn of 1967 Soviet An-12s and An-22s flew to Egypt and Syria, delivering fighters and fighter-bombers supplied as attrition replacements after the third Arab-Israeli war, better known as the Six-Day War (5th-11th June 1967). A similar air bridge was organised in 1973 immediately before the Holy Day War, aka Yom Kippur War (6th-24th October), when more aircraft and T-54 tanks were delivered. These missions were risky; on one occasion a Soviet Air Force *Cub* taking off from Hodeidah, Syria, was nearly shot down by four Israeli Defence Force/Air Force McDonnell Douglas F-4E Phantom IIs. Apart from transports, a squadron of An-12PP ECM aircraft was detached to Syria from Siauliai (Lithuanian SSR) to disrupt the operation of Israeli air defences, protecting Syrian strike aircraft that attacked Israeli SAM sites. For appearance's sake the *Cub-C*s were wearing Syrian Air Force insignia but were flown by Soviet crews.

Also in 1967, a coup d'état occurred in Nigeria, setting off a bitter three-year civil war between the separatists in the so-called State of Biafra (a maverick province in the east) and the federal government. The latter was compelled to obtain jet combat aircraft from the Soviet Union, and the jets were delivered to Nigeria by Soviet Air Force An-12s, which made a total of 86 flights. On 20th August 1968, VVS An-12s were heavily involved in the

Soviet invasion of Czechoslovakia to squash an incipient anti-Communist uprising. There was more action in November-December 1977 when Soviet An-12s and IL-76Ms airlifted supplies to Ethiopia, which was trying unsuccessfully to stamp out separatism in the Eritrea and Ogaden provinces. Cuba also extended assistance to Ethiopia, putting up a 20,000-strong military contingent which was airlifted by the Soviet transports.

However, the An-12's most significant involvement in actual warfare was arguably the Afghan War of 1979-91 – the first major conflict in which the Soviet Union openly participated after the Second World War. Soviet forces entered Afghanistan on 25th December 1979 when the Soviet government decided to cement its influence in this country. During the associated 47-hour airlift operation on 25th-28th December the VTA made 343 flights into the country, transporting 7,700 servicemen, 894 vehicles and 1,062 tons (2,341,270 lb) of assorted cargoes. The An-12 bore the brunt of this opening operation, making 200 flights; in contrast, 77 flights were performed by IL-76s and another 66 by An-22s.

During the war, quasi-civilian grey-painted An-12BPs and 'BKs were mostly used for resupply and in-country troop redeployment missions in the interests of the 40th Army (the Soviet task force in Afghanistan). A squadron of ten An-12s commanded by Col. Ishmuratov was stationed at Bagram. The unit reported directly to the Chief Soviet military advisor in Afghanistan and occasionally operated for the Afghan government troops loyal to President Najibullah; the aircraft were flown by both Soviet and Afghan crews. Later the aviation element of the 40th Army was augmented by several more units, including the 50th OSAP. As the name implies, the regiment operated a 'mixed bag' of aircraft and helicopters, including four An-12s.

In Afghanistan the *Cub* quickly proved its worth as an indispensable workhorse. True enough, the IL-76MD could lug twice the payload, but the An-12 could do what the *Candid* could not – it could operate into and out of mountain airfields with short dirt strips. Another virtue much appreciated in Afghanistan was the *Cub*'s sturdiness and high combat survivability. More than once the An-12s managed to get away from an airfield under attack by the Mujahideen rebels and make it safely back to base with hundreds of bullet holes, dead systems and wounded crewmembers on board.

Unfortunately, the An-12 suffered combat losses, as did most Soviet aircraft used in the Afghan War; most of these losses were attributed to man-portable air defence systems (MANPADS). The first *Cub* was shot down on 30th September 1980; all 45 occupants perished. Other shootdowns occurred on 25th

Above: Four lines of paratroopers inside the cabin of an An-12 wait until it's time to hit the silk.

Above: As paratroopers dropped by the previous wave of An-12s float earthwards, the next wave is coming in.

A PGS-500 pallet with a wheeled vehicle (possibly a BTR-40 light armoured personnel carrier) is paradropped by an An-12B coded '67 Blue'.

April 1983, in May 1983 and 11th November 1984. On 29th November 1986 a 50th OSAP/1st Sqn An-12 bound for Jalalabad was hit by a Stinger SAM 24 km (15 miles) from Kabul airport as it climbed through 6,400 m (21,000 ft). The aircraft's load of ammunition detonated and blew it apart, leaving no chances of survival for the crew commanded by Capt. Khomootov and the 27 passengers.

In Kandahar there was a case when a *Cub* came under fire during final approach; apparently the captain was killed and the co-pilot couldn't cope with the aircraft for some reason. The An-12 overran, crashing into a parked Mil Mi-6 heavy transport helicopter, and both aircraft were destroyed by the ensuing fire. In 1987 another An-12 had a narrow escape when a Stinger scored a direct hit but failed to detonate as the aircraft was cruising above 9,000 m (29,530 ft) near Gardez. The unexploded missile tore away more than one-third of the lower skin on one of the stabilisers and ripped away the oxygen bottles in the aft fuselage; nevertheless the aircraft pressed on towards Kabul, making a safe emergency landing.

Of course, due credit has to be given to the crews who managed to keep their heads cool in such situations and did their best to bring the aircraft home. One such incident occurred at Farah, the capital of the province of the same name, in 1983. As a *Cub* captained by Maj. Zalyotinskiy was offloading supplies the Mujahideen launched a mortar attack on the airfield. Mortar shells began exploding all over the hardstanding; shell fragments struck down the aircraft's navigator and punctured the rear underfloor fuel tank. Zalyotinskiy immediately ordered the crew to start the engines and take off. As soon as the No.1 engine had reached ground idling rpm the crew opened the throttle and commenced taxying, starting the Nos. 4 and 3 engines en route. Before the last engine could be started another mortar round exploded right next to the runway; it became clear that the next one

would fall squarely on the runway and there was no choice but to get out of there immediately. Even though every single man aboard was wounded, the crew managed to take off on three engines and escape to Kabul; the aircraft and the crew were saved.

On another occasion a Stinger knocked out the No.1 engine, causing a massive fire. Showing considerable bravery and skill, the crew managed a safe landing with much of the port flap consumed by the fire. Yet the joy of making it back in one piece was muted by the tragic death of the youngest member of the crew – the tail gunner who, unable to bear the immense stress, baled out immediately after touchdown.

Of course the commanders of the 40th Army were not going to put up with these losses. Previous combat experience was carefully analysed and countermeasures were developed. Firstly, in the case of the An-12, tandem 30-round ASO-2 chaff/flare dispensers were installed on the forward fuselage for protection against heat-seeking missiles, which required some local reinforcement of the airframe. If you see a *Cub* with what looks like shallow strakes low on the forward fuselage sides, you can be sure this one is an Afghan veteran. The tail gunner acted as an observer, firing the flares after spotting an incoming missile; the flares were fired at preset intervals. Secondly, from then on the crews of Soviet military transports used a new piloting technique similar to the 'Khe Sanh tactical approach' introduced by the USAF in Vietnam. This involved staying around 5,400 m (17,700 ft) above ground level – that is, out of range of MANPADS – until the aircraft entered the airfield's security zone measuring approximately 4 x 6 km (2.5 x 3.75 miles), then descending in a tight spiral to minimise the danger of being fired upon. The sink rate during this manoeuvre reached 20-25 m/sec (3,940-4,920 ft/min), which was about three times the normal rate. The climbout on the return trip was also in a tight spiral. Of course,

such fighter-style approaches required the flight manual to be disregarded in certain areas – but then, the crews would rather bend the rules than bend the aircraft! For instance, during the 'Afghan tactical approach' the pilots were forced to retard the throttles all the way to ground idle, otherwise the aircraft would descend all too fast.

Avenues of approach were changed for each single flight; the rebels were avid mountain-climbers who could lug heavy armament to vantage points, and even using the same route twice involved a considerable risk of being ambushed. Finally, extra attention was paid to crew training, including the psychological aspect; crew coordination was crucial during such manoeuvres with extreme pitch and bank angles in mountainous terrain.

Countermeasures and new tactics notwithstanding, a pair of Mi-24 gunship helicopters always provided cover for the heavy transport during take-offs and landings. The Mi-24s also fired IRCM flares and could promptly attack a Mujahideen ambush on the outskirts of the airport.

An-12 operations in the hot and dusty climate of the mountainous regions of Afghanistan were a sore trial for the crews, considering that, unlike the smaller An-26, the *Cub* did not have a cooling turbine in the cabin ventilation/pressurisation system. The control wheels and electric switches got hot enough to burn the fingers, while the headsets dribbled molten fat all over your ears, as the pilots in Afghanistan used to say.

Whereas the An-12s brought fresh personnel, heavy equipment and supplies to the Soviet bases in Afghanistan, one of the most common loads on the return trip was wounded personnel going to 'Unionside' hospitals. The An-12 crews also had to fill the hated role known in Soviet Army/Afghan contingent slang as **chornyy tyul'pahn** (Black Tulip). This appellation, whose origin is unknown, applied to any aircraft carrying the bodies of servicemen killed in action back to

For appearance's sake the Soviet An-12s operating in the Afghan theatre (such as these five An-12BKs, including CCCP-11724) were always quasi-civil. Note the ASO-2 IRCM flare launchers.

Soviet territory for burial. The bodies themselves were euphemistically called *grooz dvesti* ('cargo 200'), in a similar vein any wounded personnel were referred to as *grooz trista* ('cargo 300').

Aircraft designers also learned a thing or two from Afghan experience. Firstly, all Soviet Air Force transport aircraft operating into Afghanistan (and many others as well) were equipped with either permanently installed or removable IRCM flare dispensers. Secondly, inert gas pressurisation systems were retrofitted (or upgraded where already present) to pressurise the fuel tanks, reducing the hazard of explosion if hit by enemy fire. Also, the An-12's flap tracks and carriages were reinforced to withstand the augmented loads during the famous tactical approaches.

Of course, the VTA top command drew some important conclusions as well. Changes were made to the VTA crews' combat training programme to include the 'Afghan tactical approach' and IRCM techniques. Most of the Soviet Air Force's transport aircraft pilots – first and foremost the highly skilled ones – had a tour of duty in Afghanistan. All of this allowed the VTA's combat potential to be improved dramatically by the late 1980s.

Sadly enough, the An-12 was also involved in several wars on home ground – to be precise, the Commonwealth of Independent States (CIS). Shortly before and immediately after the break-up of the Soviet Union a spate of ethnic conflicts erupted down in the southern republics, one of them being the Georgian-Abkhazi civil war of 1992-94. In the course of this conflict a pair of Ukrainian Air Force An-12s delivered humanitarian aid and evacuated ethnic Georgian refugees from the war zone in October 1993. In so doing the aircraft were repeatedly fired upon by the Abkhazi side but got away unharmed.

The An-12 was used in the First Chechen War (1994-96) as the Russian federal government strove to restore law and order in this republic which had turned into a loose cannon. Together with other Russian Air Force transports, the *Cubs* delivered personnel and materiel to Groznyy-Severnyy airport and Mozdok (Ingushetia) from all over Russia.

Not only Soviet/Russian *Cubs* saw action; those supplied to the air arms of various 'friendly nations' had their share of combat, too. The war in Afghanistan continued after the Soviet pullout in 1989; Najibullah's government used the military hardware donated by the USSR quite actively against the 'irreconcilable opposition' (the Mujahideen). This included several An-12s that were used, among other things, as auxiliary bombers; flying high and out of range of the Stingers they performed carpet bombing of Mujahideen positions. When the opposition seized Kabul

An air-to-air of Russian Navy An-12PS '16 Yellow' (c/n 7344702).

in May 1992, the various warlords scrambling for power tore the Afghan Air Force apart and started using the aircraft against each other. Later, several An-12s were appropriated by the new Afghan opposition – the fundamentalist Taliban militia notorious for its affiliations with the al-Qaeda terrorist group and the destruction of 'non-Islamic' culture. Little is known about the operations of Taliban *Cubs*, except that one such aircraft crashed near Quetta, Pakistan, on 13th January 1998.

Starting in 1977, Ethiopia obtained sixteen second-hand An-12s from the Soviet Union and immediately put them to good use in repelling an aggression from neighbouring Somalia. The *Cubs* were also actively used against the separatists in Eritrea and Ogaden – again both as transports and as auxiliary bombers. One of them, an An-12B serialled 1506 (c/n 402002), was blown up by Eritrean guerillas who overran the airfield at Tesenni on the night of 15th January 1984; another *Cub* reportedly crashed while taking off from the Eritrean capital Asmara in 1987. Still another was damaged beyond repair prior to May 1984, overshooting the runway at Addis Ababa during an attempted hijack.

In 1962-67 Egypt was involved in the civil war in Yemen, supporting the Republicans who had overthrown the king. At least eight EAF *Cubs* were destroyed on the ground at Cairo-West by Israeli air strikes on 6th June 1967, the second day of the Six-Day War; these reportedly included An-12Bs 1217 (c/n 402303) and 1218 (c/n 402304). Egyptian An-12s were active during the Yom Kippur War, deploying troops and flying to the Soviet Union to pick up fresh consignments of weaponry. Later, they brought the main part of the United Nations Peace Force troops deployed in the Middle East (except for the Polish UNPF contingent which arrived in a Polish *Cub*).

The Indian Air Force holds the distinction of being the world's first air arm to use the

An-12 in actual combat. Frictions between India and China had started in 1959 after the Khampa rebellion against the Chinese occupation of Tibet, when the Dalai Lama fled to the Indian town of Tawang. On 20th October 1962 the tension escalated into outright military conflict when Chinese troops infiltrated Indian territory, attacking and encircling several Indian Army outposts along the Himalayan border. India's An-12As flew supply missions, paradropping food and ammunition to the besieged garrisons. Remarkably, only 5% of the cargo was lost, despite the fact that the drop zones lay in difficult mountainous terrain.

Besides resupply missions, the An-12s were used alongside IAF Fairchild C-119G Flying Boxcars to deploy the 114th Infantry Brigade to the area, flying from Chandigarh to Chushul, a small mountain airfield with a perforated steel plate (PSP) runway that became unserviceable every now and then. The 114th Infantry Brigade was heavily outnumbered and would have been defeated, had it not been for a troop of French-made AMX-13 light tanks and field guns that the *Cubs* airlifted to the area. The Chinese Air Force did not put up any opposition to these operations, and no An-12s were lost. Finally, on 20th November China called a ceasefire.

The IAF An-12s saw a lot of action during two Indo-Pakistani conflicts over the State of Kashmir – in December 1965/January 1966 and December 1971. The 1971 conflict was also the first time when the An-12 was used as a bomber, dropping up to forty 450-kg (992-lb) bombs or 200-litre (44-Imp gal) napalm tanks; during several successful night raids against targets in western Pakistan the bomb load reached 16 tons (35,270 lb)! On one occasion a *Cub* bomber was intercepted by a Pakistani Air Force Dassault Mirage III but managed to get away. Finally, the Indian An-12s were also used in the Indian Peacekeeping Force operation carried out in northern Sri Lanka in the late 1980s/early 1990s – a futile attempt to stop the prolonged civil war between the Dhaka government and the Tamil separatists known as the Liberation Tigers of Tamil Eelam (LTTE).

Iraqi Air Force An-12BPs saw a lot of action both during Saddam Hussein's punitive operations against the Kurdish minority in the northern regions of the country and during the Iran-Iraq war of 1980-1988. Their missions included flights abroad to pick up weapons, maritime reconnaissance over the Persian Gulf and the Red Sea, and even in-flight refuelling of IrAF Dassault Mirage F1EQ-200 fighter-bombers as well as Mikoyan MiG-23BN attack aircraft retrofitted locally with IFR probes. IrAF An-12s presumably also participated in the Iraqi invasion of Kuwait in early August 1990. Two of them were destroyed on the ground by Royal Navy Blackburn Buccaneer S.2 strike aircraft toting 'smart bombs' on 27th February 1992 during the Gulf War (Operation Desert Storm).

The Cuban Air Force reportedly had a few An-12s and used them alongside Soviet Cubs to extend military help to the pro-Communist Angolan government of José Eduardo dos Santos between 1975 and the late 1980s. It is indeed known that in the crucial autumn days of 1975, when the South African Defence Force (SADF) supporting the opposition was advancing on Luanda, two An-12s brought urgently needed ammunition and military advisors, enabling the government troops to stem the assault. Operating into Angolan airfields, the An-12s were frequently fired upon by UNITA rebels but suffered no losses – as yet. Later, however, the rebels obtained a sufficient number of MANPADS and started using them indiscriminately against any aircraft that came within range. Civil aircraft shot down in Angola included several Cubs – An-12B ER-ACE (c/n 402812) downed at

Lukapa on 27th February 1996 while operating for the local airline Aerotropical, Lda and Khors Aircompany An-12BP UR-11319 (c/n 4342510) shot down near Cuito Cuanavale on 14th December 1999.

Now we have to focus our attention on Sri Lanka again. In 1991 the government in Colombo struck close ties with mainland China which at the time was the only nation willing to extend any tangible support – including military support. Arms deliveries began that same year; these included two Shaanxi Y8D transports for the Sri Lankan Air Force (SLAF), followed by a second-hand Y8B in 1994. The second aircraft, serialled CR-872, exploded in mid-air shortly after take-off on 5th July 1992, killing all 20 persons on board; there is speculation that the aircraft was carrying a load of ammunition which became dislodged and detonated.

In 1995 the LTTE called a ceasefire – only to regroup forces and acquire additional weapons, as it turned out. In April 1995 the hostilities resumed with renewed fury, now that the rebels had North Korean-built 9M319 Igla-1E (Needle; NATO SA-18 Grouse) MANPADS at their disposal. The SLAF's 1st Transport Wing (especially the 2nd Heavy Transport Sqn) was the hardest hit, losing five aircraft to the SAM that year, including Y8D CR-871 which was shot down on approach to Palaly AB on 18th November.

Sudanese Cubs were used in the struggle against the National Liberation Army (NLA) rebels terrorising the southern regions of Sudan (El Istwâ'ya province) in the 1970s. Algerian Air Force An-12Bs also took part in a civil war – this time in neighbouring Morocco, supporting the anti-government Polisario Front. Finally, the two Yugoslav Air Force An-12BPs played an important part in evacuating federal government troops from Bosnia, Slovenia and Croatia into Serbian ter-

ritory as the country disintegrated into a collection of belligerent states.

In Civil Service

The An-12's career with Aeroflot started with several celebrated missions to the Arctic regions and to Antarctica to support Soviet Polar research stations. Reliable aircraft were needed to fly these demanding missions, and the four-engined Cub fitted in ideally here.

Regular flights to the drifting research stations in the Arctic Ocean began on 5th April 1960 when an early-production Cub carrying a load of more than 8,500 kg (18,740 lb) departed from one of the Arctic airfields to the research station SP-8 (**Severnyy polyus** – North Pole). In press reports the aircraft was referred to as 'a cargo-configured An-10' because the true designation was still classified back then. The airstrip was prepared on a stretch of icefield 1,300 m (4,260 ft) long; the heavy An-12 performed the landing flawlessly. Interestingly, the aircraft was unloaded within just 15 minutes. If the same load were to be delivered by the piston-engined IL-14G, six such aircraft would have been required.

As already mentioned, on 15th December 1961 the unique An-12TP-2 transport/geophysical survey aircraft (CCCP 04366) departed from Moscow to Ice Station Mirnyy in the Antarctic in company with a suitably modified IL-18V, CCCP-75743. The mission was led by Mikhail I. Shevelyov (Hero of the Soviet Union), head of Aeroflot's Polar division. The An-12's crew comprised captain Boris S. Osipov, first officer P. Rogov, navigator V. Steshkin, flight engineer I. Naïkin, technician V. Sergeyev and radio operator N. Starkov – all airmen with a lot of experience of flying in polar regions.

The route, which was 26,423 km (16,411 miles) long, took the aircraft across four continents and two oceans. The An-12 covered this distance in 48 hours 7 minutes, clocking an average speed of 532 km/h (330 mph). Refuelling stops were made in Tashkent, Delhi, Rangoon, Jakarta, Darwin, Sydney, Christchurch and at the US Antarctic research station McMurdo. The last-but-one leg of the journey (from Christchurch to McMurdo) turned out to be the hardest because the American radio officer would not answer the radio calls of the Soviet crews who needed meteorological and navigation information. Still, despite lacking the all-important weather report, the crews of both aircraft maintained the planned route without deviating. Having nothing but their weather radars and astro-sextants to rely on, they circumnavigated tall mountains obscured by clouds, including the 3,743-m (12,280-ft) Mt. Erebus, and made a precision approach to McMurdo's airstrip.

The two aircraft spent a full month on the glacial continent. On arrival at Mirnyy the Cub

CCCP-04363 was one of several An-12As operated by the Polar Aviation branch. It was painted silver with a red cheatline.

The An-12 was used a lot for various relief missions. Here, An-12BP RA-13341 owned by the Komsomol'sk-on-Amur aircraft plant (KnAAPO) was used by the United Nations High Commission for Refugees (UNHCR) in 1994.

was refitted with non-retractable skis, making several survey flights over unexplored areas of the Antarctica for the purpose of measuring the Earth's magnetic field. Several landings were made on suitable clearings spotted from the air. CCCP 04366 also made a dozen take-offs and landings specifically to determine the suitability of the skis for operation from airfields covered by deep snow (no small matter, since preparing the hard-packed runways in the Antarctica is a back-breaking job).

On 2nd February 1962 the An-12TP-2 returned to Moscow, spending a total of 90 hours in the air during the expedition. The success of the mission proved that aircraft could resupply the Antarctic research stations much quicker and at less cost as compared to the traditional delivery by sea. All participants of the expedition were awarded government orders; additionally, B. S. Osipov and A. S. Polyakov (the captain of the IL-18) received the Hero of Socialist Labour title.

Originally Aeroflot had to rely on An-12s 'chartered' from the Air Force. Gradually, as the needs of the Soviet military were met, Aeroflot started taking delivery of its own Cubs – both factory-fresh aircraft and second-hand examples transferred from the VTA. The An-12 was operated by 14 of the Soviet Union's Civil Aviation Directorates (CADs). These included the Central Directorate of International Services (TsUMVS – *Tsentrahl'noye oopravleniye mezhdunarodnykh vozdooshnykh so'obschcheniy*)/64th Flight, Komi Civil Aviation Directorate/Syktyvkar United Air Detachment/318th Flight, Komi CAD/Vorkuta UAD/366th Flight, Krasnoyarsk CAD/Krasnoyarsk UAD/214th Flight, Krasno-

yarsk CAD/Noril'sk UAD/329th and 434th Flights, Leningrad CAD/1st Leningrad UAD, Leningrad CAD/Penza UAD, Magadan CAD/1st Magadan UAD/181st Flight (1st and 2nd Squadrons), Moscow Territorial CAD, North Caucasian CAD/Rostov UAD, Siberian (later East Siberian) CAD/Irkutsk UAD/134th Flight, Tyumen' CAD/2nd Tyumen' UAD/ 435th Flight, Urals CAD/Chelyabinsk UAD, Urals CAD/Sverdlovsk UAD, Volga CAD/ Kuibyshev UAD/368th Flight and Yakutian CAD/Yakutsk UAD/139th Flight.

Aeroflot *Cubs* carried all manner of civilian cargoes. These included heavy construction and earth-moving equipment, livestock, foodstuffs (including tangerines and oranges for the workers of Siberian oil and gas fields, which gave rise to the slang phrase *mandarinovyy reys* – 'tangerine flight'), money and other valuables, and humanitarian aid. Originally the cargoes were carried in bulk or at best in their own packaging. In October 1977, however, the An-12 introduced containerised cargo transport on Aeroflot's routes, which was much more convenient and civilised, reducing the risk of damage – or theft. The cost of such transport was an all-time low in the airline's practice – 10 kopecks per tonne-kilometre (one kopeck is 1/100th of a rouble).

On 3rd February 1966 a TsUMVS *Cub* inaugurated Aeroflot's first international cargo service from Moscow-Sheremet'yevo to Paris via Riga; the flight time was 5 hours 30 minutes. A second route – the first transcontinental route from Vladivostok in the Far East to Amsterdam with several staging points – was opened in July 1969; others followed quickly. In due course the An-12 was supplemented in service

with Aeroflot by the larger IL-76, just as had been the case in the Soviet Air Force.

Apart from Aeroflot, the An-12 was operated by various enterprises within the frameworks of MAP, the Ministry of General Machinery (MOM – *Ministerstvo obschchevo mashinostroyeniya*) responsible for the Soviet space and missile programmes, the Ministry of Shipbuilding (MSP – *Ministerstvo soodostroitel'noy promyshlennosti*) and the Ministry of Electronics Industry (MRP). MAP *Cubs* belonged to the aircraft factories in Arsen'yev, Irkutsk, Kazan' (No.22), Komsomol'sk-on-Amur, Kuibyshev, Kumertau, Omsk, Tashkent, Ulan-Ude, Ul'yanovsk and Voronezh, the Zaporozh'ye Engine Factory (now Motor-Sich), the Transport Aviation Production Association and the Antonov OKB itself.

An-12 operators in the MOM system were the Kirov Machinery Production Association and Zlatoust Machinery Plants (divisions of NPO Energiya), the Kuibyshev Engine Production Association named after Mikhail V. Frunze, the Omsk Engine Production Association and the Orenburg 'Strela' Production Association. Known MRP divisions operating the type were the Kamensk-Ural'skiy Radiotechnical Plant, NPO Vega-M in Moscow and LNPO Leninets. MSP An-12 operators included the Amur Shipbuilding Plant in Komsomol'sk-on-Amur.

The An-12 was used a lot for humanitarian missions, since its robust airframe, high payload and ability to operate into semi-prepared fields made it an ideal aircraft for such tasks. Originally such missions were performed by Soviet Air Force An-12s flown by highly skilled

The wreckage of An-12BP CCCP-11107, a TsUMVS/64th Flight aircraft, which overran and burnt out after an aborted take-off from Novyy Urengoy on 24th April 1982.

crews. Such aircraft ostensibly wore civil registrations and Aeroflot titles, while the crews were issued Aeroflot uniforms. The reason is obvious; imagine red-starred An-12s landing somewhere in Europe in the Cold War days! It would be pretty hard to convince everyone World War Three had not begun yet! One of the earliest known episodes of this kind was in July 1970 when a devastating earthquake hit Peru, flattening cities and causing a large death toll. Among other Soviet aircraft, a group of thirty-five 3rd GvVTAD An-12s commanded by the division's CO Maj.-Gen. N. F. Zaïtsev delivered medicines and food from Moscow to Lima, staging through Iceland, Canada, Cuba and Colombia.

In post-Soviet days such missions were largely performed by civil machines chartered by the United Nations World Food Programme (WFP), the UN High Commission for Refugees (UNHCR) and the International Committee of the Red Cross (ICRC). For example, in 1993 Tyumen' Airlines An-12BPs RA-11112 and RA-12976 were operated by the WFP in Angola and Ethiopia, wearing the all-white UN colours and appropriate titles; An-12A UR-11833 was also used in a similar capacity in Angola in January 1994. In October 1994 Russian Air Force An-12s delivered medicines, food, tents and diesel-powered generators to Iturup Island in the Kuriles which had been hit by a powerful earthquake.

The biggest problem associated with An-12 operations today is the maintenance and overhaul issue. According to Soviet practice one or two aircraft overhaul plants (ARZ – *aviaremontnyy zavod*) would repair all aircraft of a given type, regardless of where they were based. Thus, ARZ No.412 in Rostov-on-Don traditionally handles civil An-12s. Military *Cubs* are dealt with by two Russian Air Force

plants – ARZ No.123 in Staraya Roossa near Velikiy Novgorod and ARZ No.325 in Novocherkassk; some repair and conversion work is also done by ARZ No.308 at Ivanovo-Severnyy AB. All of these plants are situated in Russia, which makes it pretty hard for the foreign operators – especially military ones – to keep their *Cubs* fit and healthy. One of the opportunities is at Sharjah in the United Arab Emirates – a major cargo hub frequented by Soviet types (including the An-12), and a special maintenance base for these has been set up there. One of the most important aspects of the problem is service life extension, considering the aircraft's advanced age. In the mid-1990 the Antonov OKB subjected one of the high-time airframes to fatigue tests; as a result, the type's service life is currently set at 43,000 hours, 16,000 cycles and 40 years.

Regrettably the An-12 had a fairly high accident rate – for various reasons. Powerplant failures were one; among other things, the feathering mechanism of the AV-68 propellers proved rather troublesome at first. For example, on 7th December 1963 An-12B CCCP-11347 (c/n 401803) of the East Siberian CAD crashed in Kirensk, Russia, when both engines on the port wing flamed out immediately after take-off due to a vapour lock in a fuel line. The propellers did not feather automatically, causing tremendous drag; with the two live engines running at full power, the result was inevitably an irrecoverable departure. Yawing and rolling to port, the aircraft plunged into the ground; all six crew were killed.

In many cases, however, the aircraft was not to blame; many of the accidents were caused by human error or simply negligence. Thus, on 28th October 1980 CCCP-11104, a TsUMVS/64th Flight 'civil' An-12BP (c/n 01347710), was en route from Sofia-

Vrazhdebna to Kabul via Mineral'nyye Vody and Tashkent on flight SU1531. On the last leg of the journey the crew encountered bad weather with low cloud and rain; yet the pilots persisted with the approach, descending below the minimum safe altitude. As a result, at 10:32 local time the aircraft smacked into Mt. Vaïsi-Karnibaba 25 km (15.5 miles) from Kabul airport, disintegrating utterly; all six crew were killed, of course.

An even worse case occurred on 16th May 2003. The day before, Angolan Air Force An-12 T-307 suffered an engine failure, force-landing at Meninguie, Angola. Instead of summoning a repair team, the devil-may-care crew chose to fly back to Luanda on three engines for repairs. As the aircraft took off, one more engine quit and the freighter crashed, killing the crew.

The crash on 4th December 1974 when 'civil' An-12BP CCCP-12985 (c/n 00347110) of the East Siberian CAD/Irkutsk UFD/134th Flight collided with An-2 CCCP-49342 (c/n 1G1226) of the East Siberian CAD/Irkutsk UFD/190th Flight over Irkutsk airport was caused by ATC incompetence. Quite simply, the feeder traffic ATC officer had cleared the biplane to take off into the An-12's flight path without informing the airport's approach controller who was tracking the freighter. All 17 occupants of the An-2 were killed; the An-12 made a successful belly landing with no fatalities but was a write-off.

Most aircraft find their way into museums sooner or later. For example, the Central Russian Air Force Museum in Monino boasts an Irkutsk-built An-12A coded '04 Blue' (c/n 8900203); an Indian Air Force example serialled BL727 (c/n 2401205) is preserved in the IAF Museum at Palam AFB, while Aeroflot An-12B CCCP-11355 (c/n 402712) was preserved on a plinth at Magadan-Sokol airport in the late 1970s as a tribute to the sterling service rendered by the type. Other *Cubs* served as ground instructional airframes at various educational and training establishments in the Soviet Union.

Yet even as of this writing the *Cub* is still going strong, serving with a multitude of airlines in and outside the CIS. The An-12 is cheap on the used aircraft market, which means pretty high revenues for the operator, and stocks are reasonably large. Moreover, the An-12 is enjoying something of a revival these days; old it may be, but it conforms to ICAO Annex 16 Chapter 3 noise regulations enacted on 1st April 2002, while the D-30KP-powered versions of the IL-76 do not.

Even though largely supplanted by more modern types, the perennial An-12 still enjoys well-earned respect from the people who fly it. This was clearly demonstrated in 1999 when the Russian peacekeeping forces contingent in Kosovo used *Cubs* along with Il-76MDs.

Chapter 6

The *Cub* Worldwide

While the Soviet Union was by far the largest operator of the type, the An-12 was supplied to a number of 'friendly nations'. With the demise of the Soviet Union and the disintegration of Aeroflot, the Soviet *Cubs* continued in service with the air forces and the numerous airlines of Russia and most of the other CIS republics. Additionally, some An-12s were resold to operators in third-world countries (often obscure ones), not to mention short-term leases and charters; the latter included nations which did not normally operate Soviet/Russian aviation hardware. Thus, if one includes the CIS republics, the An-12 has seen service in more than 50 nations in Europe, Asia, the Middle East, Africa, Central and South America. Of these, 17 customer nations took delivery of new (or, more rarely, used) *Cubs* directly from the Soviet Union.

For each country, operators are listed in alphabetical order, with each airline's two-letter IATA designator and three-letter ICAO designator where applicable. Aircraft no longer operated are shown in italics in the fleet lists (except in cases when the airline itself no longer exists and/or all of its An-12s have been sold or retired). Aircraft built with a tail gunner's station are marked (+); those with a commercial tailcone are marked (–).

AFGHANISTAN

• The **Afghan Republican Air Force** (*Afghan Hanai Qurah*) operated at least 11 ex-VVS 'military' An-12Bs and 'BPs, apparently serialled consecutively 380 Black through 390 Black. Some of these later passed to the anti-Taliban coalition headed by Gen. Abdul Rashid Dostum known as the Northern Alliance. To date only one example (An-12BP '387 Black', c/n 4342205) has been identified by construction number. An-12BP '390 Black' was written off in an accident near Termez, Uzbekistan, on the night of 10 February 1993.

• The Afghan flag carrier **Ariana Afghan Airlines [FG/AFG]** had two *Cubs* – 'civil' An-12BP YA-DAA (c/n unknown) in full Ariana livery and 'military' An-12BP YA-DAB (ex-Polyot Airlines RA-11325, c/n 5342801) in ex-Polyot colours bought in late 1997. In addition to hauling cargo the aircraft were reportedly used on passenger services due to the scarcity of true airliners, for which purpose seats were installed in the hold.

The aircraft were locked inside the country when the UN imposed a ban on Ariana's international flights in 2000 due to the activities of

Ariana Afghan Airlines An-12BP YA-DAA seen during a visit to Sharjah.

the Taliban militia; both were eventually destroyed at Kabul International Airport by US bombing strikes in November 2001 during Operation Enduring Freedom (a massive military operation against the Taliban and al-Qaeda in the wake of the 11th September 2001 terrorist attacks against New York and Washington, D.C.).

• **Pamir Airlines** operated An-12BP YA-PAA (ex-Special Cargo Airlines RA-11321, c/n 9346801?) and YA-PAB, a demilitarised An-12BK re-equipped with an ROZ-1 radar (ex-Air Cess EL-AKW, ex-RA-12191, c/n 8346202), in 1996. Both aircraft retained basic Special Cargo Airlines colours. In 1996 YA-PAA was sold to Santa Cruz Imperial as EL-ALF, while YA-PAB followed suit in 1997 as EL-ALJ.

• **The Taliban militia** had at least one ex-Afghan Republican AF *Cub* (identity unknown); the aircraft crashed near Quetta, Pakistan, on the night of 13th January 1998.

• A *Cub* serialled 00406 belonged to an unknown Afghan operator in April 2002; it has been reported as ex-YA-PAA.

ALGERIA

The Soviet Union began providing military assistance to Algeria in 1962 when the country gained independence from France. In early 1966 the **Algerian Air Force** (*Force Aérienne Algérienne/al Quwwat al Jawwiya al Jaza'eriya*) took delivery of eight Voronezh-built 'military' An-12Bs. The aircraft were operated by the 35th Transport Squadron at Boufarik AB. Interestingly, the *Cubs* wore civil registrations along with Algerian Air Force insignia and military serials.

In the early 1970s, however, President Col. Houari Boumedienne switched allegiance to the West and the Algerian Air Force started re-equipping with Western hardware. The An-12s were placed in storage and supplanted by 'short' Lockheed C-130H and 'stretched' C-130H-30 Hercules transports. At least four of the aircraft were ultimately sold (one of them to the Angolan Air Force).

Registration	Serial	C/n	Notes
7T-WAA	560	402607	
7T-WAB	566	402606	Sold to Mikma (?) as ER-ACC
7T-WAC	514	402605	Sold to Mikma as ER-ACD by 5-95
7T-WAD	?	?	No roundels and no c/n on aircraft. C/n sometimes reported in error as 402608, which is CCCP-11378!
7T-WAE	550	402810	Reportedly sold to an unknown Russian operator as RA-11119 by 12-95? *
7T-WAF	?	402811	
7T-WAG	591	402812	Sold to Mikma as ER-ACE by 6-95
7T-WAH	516	402809?	

* The original CCCP-11119 (c/n 02348101), a 'civil' An-12B, was still operational at the same time! Other sources say, however, that 7T-WAE was sold to the Angolan airline ALADA to become D2-FAR.

• The **Angolan Air Force** (FAPA – Força Aérea Populaire de Angola) operated at least eleven An-12s. Apart from military serials, they had ATC callsigns in the D2-M** range (M for military).

Serial/ registration	Version	C/n	Notes
T-300	?	?	Basic Aeroflot c/s, in service 2001
T-301	An-12B (+)	5343405	Ex-Tiramavia ER-ADM, in service 2001. Became, see next line
D2-MAZ			
T-302	?	?	Basic Aeroflot c/s, in service 2001
T-303	An-12B (+)	3340903	All-white c/s, in service 2001
T-304	?	?	In service 2001. Crashed on landing Kanyengue 27-1-02
T-305	?	?	In service 2003
T-306	An-12TB	402007	Ex-Tiramavia ER-ADB; ATC callsign D2-MBE. In service 2003
T-307	?	?	Ex-Tiramavia ER-ACH; ATC callsign D2-MBH. In service 2003. Crashed on take-off Menongue 16-5-03
T-308	?	?	In service 2003
T-309	An-12B (+)	4342209	In service 2003
T-310	?	?	In service 2003
T-311	An-12BK	7345410	Ex-Adala Airways 9Q-CEN; ATC callsign D2-MBI. In service 2005
D2-MBD	An-12A (+)	2340608	Ex-Tiramavia ER-ACB, bought 2004;ATC callsign applied as registration for overhaul, serial unknown

• The **Angolan government** operated three An-12s registered D2-EAC, D2-EAD and D2-EAE (c/ns unknown). In reality they, too, almost certainly belonged to the Angolan Air Force. D2-EAD reportedly crashed on 19th September 1984. (Incidentally, if you omit the digit from the registration, you get the word 'dead'… talk about unlucky reggies!)

• An airline called **Aerotropical, Lda** leased 'military' An-12B ER-ACE (c/n 402812) from Mikma in 1996. Sadly, the aircraft was shot down by a missile on finals to Lukapa on 27th February 1996 while operating for Aerotropical.

• **Air Mapeko** operated An-12BK D2-FBK (ex-Gromov Air RA-83962, c/n 402210) bought in 1998. On 25th (some sources say 26th) October that year the aircraft vanished without trace over Lunda Norte Province, Angola; there were speculations that it had been shot down by UNITA rebels or hijacked.

• **Air Nacoia Exploraçao de Aeronaves [–/ANL]** based in Luanda leased 'military' An-12BP RA-11531 (c/n 6344506), a former weather research aircraft, from GosNII GA in June 1994. In 1996 the aircraft was sold to Air Nacoia and transferred to the Angolan register as D2-FVG No.1. Unfortunately, on 12th March 1997 it crashed in Lukapa, Angola, whereupon its registration was reused (see below).

• In 1999 an airline called Hellier International acquired a demilitarised An-12BK re-equipped with an ROZ-1 radar (D2-FBZ, ex-Special Cargo Airlines RA-11329, c/n 8346010); in 2001 the aircraft was sold to Space Cargo as 3C-QRD. Earlier Hellier International had leased D2-FBY form Savanair (see below).

• **ALADA – Sociedade de Transportes Aéreos [–/RAD]**, also based in Luanda, had eight *Cubs*.

Registration	Version	C/n	Notes
D2-FAJ		?	
D2-FAO	An-12B (+)	?	Bought ?-96. Reported as ex-Algerian Air Force 7T-WAG/591 (c/n 402812) but this cannot be true (see Moldova/Mikma)
D2-FAR	An-12B (+)	402810	Ex-RA-11119 No.2, ex-Algerian Air Force 7T-WAE/550? Bought ?-96; scrapped mid-2004
D2-FAW	An-12B (+)	402605	Ex-Mikma ER-ACD, bought by 1998
D2-FAY	An-12BP (+)	8345810	Ex-Russian Air Force '37 Red'
D2-FAZ		?	Damaged beyond repair Saurimo 11-8-98
D2-FBJ	An-12B (+)	401711	Ex-SVGAL (North-East Cargo Airlines) RA-11421, bought ?-99
D2-FRG	An-12BP (–)	00347202	Ex-Chelyabinsk Air Enterprise RA-12987, bought 7-98. Scrapped by mid-2004

• **Loex Air Cargo** leased An-12BP RA-11531 from GosNII GA in November 1993, returning it to the lessor in May 1994.

• **National Commuter Airlines** bought 'civil' An-12BP RA-11526 (c/n 02348207) from Komiinteravia and 'civil' An-12BP RA-11114 (c/n 01347909) from Special Cargo Airlines; the aircraft was were reregistered D2-FDB and D2-FDC respectively. By May 2001 D2-FDC had been sold to the Moldovan airline Tiramavia as ER-ACJ.

• **Savanair, Lda [–/SVN]** owned two *Cubs* – 'civil' An-12BP D2-FBY (ex-Komiinteravia RA-12959, c/n 8345510) and 'military' An-12B D2-FRT (ex-Russian Air Force '10 Red', c/n 3341408). In 2000 the former aircraft was sold to the Moldovan carrier Airwest, becoming ER-ACW, while D2-FRT was sold to British Gulf International as S9-CAQ. Additionally, Savanair leased 'military' An-12A EL-ASA (c/n 3340909) from Santa Cruz Imperial in early 1999; on 2nd February 1999 the aircraft crashed fatally in Luanda. 'Civil' An-12BP TN-AFR (/n 8345502) leased from an unidentified airline was just as unlucky – it was shot down near Luzamba on 1st July 1999.

• **Voar Airlines** ('voar' means 'to fly' in Portuguese) leased 'civil' An-12B RA-11527 (c/n 02348208) from Pulkovo Avia in 1994.

• In 1995 **Von Haaf Air** acquired 'military' An-12A D2-FVD (ex-RA-98101, c/n 1901706) from NPO Energiya; the aircraft was grey overall with a blue cheatline. The following year it was sold to Air Cess as EL-AKN and a new *Cub* was bought instead, namely ex-Moscow Airways 'military' An-12B RA-11318 (c/n 401908) which became D2-FVG No.2. However, in 1998 this aircraft was also sold, going to Congo as TN-AFJ.

• 15 more Angolan *Cubs* – D2-FBB, D2-FBC, 'military' An-12BP D2-FBD (ex-Ukraine AF UR-12423, c/n 4342610), D2-FBG, An-12AP D2-FBM, D2-FBS, D2-FBT, 'military' An-12TA D2-FBV (ex-ER-ACK No.2, c/n 2340604), 'military' An-12A D2-FCU (c/n 2340503), 'military' An-12B D2-FCV (ex-Magadan-Aerogrooz RA-11986, c/n 401901), 'military' An-12BP D2-FDT (ex-NAPO-Aviatrans RA-12192, c/n 5343305), 'military' An-12BPs D2-FRC (ex-Penza Air Enterprise RA-11338, c/n 3341506), D2-FRI (ex-Belorussian Air Force '10 Yellow', c/n 7345210) and D2-FRK – were operated by unidentified Angolan carriers, lacking any insignia other than the registration. (This sure tells a thing or two; if the operator is so reluctant to identify itself, chances are that it is involved in illegal operations, such as arms trafficking!)

Two of these aircraft returned to the CIS: D2-FBD was sold to Mikma by May 1998 as ER-ADL, while D2-FCU became ER-ADE with Aerocom. D2-FBD was acquired by Vega Airlines as LZ-VED in 2001;

D2-FCV and D2-FDT went to São Tomé & Principe in 2001 as S9-CDB and S9-BOT respectively. D2-FBV crashed at N'zaki, Angola, at an unknown date.

ARMENIA

• **Air Armenia [QN/ARR]** established in 2003 and based at Yerevan operated three *Cubs*.

Registration	Version	C/n	Notes
EK-11001 No.1	An-12BP (+)?	5343408	Reported as An-12BK but batch seems too low for that. Ex-9L-LEA, in service 12-03 to 3-04. Sold to GST Aero as UN 11009.
EK-11001 No.2	An-12BK	8346107	Ex-Soviet Air Force CCCP-11244. Bought 2004
EK-12001	An-12B (+)	401801	Demilitarised; ex/to RA-11345, leased from Avial'-NV 9-03 to 6-04; basic Avial' c/s

• An An-12BK with the non-standard registration EK-46741 (c/n 8345408) was operated by an airline called **Aviatek** at an unknown date. Note: the 46xxx block is allocated to the An-24 airliner, and there was previously a Kiev-built An-24 *sans suffixe* registered CCCP-46741 (c/n 47300803).

• In 1998 the same An-12BK EK-46741 was operated by **Armenian Airlines [R3/RME]**, the then Armenian flag carrier. By 2001 the aircraft had been sold to Phoenix Avia.

• **Dvin-Avia Cargo [–/DVN]** (aka Dvin-Air) based at Yerevan-Erebuni operated seven An-12s until it suspended operations in November 2001.

Registration	Version	C/n	Notes
EK-11028	An-12BK	8345310	Ex-Soviet Air Force '29'. Bought ?-00; sold to Azza Air Transport 2006 as ST-ARV
EK-11029	An-12BP (+)	7344908	Demilitarised; ex-RA-11029, bought ?-98
EK-11030	An-12BP (+)?	9346208	Reported as An-12BP but may be An-12BK. Ex-Ukrainian Air Force 22 Blue
EK-11304	An-12A (+)	0901304	Ex-Lasare Air 4L-11304; resold to original owner?
EK-11351	An-12BP (+)	4341910	Ex-Ukrainian AF UR-11351; sold to Ararat-Avia ?-98
EK-11660	An-12BP (+)	5343209	Bought ?-00
RA-48984	An-12B (+)	402913	Leased from Voronezh aircraft factory (VASO) ?-97 to ?-??; transferred to Ukraine Air Alliance as UR-48984

• **Ararat-Avia** purchased An-12BP EK-11351 from Dvin-Avia in mid-1998. By May 2004 the aircraft had been sold to Pnac Cargo (see end of chapter).

• **Phoenix Avia [–/PHY]**, the Armenian sister company of Phoenix Aviation (see Kyrghyzstan), operated An-12BP EK-12148 (ex-RA-11516, c/n 4341906, named 'Albatros') and An-12BK EK-46741 named 'White Bird'. The latter aircraft crashed on take-off at Payam, Iran, on 28th March 2006.

• Sharjah-based **South Airlines [–/STH]** has a single 'civil' An-12BP, EK-12777 (ex-Lotus Airways 3C-ZZD, c/n 00347305), bought in 2004. The aircraft was briefly leased to Sarit Airlines that year as ST-SAE.

Above: An-12B EK-11351 in the smart livery of Armenian carrier Ararat Avia; the image of Mt. Ararat was the airline's logo.

An-12B EK-12148 of Phoenix Avia, the sister airline of the Kyrghyz carrier Phoenix Aviation, had an extremely restrained livery and was named Albatros.

• **Veteran Aircompany Ltd. [–/RVT]** established in 2001 took over from the defunct Dvin-Avia, operating An-12s EK-11028, EK-11029 and EK-11660.

• The following Armenian-registered An-12s were operated by unidentified carriers.

Registration	Version	C/n	Notes
EK-11102	?	?	
EK-11132	An-12BP (+)	5343307	Ex-Sarit Airlines ST-SAD
EK-11772	An-12BP (+)	5342903?	
EK-12201	An-12BK	7345201	Ex-Air Bridge Group ER-AXE
EK-12222	An-12BK	00347606	Ex-Volga-Dnepr CCCP-11341 No.2, in service 2003. Sold to Sarit Airlines 2004 as ST-SAF
EK-12333	An-12BP (+)	8346006	Ex-Bright Aviation Services LZ-BRA, bought 2004; sold to Click Airways same year as EX-031

AZERBAIJAN

• The **Azerbaijan Air Force** operated at least one ex-VTA An-12 registered 4K-12425 (c/n 2401103) and based at Nasosnaya AB near Baku.

• **Azerbaijan Airlines** (AZAL, or Azerbaijan Hava Yollari) **[J2/AHY]** based at Baku-Bina airport operated An-12A 4K-48971 (ex-Volga Dnepr Airlines RA-48971, c/n 1340107) around 1995.

• **AZAL Cargo [–/AHC]**, the specialised cargo division of Azerbaijan Airlines established in 1998, operated at least three An-12s.

Registration	Version	C/n	Notes
UK 11418	An-12BK	7344705	Ex-CCCP-11418 No.2, leased from Avialeasing in 2000; now returned
4K-AZ18	An-12BP (+)	9346308	Ex-Gromov Air RA-12108. Sold to Shovkovyy Shlyakh 2003 as UR-CBU
4K-AZ32	An-12BP (+)	5343006	Ex-Soviet Air Force CCCP-11430, in service 2003. Sold 7-05 as 4L-12005

• The Baku-based airline **Imair [IK/ITX]**, a division of the Improtex trading company, operates passenger and cargo aircraft, mostly leased in other CIS republics as required. These included 'civil' An-12BP 4K-12999 leased from Ural Airlines from December 1995 to 1997 (ex-RA-12999, c/n 01347701); the aircraft wore basic Ural Airlines colours with an Azeri flag and Imair titles.

• Starting in August 2002, **Silk Way Airlines [ZP/AZQ]** operated at least four demilitarised An-12s. None remain in the fleet by now, having been superseded by IL-76TDs.

Registration	Version	C/n	Notes
4K-AZ21	An-12BK	8345609	Registration painted on in error as 4KAZ-21. Crashed Kome, Chad, 7-11-02
4K-AZ23	An-12BK	8345605	Registration painted on in error as 4KAZ-23, later corrected
4K-AZ30	An-12BP (+)	5343410	Ex-Soviet Air Force CCCP-11404. Leased to Sarit Airlines
4K-AZ33	An-12BK	8346201	
4K-AZ56	An-12B (+)	3341209	Ex-Aerofreight RA-11408, bought 7-04
4K-AZ60	An-12BP (+)	5343510	Ex-Russian Air Force RA-11400, bought 2006
4K-AZ63	An-12TBK	9346308	Ex-Shovkovyy Shlyakh UR-CBU, bought 2006

• The following An-12s were operated by as-yet unidentified Azeri airlines.

Registration	Version	C/n	Notes
4K-AZ35	An-12BK	00347102	Ex-Tiramavia ER-ACA, bought by 8-03; to Global Georgian Airways as 4L-AIR
4K-AZ36	An-12BK	8345807	Ex-Soviet Air Force CCCP-11846. Sold 2005 as EX-084
4K-AZ37	An-12BK	00347506	Ex-Soviet Air Force CCCP-11938
4K-AZ59	An-12TA	2340801	Ex-Antex-Polyus RA-11098. Sold 2005 as EX-085

BANGLADESH

Bismillah Airlines [–/BML] leases An-12s from other airlines as required. For instance, in January 1999 – March 2000 it operated 'civil' An-12BP RA-12988 (c/n 00347206) leased from the now-defunct Baikalavia. In 2006 'civil' An-12BP XU-365 No.2 and An-12BK XU-395 No.2 were leased from/jointly operated with Imtrec Aviation of Cambodia. An-12BP UN-11650 (c/n 6344506) was leased from Almaty Avia Cargo in the summer months of 2006.

BELARUS (BELORUSSIA)

• The **Belorussian Air Force** had seven An-12s on strength, operated by the 2nd Squadron of the 50th OSAP; six have been identified so far.

Originally based at Lipki AB near Minsk, the unit moved to Machool-ishchi AB (also near Minsk) in 1994 and was transformed into the 50th Air Force Base; a second reorganisation took place on 26th March 1996 when the unit became the 50th Transport Air Base. By then only a single *Cub* ('12 Yellow') remained with the unit. The aircraft wore the overall grey finish standard for Soviet Air Force An-12s, with faded VVS star insignia and the red/green Belorussian flag (strongly reminiscent of the flag of the former Belorussian Soviet Socialist Republic) aft of the flightdeck.

C/n	Version	Tactical code	Notes
4342010	An-12BP (+)	07 Yellow	Code removed by 5-96; sold to Techaviaservice as EW-11368
4342108	An-12BP (+)	08 Yellow	Code removed by 5-96; sold to Techaviaservice as EW-11371
5343109	An-12BP (+)	09 Yellow?	Sold to Techaviaservice as EW-11365
7345210	An-12BP (+)	10 Yellow	Sold to Angola by 6-05 as D2-FRI
7345410	An-12BK	11 Yellow	Sold to Adala Airways 10-01 as 9Q-CEN
00347107	An-12BK	12 Yellow	Reported as such but see Ukrainian Air Force!

• In mid-2006 the Gomel'-based airline **Gomelavia [YD/GOM]** purchased An-12PS EX-096 (c/n 6344608) from Reem Air. The aircraft was reregistered EW-245TI under the new Belorussian alphanumeric system, the suffix letters denoting the operator.

• In 1996 the airline **Techaviaservice [–/BTS]** based in Vitebsk acquired three Belorussian Air Force An-12BPs which were registered EW-11365, EW-11368 and EW-11371 (see above). The aircraft were operated for the Russian petroleum company LUKoil. EW-11368 crashed near Kalomboloka, Angola, on 26th August 1998.

• An airline called **Wings [–/VGS]** had at least one An-12A, EW-11322 (c/n 0901409).

BOSNIA-HERZEGOVINA

In 2000 the Bosnia-Herzegovenian cargo airline **BIO Air Company [–/BIO]**, a division of the Bosnian Investment Organization, leased An-12BP UR-11332 (c/n 4342202) from Khors Aircompany; the aircraft was reregistered T9-CAD.

BULGARIA

• The cargo airline **Air Sofia [CT/SFB]** operated sixteen An-12s, often wet-leasing them to other airlines.

LZ-ITA, the first An-12BP operated by Inter Trans Air.

Registration	Version	C/n	Notes
LZ-SFA	An-12BP (–)	02348007	Ex-SiGi Air Cargo LZ-SGA, ex-YU-AIC, basic SiGi Air Cargo blue/white c/s
LZ-SFC	An-12B (+)	402913	Ex-SiGi Air Cargo LZ-SGC, ex-CCCP-48984; D/D 15-2-92. To RA-48984. C/n also reported in error as 402513
LZ-SFE	An-12BP (+)	5342708	Demilitarised. Ex-Soviet AF CCCP-11230, bought 6-92. Sold to Bulgarian Flying Cargo ?-93 as LZ-BFA
LZ-SFF	?	?	Seen on two occasions but existence denied by airline!
LZ-SFG	An-12P (+)	3341605	Demilitarised. Ex-Soviet AF CCCP-11145 No.2 (CCCP-11145 No.1 was an An-10), D/D 16-6-92. Crashed Lajes, Azores, 4-2-98 while operating in own colours
LZ-SFI	An-12B (+)	3341606	Ex-Soviet AF CCCP-11511, D/D 16-6-92.
LZ-SFJ	An-12BP (+)	4342105	Ex-Czech Air Force 2105 Black, D/D 10-9-97; not in 2002 fleet list, fate unknown
LZ-SFK	An-12B (+)	2341901	Demilitarised. Ex-Soviet AF CCCP-11511, D/D 16-6-92.
LZ-SFL	An-12BP (+)	4342101	Demilitarised. Ex-Soviet AF CCCP-11908 No.1, D/D 16-6-92. Was leased to Avioimpex Macedonia 6-95 to 7-96 as Z3-AFA
LZ-SFM	An-12P (+)	401705	Demilitarised. Ex/to UR-11765, leased from Antonov Design Bureau 1993-98
LZ-SFN	An-12B (+)	2340806	Demilitarised. Ex-Phoenix Air Cargo LZ-FEA, bought 13-10-94. Was leased to Pecotax-Air 1-03 to 6-05 as ER-AXM
LZ-SFR	An-12B (+)	401801	Ex-Avial'-NV RA-11345, bought late 2004
LZ-SFS	An-12BP (+)	6344308	Demilitarised. Ex-Polish Air Force SP-LZB/51 Red, bought 2-95
LZ-SFT	An-12BP (+)	9346904	Demilitarised. Ex-Solis Aviation LZ-SAA, bought ?-01. Sold to Airline Transport Inc. 2004 as ER-AXY
LZ-SFW	An-12A (+)	2340507	Ex-Russian Air Force RA-11936, bought ?-01. Sold to AeroVis Airlines 2005 as UR-CCP
RA-12108	An-12BP (+)	9346308	Demilitarised. Leased from Aeroflot in 1994

Note: The registrations LZ-SFB, LZ-SFO and LZ-SFQ have not been noted; LZ-SFD was an An-22 sans suffixe, LZ-SFH is an An-26 and LZ-SFP is an An-24B.

With the exception of LZ-SFA which retained the basic blue/white colours of ex-owner SiGi Air Cargo, the aircraft were painted white overall. Not infrequently, however, Air Sofia An-12s leased abroad were repainted in the colours of the lessor. Also, in August 1997 LZ-SFK received a 'Noah's Ark look' with various animals painted on the aft fuselage and a black-striped fin fillet.

A curious feature of Air Sofia's An-12s is that most of them had the radar removed and the radar bay faired over. One can only guess why, and how the crews managed to do without weather radar!

• A Sofia-based airline called **Aviostart [–/VSR]** acquired a single demilitarised An-12B registered LZ-ASY (ex-Sakha Avia RA-11991, c/n 402006) in early 2000. The aircraft wore basic Aeroflot red/white polar colours without titles or logo. By 2002 it had been sold to Congo-Brazzaville as TN-AGK No.2.

• **Balkan Bulgarian Airliness [LZ/LAZ]** the then national flag carrier, was the first An-12 operator in Bulgaria, operating 12 of the type. In the late 1990s Balkan started suffering major financial troubles. After an abortive attempt to rescue the airline it ceased operations in December 2002, selling off the *Cubs*.

Registration	Version	C/n	Notes
LZ-BAA	An-12BP (–)	8346001	Crashed somewhere in Egypt in 1975
LZ-BAB	An-12BP (–)	8346002	WFU Bourgas 6-6-89, to local museum 10-98
LZ-BAC	An-12BP (–)	6343708	Ex-CCCP-1100, bought by 7-80; non-standard c/s. Sold to Bulgarian Air Cargo by 4-02. To Heli Air Services as LZ-CBE
LZ-BAD	An-12BP	6344001	Ex-CCCP-110012?, bought by 3-84. Crashed Addis Ababa 24-8-84
LZ-BAE	An-12B (–)	402001	Ex-CCCP-11976 No.1, bought by 12-87; leased to HeavyLift Cargo Airlines. Sold to Vega Air 2004 as LZ-VEF
LZ-BAF	An-12B (–)	402408	Ex-CCCP-11768 No.1; named 'River of Maritza'
LZ-BAG	An-12BP (+)	6344305	Ex-RA-11650; to Bulgarian Flying Cargo by 8-97 as LZ-BFG
LZ-BAH	An-12BP (+)	9346807	Demilitarised. Ex-RA-11317, bought by 2-00; named 'River of Iskar'. To Heli Air Services as LZ-CBH
RA-11650	An-12BP (+)	6344305	Leased from Arsen'yev Aircraft Production Association 9-93; basic Aeroflot c/s, blue/white tail, 'Chartered by Balkan' titles; bought and reregistered LZ-BAG by 4-96, see two lines up!
RA-12108	An-12BP (+)	9346308	Demilitarised. Leased from Aeroflot in 1993; later to Air Sofia
CCCP-12975	An-12BP (–)	9346509	Leased from Ural Airlines 6-92 to ?-??
12999	An-12BP (–)	01347701	Lsf Ural Airlines 10-90 to ?-??, Aeroflot c/s with additional Balkan titles

• An-12BPs LZ-BAA and LZ-BAB were originally operated by **Bulair**, a sister company of TABSO (an acronym for Bulgarian-Soviet Aviation Co.). TABSO was renamed Balkan on 1st April 1968.

• **Bright Aviation Services [–/BRW]** operated five An-12s.

Registration	Version	C/n	Notes
LZ-BRA	An-12BP (+)	8346006	Ex-Inter Trans Air LZ-ITB, bought 10-01. Sold 12-04 as EK-12333
LZ-BRC	An-12BP (–)	8345510	Ex-Airwest ER-ACW, bought ?-02; basic Airwest c/s. Sold to Heli Air by 10-05
LZ-BRI	An-12BP (+)	4342103	Ex-AeroVis UR-CEX, bought 2006
LZ-BRV	An-12BP (–)	01348006	Ex-Sakhaviatrans RA-11116, bought 5-04
LZ-BRW	An-12BP (–)	01347907?	Ex-Avial'-NV RA-11112? Sold to Aerocom 2-02 as ER-AXA?

LZ-BRC was one of five An-12s operated by Bright Aviation Services.

• A start-up airline called Bulgarian Air Cargo bought An-12BP LZ-BAC from Balkan in the spring of 2002.

• Sofia-based **Bulgarian Flying Cargo** or **BF Cargo [FN/BFB]** leased An-12s from other operators as required. Six examples have been identified.

Registration	Version	C/n	Notes
LZ-BFA	An-12BP (+)	5342708	Demilitarised. Ex-Air Sofia LZ-SFE, leased 1993; to Komsomol'sk-on-Amur Aircraft Production Association 1996 as RA-11230
LZ-BFB	An-12BP (+)	6343905	Ex-Soviet AF CCCP-11789, leased 1993; to Komsomol'sk-Avia ?-96 as RA-11789
LZ-BFC	An-12BP (+)	2400502	Demilitarised. Ex/to RA-48970, leased from Kumertau Express 1994-96 (originally with Russian registration)
LZ-BFD	An-12BP (+)	5343005	Demilitarised. Ex-RA-98102, Isf Arsen'yev Aircraft Production Association ?-95; to Gromov Air by 8-01 as RA-98102
LZ-BFE	An-12TBK (+)	9346308	Demilitarised. Ex-RA-12108, leased by 1999; to Gromov Air by 10-00 as RA-12108
LZ-BFG	An-12BP (+)	6344305	Ex-Balkan LZ-BAG, leased by 8-97; to Gromov Air by 8-00 as RA-11650

• In September 1992 – July 1993 **Global Air** operated two 'civil' An-12BPs leased from Pulkovo Avia. These were temporarily registered LZ-PVK (ex/to RA-11108, c/n 01347810) and LZ-PVL (ex/to RA-11127, c/n 02348202).

• **Heli Air [–/HLR]**, primarily a helicopter operator, had five *Cubs*.

Registration	Version	C/n	Notes
LZ-BRC	An-12BP (–)	8345510	Ex-Bright Aviation Services, bought by 10-05
LZ-CBE	An-12BP (–)	6343708	Ex-Balkan LZ-BAC
LZ-CBG	An-12A (+)	2340804	Demilitarised. Ex-RA-11370, named *Bansko*; bought 2003
LZ-CBH	An-12BP (+)	9346807	Ex-Balkan LZ-BAH
LZ-CBM	An-12BP (+)	01347810	Ex/to UR-CCP, leased from AeroVis Airlines 2004-05

• **Inter Trans Air [–/ITT]** operated four An-12s. In 2005 the airline ceased operations and the two aircraft remaining by then were retired.

Registration	Version	C/n	Notes
LZ-ITA	An-12B (+)	3341004	Demilitarised; previous identity unknown. Derelict Gorna Orekhovitsa, Bulgaria
LZ-ITB	An-12BP (+)	8346006	Ex-Antey RA-11368, bought ?-00. Sold to Bright Aviation Services 10-01 as LZ-BRA
LZ-ITD	An-12PP	00347107	Converted to freighter. Ex-President Airlines RA-11301, leased 5-00; back to President Airlines 9-00 as XU-355
LZ-ITS	An-12B (+)	3341505	Ex-Skycabs 4R-SKL, bought ?-00. Derelict Gorna Orekhovitsa, Bulgaria

• **Phoenix Air Cargo** leased 'military' An-12A RA-11307 from the Russian Air Force in 1993. The aircraft was bought in the same year to become LZ-PHA but then was reregistered LZ-FEA for some reason in 1994. Finally, on 13th October 1994 it was resold to Air Sofia, with whom it became LZ-SFN.

• In 1999 **Rila Airliness [–/RAB]** of Sofia (Rila is the name of a mountain ridge in Bulgaria) acquired a single demilitarised An-12BP (RA-11959, c/n 402410) from Samara Airlines. Reregistered LZ-RAA, the aircraft was in service until 2003 when the airline shut down, selling the machine to Vega Air as LZ-VEE.

• **Scorpion Air [–/SPN]** operated at least five An-12s.

Registration	Version	C/n	Notes
LZ-MNK	An-12BK	8345802	Ex-Ukrainian Air Force '53 Red', bought 2003
LZ-MNN	An-12P (+)	0901409	Ex-UR-BYW, bought 2003
LZ-MNP	An-12BK	9346309	Ex-Ukrainian Air Force '68 Red'/CCCP-12113, bought 2003. Also reported as An-12BP, ex-AeroVis UR-CBH (c/n 8345710)
LZ-MNQ	An-12B (+)	3341402	Ex-Russian Air Force '70 Black', bought 2003
LZ-VEB	An-12BP (–)	01347701	Bought from Vega Air 2002

• **SiGi Air Cargo** operated a total of four An-12s. The airline ceased operations in 1992.

Registration	Version	C/n	Notes
LZ-SGA	An-12BP (–)	02348007	Ex-Yugoslav Air Force YU-AIC, bought 1990. Leased to Air Sofia 16-3-92 as LZ-SFA, sold to Air Sofia 23-2-98
LZ-SGC	An-12B (+)	402913	Ex-CCCP-48984, leased from Voronezh aircraft factory (VASO). To Air Sofia ?-92 as LZ-SFC
LZ-SGD	?	?	
CCCP-11129	An-12BP (–)	02348204	Leased from Aeroflot 1990, full c/s. DBR Janina, Bulgaria, 8-11-91

• **Solis Aviation [–/SOF]** of Sofia leases An-12s from other carriers as required. In 2001 it operated a demilitarised An-12BP, LZ-SAA, bought from Amuraviatrans (ex-RA-13341, c/n 9346304); that very year, however, the aircraft was sold to Air Sofia as LZ-SFT.

• Plovdiv-based **Vega Airlines [–/VEA]** had six *Cubs*.

Registration	Version	C/n	Notes
LZ-VEA	An-12A (+)	1340106	Ex-Rostvertol RA-11976, bought ?-99, named *Khan Asparukh*
LZ-VEB	An-12BP (–)	01347701	Ex-Ural Airlines RA-12999, bought ?-99; red/blue/white c/s
LZ-VEC	An-12BP (+)	6344610	Demilitarised. Ex-TAPO-Avia UK 93920, bought ?-00; black/white c/s, named *Tsar Simeon Veliki* (Czar Simeon the Great). Damaged Baghdad 11-3-05 but repaired
LZ-VED	An-12BP (–)	02348207	Ex-D2-FDB, bought ?-01
LZ-VEE	An-12B (+)	402410	Ex-Rila Airlines LZ-RAA, bought 2003
LZ-VEF	An-12B (–)	402001	Ex-Balkan LZ-BAE, bought 2004

BURUNDI

Three *Cubs* with Burundi registrations – 'civil' An-12BP 9U-BHN No.1 (ex-Renan ER-ACK No.1, c/n 8345503), 'military' An-12B 9U-BHN

No.2 (ex-D2-FRC, c/n 3341506) seen in 2002 and 9U-NHN (c/n unknown) – have been sighted to date. 9U-BHN No.1 probably received this registration in error and soon became 9U-BHO.

9U-BHN No.2 belonged to **Air Vitoria**, and so apparently did 9U-BHO. In early 2005 they were sold to the Congolese (DRC) operator Mango Airlines, becoming 9Q-CVT and 9Q-CVM respectively soon afterwards. The operator of the third aircraft is unknown.

CAMBODIA (KAMPUCHEA)

• **Cambodia Cargo** (later renamed **Kampuchean Airlines**) leased 'civil' An-12BP RA-11034 (c/n 7345010) from Aeroflot's Irkutsk division in 1993.

Registration	Version	C/n	Notes
XU-315	An-12A (–)	2400702	Ex-Avia (Yuriy Petrov's Airline) RA-11131, bought 1999. To President Airline
XU-365 No.1	An-12BK	01348005	Ex-Uzbekistan Airways UK 11109, bought 2001. Sold to unknown operator 2004 as EX-034; see next line
XU-365 No.2	An-12BP (–)	402601	Ex-Avial'-NV RA-11899, bought 7-04. Leased to/jointly operated with Bismillah Airlines
XU-395 No.2	An-12BK	01347803	Ex-Veteran Airlines UR-11305, bought 10-05. Leased to/jointly operated with Bismillah Airlines
3C-QRN	An-12BK	7344705	Ex-ER-AXB; operated twice in 2002 and 2-03 to 4-03

• **Imtrec Aviation Cambodia [–/IMT]** of Phnom Penh operated five An-12s.

• **PMT Air [U4/PMT]** (PMT stands for Progress Multitrade Co.) bought 'military' An-12B RA-11372 (c/n 401912) from NPP Vega-M in mid-2004; the aircraft was operated with the Guinean registration 3X-GDM. At the end of 2005 it was sold to Reem Air of Kyrghyzstan as EX-098. In November 2006 PMT Air bought another *Cub* (ex-Almaty Aviation UN 98102, c/n 5343005) which received the unusual registration XU-U4C.

• **President Airlines [TO/PSD]**, a subsidiary of Holiday Group Cambodia, operated three An-12s.

Registration	Version	C/n	Notes
XU-315	An-12A (–)	2400702	Ex-Imtrec Aviation
XU-345	An-12BP (+)		Ex-NAPO-Aviatrans RA-12192, bought 4-00. Became, see next line
D2-FDT			Operated as such! Sold to Sarit Airlines 12-01 as S9-BOT
XU-355	An-12BK	00347107	Converted An-12PP! Ex-Inter Trans Air LZ-ITD, bought 9-00. Sold to Sri Lanka as 4R-AIA

• **Yana Airlines** leased An-12s as required until it suspended operations in 2001. For instance, XU-315 was reportedly operated in January 1999; An-12BP XU-345 was reportedly operated in April 2000, going to President Airlines same month.

• An-12BK XU-395 No.1 (ex-Daallo Airlines EK-12555, c/n 8345607) was operated in all-white colours minus titles by an unknown airline in September-December 2002. This aircraft later became EX-029 with Click Airways.

CANADA

Toronto-based **Skylink Aviation, Inc. [–/SKK]** operates relief and ad hoc charter flights outside Canada with Russian aircraft wet-leased as required. In December 1994 it operated 'civil' An-12BP RA-11114 (c/n 01347909) leased from Komiinteravia. Later, in January-March 2004, Skylink operated An-12B 9L-LEC (ex-Trans Air Congo 3C-QQL, c/n 4341803) which became 9Q-CIH after the lease.

CENTRAL AFRICAN REPUBLIC

'Military' An-12As TL-ACJ (ex-Air Pass 3D-AKV, ex-Air Cess TL-ACV, ex-RA-48971; c/n 1340107) and TL-ACR (c/n and ex identity unknown) were registered in 1998; the former aircraft had basic Air Pass colours without titles while the other was white overall. Chances are that they belonged to **Centrafricain Airlines [GC/CET]** founded in 1998 which bought almost the entire fleet of the defunct Air Pass (see Swaziland section). Interestingly, besides Bangui (the capital of the Central African Republic), the airline was also based at Sharjah, UAE – as was Air Cess, a sister company of Air Pass (see Liberian section). Makes you wonder if all three airlines had a common owner and Centrafricain Airlines is simply the successor of Air Cess/Air Pass incorporated under a new name.

CHINA (PEOPLE'S REPUBLIC OF CHINA)

• Chinese developments paralleled those in the former USSR in that originally the huge country had just one huge airline, **CAAC (Civil Aviation Administration of China)** – the 'Chinese Aeroflot' (even the livery was extremely similar to Aeroflot's 1973-standard colour scheme). In 1984, when deregulation set in, numerous new airlines (often based on CAAC's regional divisions – the equivalent of Civil Aviation Directorates in the USSR) started appearing; a few of these took over the former CAAC *Cubs*, some of which are listed below.

Registration	Version	C/n	Notes
1151	An-12BP (+)	8345308	Preserved PLAAF Museum, Datangshan AB, Changping
B-201	An-12BP (+)	6344402	To Air China as B-3151
B-203	An-12BP (+)	8345303	To Air China as B-3152
B-1056	An-12BP (+)	7345107	Ex-PLAAF 51056 Red?
B-1059	An-12BP (+)	7345307	Ex-PLAAF 1059 Red, transferred after 1988. Preserved PLAAF Museum
B-3101	Y8F-100	1001	Registered 1985. To China Postal Airlines
B-3102	Y8F-100	1002	Registered 1985. To China Postal Airlines
B-3103	Y8F-100	1005	Registered 1985. To China Postal Airlines
B-3104	Y8B	?	
B-3105	Y8B	070802?	To ACA Air Changan Airlines
B-3196	Y8	?	Ground instructional airframe at Xian Aeronautical Institute
B-3198	Y8	?	Ground instructional airframe at Xian Aeronautical Institute
B-3199	Y8	?	Ground instructional airframe at Xian Aeronautical Institute
B-4101	Y8	?	Preserved PLAAF Museum

• **ACA Air Changan Airlines [2Z/CGN]** based in Xian operated a single Y8B registered B-3105. The aircraft was leased to the Sri Lankan Air Force as CR-873 pending the return to service of a damaged sister aircraft (CR-871) but, in the event, never returned to the lessor.

• **Air China International [CA/CCA]** (formerly CAAC's Beijing Directorate) operated two Soviet-built 'military' An-12BPs registered B-3151 (ex-B-201, c/n 6344402) and B-3152 (ex-B-203, c/n 8345303). Both were retired by 2000.

• The **Aviation Industry Corporation (AVIC)** operated a number of Y8s, including Y8C B-504L (possibly ex-'182 Black'), the Y8F-200 prototype (B-576L) and the Y8F-400 prototype (B-575L). B-576L was later converted into the KJ-200 AWACS demonstrator.

• **China Postal Airlines [–/CYZ]**, the flying division of the Ministry of Posts & Telecommunications based in Tianjin, operates five Y8F-100s registered B-3101, B-3102, B-3103, B-3109 and B-3110 (c/ns 1001, 1002, 1005 and 1303 respectively; the c/n of the last aircraft is unknown). The airline also ordered a single Y8F-400 due for delivery in 2002.

• **China Southern Airlines [CZ/CSN]** based at Huanzhou-Baiyun leased 'civil' An-12BP RA-11116 (c/n 01348006) from Baikal Airlines at an unknown date.

• **China Xinjiang Airlines [XO/CXJ]** (formerly CAAC's Xinjiang Directorate) based at Urumqi-Diwobao has a single Shaanxi Y8B, B-3105 (c/n unknown).

• **OK Air** operated at least one 'glass-nosed' Y8, B-4071 (c/n unknown), apparently an ex-PLAAF machine, outfitted as a geophysical survey aircraft with an MAD boom.

• The **People's Liberation Army Air Force** (PLAAF, or *Chung-kuo Shen Min Taie-Fang-Tsun Pu-tai*) was the largest An-12/Y8 operator in China. Known aircraft are listed below. (Note: In the five-digit PLAAF serials currently in use the first two digits may be a code denoting one of the eleven defence districts, the fourth digit a unit code, while the third and fifth digits make up the individual number of the aircraft in the unit.)

PLAAF aircraft normally carry five-digit serials which indicate the unit operating the aircraft in coded format. The first and fourth digits denote the Air Division (a special table is used for encoding/decoding this); the second digit denotes the number of the regiment within the division, while the third and fifth digits combine to give the aircraft's sequence number within the unit, acting almost as the tactical code of Soviet/CIS aircraft. For instance, the serial 31042 has the following meaning: when checked against the decoding table, 3-4 denotes the 13th Division; 1 means the first regiment in the division (that is, the 37th Regiment at Wuhan, Guangzhou Military Region), while 0-2 means second aircraft in the unit.

Serial	Version	C/n	Notes
076 Black	Y8		CFTE, probably avionics testbed
079 Black	Y8CA		CFTE, avionics testbed; also referred to as Y8CB
181 Red	Y8	?	
182 Red	Y8	?	First Shaanxi-built example. Converted to, see next line
182 Black	Y8C	001802	Prototype. Converted to, see next line
	Y8F-100	001802	Prototype
980 Black	Y8H	?	Survey aircraft or avionics testbed
982 Red	Y8	?	
983 Red	Y8	?	
987 Red	Y8	?	
989 Red	Y8	?	
4139 Red	Y8	?	Independent Transport Regiment, Dalian, Shenyang Military Region. Converted to, see next line
	Y8E	?	Prototype. Ground instructional airframe at Xian Aeronautical Institute
9104 Red?	Y8F-400 mod	?	Battlefield surveillance version prototype, opb CFTE; serial unconfirmed, may be '0134 Red'
31011 Red?	Y8	?	ECM version; serial unconfirmed!
31041 Red	Y8	?	13th Division/37th Regiment. Reported as c/n 020803/to '31046 Red'
31042 Red	Y8	?	
31043 Red?	Y8	?	Existence not proved but likely
31044 Red?	Y8	?	Existence not proved but likely
31045 Red	Y8	?	Preserved PLAAF Museum
31046 Red	Y8	020803	Ex-31041 Red? Ground instructional airframe at Xian Aeronautical Institute
31047 Red?	Y8	?	Existence not proved but likely
31048 Red	Y8	?	
31049 Red?	Y8	?	Existence not proved but likely
31140 Red	Y8	030805	
31141 Red	Y8	?	Ground instructional airframe at Beijing Aeronautical Institute
31142 Red?	Y8	?	Existence not proved but likely
31143 Red?	Y8	?	Existence not proved but likely
31144 Red?	Y8	?	Existence not proved but likely
31145 Red?	Y8	?	Existence not proved but likely
31146 Red	Y8	?	
31147 Red	Y8	?	Ground instructional airframe at Xian Aeronautical Institute
31148 Red?	Y8	?	Existence not proved but likely
31149 Red?	Y8	?	Existence not proved but likely
31240 Red?	Y8	?	Existence not proved but likely
31241 Red?	Y8	?	Existence not proved but likely
31242 Red	Y8	?	Crashed on approach to Zheng Zou AB 4-1-02 (due to icing?)
31243 Red	Y8	?	Crashed on approach to Zheng Zou AB 4-1-02 (due to icing?), second crash that day/location
31244 Red?	Y8	?	Existence not proved but likely
31245 Red?	Y8	?	Existence not proved but likely
31246 Red?	Y8	?	Existence not proved but likely
31247 Red?	Y8	?	Existence not proved but likely
31248 Red?	Y8	?	Existence not proved but likely
31249 Red	Y8	?	
31340 Red?	Y8	?	Existence not proved but likely
31341 Red	Y8	?	
32042 Red	An-12BP (+)	?	Preserved PLAAF Museum
32045 Red	An-12BP (+)	?	
51056 Red	An-12BP (+)?	7345107?	34th Division/101st Regiment, Nanyuan AB, Beijing Military Region. To CAAC as B-1056?
B-576L	KJ-200	?	First prototype, converted Y8F-200 prototype, opb CFTE
T0518 Red	Y8F-400 mod	?	AWACS with rotodome, prototype, opb CFTE
T0673 Red	KJ-200	?	Second prototype, converted Y8F-600 prototype, opb CFTE

• The **Chinese Army Aviation** also operates a limited number of Y8s. Known examples are serialled LH0001, LH4002 and LH94001; the latter aircraft belongs to the 65th Group/4th Army Aviation Regiment based at Luoyang/Henan AB, Beijing Military Region.

• The **People's Liberation Army Naval Air Force** (PLANAF) also operates the Y8 – predominantly special mission versions; the type is in service with the 1st Independent Regiment at Laiyang AB. The serials of Chinese naval *Cubs* begin with a 9 and, with one exception, end with a 1 in order to confuse the casual observer; thus, 9261 Black in reality equals 26 and so on.

Gaudily painted An-12BP TH-AHD of Natalco ir Lines is seen at a very basic airfield in Congo-Brazzaville in 2004. This aircraft wore basic Aeroflot red/white Polar colours while operated by the same airline as ST-AQF.

Serial	Version	Notes
9211 Red	Y8X (Y8MPA)	Prototype
9261 Black	Y8X (Y8MPA)	Grey c/s
9271 Red	Y8X (Y8MPA)	Grey/blue/white c/s
9281 Black	Y8J	Ground instructional airframe at Beijing Aeronautical Institute
9291 Red	Y8X (Y8MPA)	Grey/blue/white c/s
9301 Black	Y8J	
9341 Red?	Y8X (Y8MPA)	Grey/blue/white c/s
9351 Black	Y8DZ	
9361 Black	Y8DZ	
9342 Black	Y8	

COLOMBIA

The cargo airline SADELCA (Sociedad Aérea del Caqueta, Ltda) [–/SDK] based in Villavicencio and Neiva leased An-12BP RA-12980 (c/n 00347103) from Tyumen' Airlines at an unspecified date.

CONGO-BRAZZAVILLE

• **Aero Fret Business** operates An-12As TN-AGY (ex-Tiramavia ER-ADC, c/n 1340206) and TN-AHA (ex-Tiramavia ER-ACL, c/n 0901306) bought in 2004. Former Trans Air Congo An-12BK TN-AGZ was also operated in 2005-06 before being transferred to sister company EX Aero Fret Business as EX-124 No.1 in mid-2006.

• **Air Atlantis** operated 'military' An-12BP TN-AGC (ex-TN-AFW, c/n 4342305) in 1999.

• The abovementioned An-12BP TN-AFW (ex-Soviet Air Force '14 Red') has been reported as operated by **Aviaputsk**.

• **Hellier International** operated An-12BK TN-AGE (ex-Polyot Russian Airlines RA-11320, c/n 4342409) in 1999.

• **Natalco Airlines** purchased two *Cubs* in 1999. One was a 'military' An-12B registered in São Tomé & Principe as S9-BAN (ex-Sakha Avia RA-11236, c/n 402111). In 2003 the aircraft was transferred to the Congolese register as TN-AGQ; the following year it was retired at Pointe

Noire, Congo. The other example (An-12BP c/n 8345504) was originally registered ST-AQF; in 2004 it became TN-AHD.

• **Trans Air Congo [Q8/TSG]** based at Pointe Noire and Brazzaville operated at least four *Cubs*.

Registration	Version	C/n	Notes
TN-AGH	An-12B (+)	4342404	Ex-Anton Air International 7P-ANB, bought 2002. Sold to Phoenix Aviation as EX-11760
TN-AGZ	An-12BK	8345403	Ex-Tiramavia ER-ACZ, bought 2004; sold to Aero Fret Business by 12-05
3C-AAL	An-12BP (–)	00347003	Ex-KNG Transavia Cargo, bought 2004. To Groupe Rubuye
3C-QQL	An-12B	3341803	Ex-UN 11003, leased from Troika Leasing 2001; sold to DRC as 9Q-CIH

• The operators of An-12 TN-ACM, 'military' An-12B TN-AFJ (ex-Von Haaf Air D2-FVG No.2, c/n 401908), 'civil' An-12BP TN-AFR (ex-RA-12951, c/n 8345502), 'civil' An-12BP TN-AGK No.1 (ex-Mikma ER-ACG, c/n 9346504; sold to Forner Airlines as ST-AQQ) and demilitarised An-12B TN-AGK No.2 (ex-Aviostart LZ-ASY, c/n 402006) are unknown. TN-AFR was shot down near Capenda (Lunda Sul Province, Angola) by UNITA rebels on 30th June 1999.

CUBA

• The fleet of **Empresa Consolidada Cubana de Aviación [CU/CUB]**, the Cuban flag carrier (often called Cubana for short), included a single demilitarised An-12B registered CU-T827 (c/n 401504). The aircraft was built to the same specification as the Indian Air Force An-12Bs but featured additional underfloor fuel cells' thus it was sort of an An-12BP with a narrow cargo door. Unfortunately, CU-T827 was lost in a fatal crash near Mexico City on 9th February 1967.

• Some sources reported that the **Cuban Air Force/Air Defence Force** (DAAFAR – *Defensa Anti-Aérea y Fuerza Aérea Revolucionaria*) took delivery of several An-12s. However, none have been identified so far.

Above: CU-T827, the only known Cuban An-12, in old Cubana colours

CZECHOSLOVAKIA
CZECH REPUBLIC

Two Tashkent-built 'military' An-12s (c/ns 4342105 and 4342209) were delivered to the **Czechoslovak Air Force** (CzAF, or ČVL – *Československé Vojenské Létectvo*) in 1964. In keeping with the then-current (and still current) Czech practice they received serials matching the last four digits of the c/n – 2105 Black and 2209 Black respectively. The transports were based at Prague-Kbely AB.

In 1989 Václav Havel's 'gentle revolution' put an end to socialism in the country and the Czechoslovak Socialist Republic became the Federal Republic of Czechoslovakia. On 1st January 1993, however, the 'gentle revolution' was followed by an equally gentle divorce and the once-united CzAF (including the tiny An-12 fleet) was divided between the Czech Republic and Slovakia; the 'new' **Czech Air Force** (*České Vojenské Létectvo*) retained the example serialled 2105 Black. The aircraft belonged to the 1.SDLP (*smišeny dopravni létecky pulk* – composite transport air regiment).

However, operating just a single aircraft of a given type didn't make much sense. After making its final flight in CzAF service on 26 May 1996 the An-12 was placed into storage at Prague-Ruzyne International airport. The following year it was sold to the Bulgarian carrier Air Sofia (which took delivery of the aircraft on 8th October 1997) and was registered LZ-SFJ.

Czech Air Force An-12B '2105 Black' is seen here on final approach to Moscow-Sheremet'yevo.

DJIBOUTI

Daallo Airlines [D3/DAO] leased 'military' An-12BP UN 11001 (c/n 5343408) from an unknown owner in January-February 2000. In 2003 the airline operated 'military' An-12BP EK-12555 (ex-Antey RA-11367, c/n 8345607) under a UN/WFP contract; the aircraft was later sold as XU-395 No.1.

EGYPT

• The **Egyptian Air Force** (EAF, or *al Quwwat al-Jawwiya il-Misriya*) had 25 *Cubs*, including 15 Voronezh-built An-12Bs delivered in 1964-67 and ten Tashkent-built An-12BPs purchased in 1966-72. The air-

craft were operated by a single squadron (No.16?) based at Cairo-West. At first they wore a restrained civil-style colour scheme with EAF serials and large Egyptian flag fin flashes but no roundels. Civil registrations were added soon afterwards, and these were apparently changed from time to time on some aircraft for security reasons.

Serial	Registration	Version	C/n	Notes
1216	1) SU-AOJ			
	2) SU-AOS?	An-12B (+)	402302	Registration confirmed worn in 1968 Registration reported in 1969 but unconfirmed!
1217	none	An-12B (+)	402303?	Destroyed Cairo-West by Israeli air strikes 6-6-67?
1218	none	An-12B (+)	402304?	Destroyed Cairo-West by Israeli air strikes 6-6-67?
1219	SU-AOI	An-12B (+)	402305	
1220	SU-AOR	An-12B (+)	402306	
1221	SU-AOZ	An-12B (+)	402307?	
1222	SU-APB	An-12B (+)	402308	
1223	SU-AOS	An-12B (+)	402309	Was a testbed for the Brandner E-1 engine in 1962
1224?	SU-AOP	An-12B (+)	402906	
1225?	SU-AOJ	An-12B (+)	402907	
1226	1) SU-AOI?			Registration reported in 1966 but unconfirmed!
	2) SU-AOT			Registration confirmed
	3) SU-BAW	An-12B (+)	402908	Registration confirmed
1227	SU-APA	An-12B (+)	402909	
1228	1) SU-AOI			
	2) SU-APZ	An-12B (+)	402910	
1229	1) SU-AOK			
	2) SU-APC	An-12B (+)	402911?	
1231?	1) SU-AOZ			
	2) SU-ARB	An-12B (+)	402912	Not confirmed if carried EAF serial!
1233	SU-ARC	An-12BP (+)	6344107	
1234	1) SU-AOR			
	2) SU-APX	An-12BP (+)	6344108	
1240	SU-APY	An-12BP (+)	9346706	
1241	SU-ARA	An-12BP (+)	9346707	
1242	SU-ARE	An-12BP (+)	9346709	
1243	SU-ARD	An-12BP (+)	9346710	
1251	SU-ARY	An-12BP (+)	02348209	
1252	SU-AVA	An-12BP (+)	02348210	
1253	SU-ARZ	An-12BP (+)	02348302	
1254	SU-AVB	An-12BP (+)	02348305	

Starting in 1976, the *Cubs* were supplemented and gradually replaced by 23 Lockheed C-130Hs, the last of which arrived in 1982 (later augmented by three 'stretched' C-130H-30s); this was in line with Egypt's new allegiance to the West. The last of the An-12s reportedly remained in service until the early 1990s; eventually, however, all the *Cubs* were retired and progressively scrapped.

• According to *Aircraft Illustrated*, in June 1970 **United Arab Airlines [MS/MSR]** (the precursor of present-day Egyptair) ordered two An-12s. Eventually, however, the order never materialised.

EQUITORIAL GUINEA

• **Atlas Air** operated 'civil' An-12BP 3C-ZZD bought from Santa Cruz Imperial (ex-EL-ALA, c/n 00347305) in 1999; however, the aircraft was sold to Lotus Airways in September of that year.

• **KNG Transavia Cargo [–/VCG]**, a Sharjah-based subsidiary of the Russian airline CNG Transavia, operated 'military' An-12BPs 3C-AAG (ex-RA-98119, c/n 7344801) and 3C-AAL (ex-RA-98103, c/n 00347003). The latter machine was sold to Trans Air Congo in 2004.

• **Space Cargo, Inc. [–/SGO]** based at Sharjah, UAE, acquired two *Cubs* in 2001; these were demilitarised An-12BK 3C-QRD re-equipped with an ROZ-1 radar (ex-Hellier International D2-FBZ, c/n 8346010) and 'civil' An-12BP 3C-QRI (ex-Tiramavia ER-ACJ).

• **Lotus Airways** (also based at Sharjah) purchased 'civil' An-12BP 3C-ZZD from Atlas Air. In 2004 the aircraft was sold to South Airlines as EK-12777.

• Additionally, 'military' An-12BP 3C-AAQ (c/n unknown) and 'civil' An-12BP 3C-OOZ (ex-RA-12975, c/n 9346509) belong to as-yet unidentified operators. (3C-OOZ was reported for Air Cess long after the airline had ceased to exist!) In 2005 the machine was sold to RPS Air Freight Co. as UN 11007.

ETHIOPIA

The **Ethiopian Air Force** (*ye Ethiopia Ayer Hail*) operated sixteen ex-Soviet Air Force An-12BPs delivered in 1977 when Mengistu Haile Mariam seized power. Originally they wore ex-Soviet Air Force grey colours; with the exception of three aircraft lost to enemy action or in accidents, the surviving *Cubs* were repainted in three-tone green/brown camouflage by 2000.

Serial	Version	C/n	Notes
1501	An-12B (+)?	?	
1502	An-12B (+)	401802	
1503	An-12BP (+)	4342009?	
1504	An-12B (+)?	?	
1505	An-12BP (+)	5342907	
1506	An-12B (+)	4342002?	*Ex-CCCP-.... Destroyed by enemy action Tesenni 15-1-84*
1507	An-12B (+)?	?	
1508	An-12B (+)?	?	
1509	An-12B (+)?	?	*Damaged beyond repair at Addis Ababa-Haile Selassie Int'l before 5-84, derelict*
1510	An-12B (+)?	?	
1511	An-12B (+)?	?	
1512	An-12BP (+)	5343206	
1513	An-12B (+)?	?	
1514	An-12B (+)?	?	
1515	An-12B (+)?	?	
1516	An-12B (+)?	?	

FIJI

• **Hellier International** operated 'civil' An-12BP D2-FBY bought from Sakha Avia (ex-RA-12959, c/n 8345510) in 1999. Another Fijian-registered *Cub*, 'military' An-12B DQ-FBS (ex-Ukraine Air Alliance UR-UAF, c/n 3341108) probably also belonged to this airline; it was sold to Moldova in 2001 as ER-ACP.

• **Pacific Express** operated An-12BK ER-AXE (c/n 7345201) on lease from Air Bridge Group in March 2003 – May 2004.

FRANCE

• In May 1999 'military' An-12BP EX-11001 (c/n 6344104?) was operated by the French petroleum company **Motul**, with appropriate titles.

Lasare Air An-12B 4L-11304 touches down on runway 07R at Moscow-Sheremet'yevo.

• The airline **Heli-Union [–/HLU]** based in Paris, Grenoble, Tarbes and Île d'Yeu wet-leased An-12BP UR-11819 (c/n 6344009) from Vitair in 1995.

GEORGIA

• The all-Antonov fleet of **Global Georgian Airways [–/GGZ]** founded in 2004 included An-12BK 4L-12003 (ex/to 4K-AZ33, c/n 9346201) leased from Silk Way Airlines in 2005-06, An-12BP 4L-12008 (ex-Yermolino Airlines RA-11768, c/n 5343103) and An-12BK 4L-AIR (ex-4K-AZ35, c/n 00347102). Only the second aircraft remains now; the first machine has been returned to the lessor, while 4L-AIR has been sold to Tbilaviamsheni.

• **Lasare Air [–/LRE]** flew demilitarised An-12A 4L-11304 (c/n 0901304) in 1995-97 before selling it to Dvin Air Cargo as EK-11304. (However, the 2002/03 edition of the JP Airline-Fleets yearbook lists 4L-11304 for Lasare Air as ex-EK-11304!) Later the airline acquired 'military' An-12B 4L-11241 (ex-Russian Air Force RA-11241, c/n 402102); this aircraft was subsequently reregistered 4L-CAA and then leased to Sarit Airlines in October 2000 as ST-SAR.

• **Tbilaviamsheni [L6/VNZ]**, the flying division of the Tbilisi Aircraft Manufacturing Co. (Tbilaviamsheni is the Georgian name), bought the abovementioned An-12BK 4L-AIR in December 2004. By April 2006 the aircraft had been sold as EX-086 No.2.

• An unknown airline operated An-12BP 4L-12005 (ex-AZAL Cargo 4K-AZ32, c/n 5343006) in September 2005. Barely a month later the aircraft was sold as EX-086 No.1. Another unidentified airline operated an all-white An-12BP registered 4L-TAS (c/n 00347408) reportedly) in late 2003/early 2004. It was reported as being an An-12AP and ex-7P-ANA but this cannot be correct (7P-ANA is indeed an An-12AP with a narrow cargo door, c/n 2340709, whereas 4L-TAS had a wide cargo door!). The machine was sold as EX-119 in 2006.

GHANA

• On 4th October 1961 **Ghana Airways [GH/GHA]** took delivery of an Irkutsk-built 'military' An-12A registered 9G-AAZ (c/n 024009). Among other things the freighter was used for flights to the UK to pick up spares for Ghana Airways' fleet of Bristol Britannia 309s, Vickers Viscount 838s and Vickers VC.10 Srs 1102s.

The *Cub*'s career in Ghana proved to be brief. In 1962 the aircraft was withdrawn from use at Accra – to quote the Royal Air Force Flying Review magazine, 'owing to its inadequate operating economy'. In 1963 the machine was restored to airworthy condition and returned to the Soviet Union; its subsequent fate is unknown.

• According to Royal Air Force Flying Review, in 1961 the **Ghanaian Air Force** received three more An-12s donated by the Soviet government. No serials are known.

GUINEA

• Four 'military' An-12BPs registered 3X-GBA through 3X-GBD (the c/ns of the first three aircraft are 02348008, 02348009 and 7345001) were delivered to Guinea. 3X-GBD has been variously reported as c/n 7345002 (ex-CCCP-11030) and 02348301, but both of these are incorrect (the former aircraft crashed and the latter c/n is an An-12BK-PPS ECM aircraft which was still in Soviet Air Force service in 1990). Though nominally owned by flag carrier **Air Guinée [GI/GIB]**, they were in fact operated by the **Guinea Air Force** (*Force Aérienne de Guinée*).

• Conakry-based Aero Trans Guinée leased 'civil' An-12BP RA-12986 (c/n 00347201) from Samara Airlines in June 1993.

• An obscure company named Minenta Labell Guinée leased demilitarised An-12TB RA-11049 (c/n 9346109) from Yermolino Airlines in early 2002.

INDIA

The **Indian Air Force** (IAF, or *Bharatiya Vayu Sena*) was the first export customer, ordering an initial eight An-12s in 1961; No.44 Sqn 'Mountain Geese' at Agra, Uttar-Pradesh, took delivery of the first *Cub* on 1st March. A second batch of eight was ordered in 1962 for delivery to No.25 Sqn 'Himalayan Eagles' at Chandigarh, Uttar-Pradesh. The IAF was also the largest foreign customer; according to available sources, 46 aircraft built by all three factories producing the type were delivered to the two squadrons but more than 50 serials have been reported. Of course, it is possible that some of the *Cubs* were reserialled.

Serial	Version	C/n	Notes
BL532	An-12A (+)	024001	Grey c/s
BL533	An-12A (+)	024002	F/n 1601. Grey c/s. Damaged 15-8-61 but repaired; later crashed
BL534	An-12A (+)	024003	Crashed in India 8-2-68
BL535	An-12A (+)	024004	
BL536	An-12A (+)	024005	F/n 1603. No.25 Sqn. Crashed Chandigarh AB 5-8-61
BL537	An-12A (+)	024006	
BL538	An-12A (+)	024007	
BL539	An-12A (+)	024008	
BL711	?	?	Coded 'C', grey/white c/s; probably reserialled later
BL726	An-12A (+)	2401204	
L727	An-12A (+)	2401205	Later reserialled BL727. Coded 'G', grey/white c/s, later 'I', grey c/s; preserved IAF Museum, Palam AB

Serial	Version	C/n	Notes
BL728	An-12A (+)	2401206	
BL729	An-12B (+)	2401301	Grey/white c/s
BL730	An-12B (+)	2401302	Coded 'P', grey c/s
BL731	An-12B (+)	2401303	Coded 'U', later 'Z', still later 'Q', grey/white c/s
BL732	An-12B (+)	2401304	Grey/white c/s
BL733	An-12B (+)	2401305	
BL734	An-12B (+)	2401306	Crashed Palam AB 16-7-63
BL735	An-12B (+)	2401401	
BL736	An-12B (+)	2401402	Coded 'N', later 'U'
BL737	An-12B (+)	2401403	Coded 'B'
BL738	An-12B (+)	2401404	Coded 'C', grey/white c/s
BL739	An-12B (+)	2401405	Coded 'D', callsign VU-FPG
BL740	An-12B (+)	2401406	Coded 'L'
BL741	An-12B (+)	2401501	Coded 'Q', later 'F', still later 'G'
L742	An-12B (+)	2401502	Later reserialled BL742. Coded 'E', later 'T', grey/white c/s
BL743	An-12B (+)	2401503	Coded 'D'
BL748?	?	?	Probably reserialled later or mis-sighting
BL913	An-12B (+)	?	Reported as c/n 401504/sold to Cubana as CU-T827 but this is doubtful!
BL914	An-12B (+)	2401505	Coded 'M', later 'Z', callsign VU-PGH
BL915	An-12B (+)	2401506	Coded 'R', grey/white c/s
BL916	An-12B (+)	401601	
BL917	An-12B (+)	401602	
BL918	An-12B (+)	401603	
BL919	An-12B (+)	?	
BL920	An-12B (+)	?	
L450	?	402903?	
L451	?	?	
L452	?	?	
L645	An-12BP (+)	6344205	Coded 'H', later 'S', callsign VU-PPA, grey c/s
L646	An-12BP (+)	6344206	Coded 'J', later 'W', still later 'G', callsign VU-PPB, grey c/s
L647	An-12BP (+)	6344207	Coded 'K', later 'Q', still later 'X', grey c/s
L648	An-12BP (+)	6344208	Coded 'B'
L649	An-12BP (+)	6344209	Coded 'X', later 'J', still later 'Q', grey c/s
L650*	An-12BP (+)	6344210	Coded 'M', grey c/s
L651	An-12BP (+)		Coded 'T'; probably reserialled later
L652	An-12BP (+)		Coded 'M'; probably reserialled later
L653	An-12BP (+)		Coded 'Y'; probably reserialled later
L1471	An-12BP (+)	?	
L1472	An-12BP (+)	?	
L2170	An-12BP (+)	5343101	Coded 'J', grey c/s
L2171	An-12BP (+)	5343302	Coded 'K'?
L2172	An-12BP (+)	5343401	Coded 'L', grey c/s; No.25 Sqn
L2173	An-12BP (+)	6343710	
L2174	An-12BP (+)	6343806	Crashed after 3-83

* Some sources claim L650 was sold to the Iraqi Air Force as I.A.F.685 but this is wrong (see Iraqi section).

Some of the *Cubs* wore overall medium grey camouflage with a white top to the flightdeck to prevent it from turning into a steam bath for the crew, while others sported a more high-viz colour scheme with a white upper fuselage/vertical tail, a grey belly and a thin black cheatline. Individual quick-identification tail codes within each unit were introduced soon after service entry; these were very conspicuous and were thus changed from time to time for security reasons.

In 1984 the IAF decided to replace the An-12 which had done sterling service but was getting long in the tooth in order to meet the HETAC (HEavy Transport AirCraft) requirement; the decision was speeded by the discovery of fatigue cracks in the wing spars of some *Cubs*. The choice fell on the IL-76MD four-turbofan transport; deliver-

Indian Air Force An-12BP L649/'Q' at rest. Note the white top to the crew section, meant to stop it from getting excessively hot in sunny weather.

ies began in February 1985 and the two squadrons gradually phased out the An-12 as deliveries progressed.

INDONESIA

• In August 2004 **Air Mark Indonesia** leased 'civil' An-12BP LZ-SFA (c/n 02348007) from Air Sofia. Additionally, An-12BP UN-11650 (c/n 6344506) was leased from Almaty Avia Cargo in the autumn of 2006.

• When President Soekarno was in office, Indonesia was on fairly good terms with the Soviet Union and enjoyed Soviet military aid. In 1964 the **Indonesian Air Force** (AURI – *Angkatan Udara Republik Indonesia*) bought nine An-12s serialled T-1201 through T-1209; no c/ns are known. T-1205 was named 'Ardjuna' after a famous warrior in the Hindu religion. The first six aircraft became quasi-civil at some stage, receiving the registrations PK-PUA through PK-PUF and 'Ministry of Air Communication' titles; PK-PUB was ex-T-1205, retaining the name 'Ardjuna'.

In 1966, however, Dr. Soekarno was overthrown by the staunchly anti-Communist Gen. Soeharto. A wave of repressions against Communists swept through Indonesia, and Soviet support was promptly withdrawn. Predictably, all Soviet-built aircraft were soon grounded by lack of spares. An-12s PK-PUA, -PUB, -PUD and -PUF had crashed by then; the five surviving aircraft were returned to the USSR and their fate is unknown.

• **Mandala Airlines [RI/MDL]** based in Jakarta wet-leased two *Cubs* – 'civil' An-12BP LZ-SFA (c/n 02348007) and 'military' An-12BP LZ-SFL (c/n 4342101) – from Air Sofia in October-December 1997 and March-May 1998 respectively.

• An-12B CCCP-11236 (c/n 402111) and 'civil' An-12BP CCCP-11130 (c/n 02348205) were leased by a Jakarta-based airline with the almost-unprintable name of **Penas Air Cargo [–/PNS]** in May 1992.

IRAN

• **Bon Air (Bonyad Airlines) [–/IRJ]** operated two Y8F-100s registered EP-BOA and EP-BOB (c/ns unknown) in 1998. There have been reports of a Y8 registered EP-ART and purportedly previously operated by Bon Air.

• **Payam Air [–/IRP]**, aka Payam Aviation Services Co. (formerly IPTAS – Iran Postal & Telecommunications Aviation Services) oper-

ates two Y8F100s registered EP-TPQ and EP-TPX (c/ns 110801 and 110802).

IRAQ

In 1961, 1965, 1966 and 1968 the Iraqi Air Force (IrAF, or al Quwwat al-Jawwiya al-Iraqiya) took delivery of 11 An-12s equipping a single squadron. In the early 1970s five of the *Cubs* were transferred to the civil register, receiving a civil-style colour scheme with Iraqi Airways [IA/IAW] titles/logo to facilitate flights abroad (typically to pick up spares for IrAF combat aircraft).

Serial	Version	C/n	Notes
505	An-12A (+)	024010	Grey c/s
506	An-12A (+)	024011	Grey c/s
507	An-12A (+)	024012	Grey c/s
I.A.F.636?	An-12B (+)	402709	Reported as 636 (exact serial presentation and c/s not known)
I.A.F.637	An-12B (+)	402710	Grey/white c/s
I.A.F.638	An-12B (+)	402711	Grey/white c/s
I.A.F.685	An-12BP (+)	6344305	Grey/white c/s. To YI-AES by 1974. Returned to the USSR by 2-81 as CCCP-11650 No.2
I.A.F.686	An-12BP (+)	6344306	Grey/white c/s. To YI-AGD by 1976; to Royal Jordanian Air Force as 352?
I.A.F.805	An-12BP (+)	8345909	Grey/white c/s. To YI-AEP by 1970; sold to the Sudan Air Force 1992 as ST-ALV No.1
I.A.F.806	An-12BP (+)	8345910	Grey/white c/s. To YI-AFJ by 1973
I.A.F.807	An-12BP (+)	8345908	Grey/white c/s. To YI-AER by 1973; sold to the Sudan Air Force as 988

As already mentioned, one of the *Cubs* was converted locally into a flight refuelling tanker but its identity is not known.

IVORY COAST

Air Afrique [RK/RKA] wet-leased five An-12s from Air Sofia at different times. These were An-12B LZ-SFC (leased in February 1992 and returned before 1997), An-12P LZ-SFG (September-October 1994), An-12B LZ-SFK (January-September 1994), An-12BP LZ-SFL (November 1992 to October 1993) and An-12B LZ-SFN (March 1996 to September 1999).

Part of the Iraqi Air Force's An-12 fleet, including An-12BP I.A.F.806, sported grey/white colours; others were painted grey overall.

Note: Air Afrique is the multinational state carrier of Benin, Burkina Faso, Chad, Congo-Brazzaville, Ivory Coast, Mali, Mauritania, Niger, Senegal and Togo. However, since Air Afrique's own fleet is entirely registered in the Republic of the Ivory Coast, the airline is listed here under this country.

JORDANIA

The **Royal Jordanian Air Force** (RJAF, or *al Quwwat al-Jawwiya al-Urduniya*) operated two An-12BPs serialled 351 and 352 in the early 1980s. The transports, which were reportedly ex-Iraqi aircraft, were operated by the No.3 Sqn in Amman, serving alongside three C-130Bs and four C-130Hs. 352 (c/n 6344306?) eventually ended up in Iraq again and was destroyed at Samarra by a US bomb strike.

KAZAKSTAN

• **Ak-Kanat [–/KAN]**, an airline from Almaty, operated ex-Kazakstan Air Force An-12BP UN 11373 (c/n 02348304) and An-12B UN 11374 (c/n 3341501) in 1999.

• **Almaty Aviation [–/LMT]** had two An-12BPs purchased from Gromov Air – UN-11650 (ex-RA-11650, c/n 6343405) and UN-98102 (ex-RA-98102, c/n 5343005) bought in November 2002. The latter aircraft was sold to PMT Air of Cambodia in 2006 as XU-U4C. UN-11650 was leased to several foreign operators, including Air Mark.

• An airline called **ATMA** operated 'military' An-12BP UN 11003 No.2 (ex-Avial'-NV RA-69314, c/n 5343004) since at least February 2005. On 25th April 2005 the aircraft was written off in a crash landing at Kabul airport.

• **Avia-Pusk [–/GFR]**, an airline based in Almaty, had a demilitarised An-12BP registered UN 11001 (c/n 5343408).

• **GST Aero** (Gulf Sand Tours Cargo) **[–/BMK]** operated An-12B UN-11002 (c/n 4341705) in 2001-02 and An-12BP UN 11009 (ex-EK-11001, c/n 5343408) in early 2006.

• The **Kazakstan Air Force** operates a number of *Cubs*.

Registration/ tactical code	Version	C/n	Notes
UN 11367	An-12B (+)	3341201	Ex-Soviet Air Force '11 Blue'; basic Aeroflot c/s with Kazakstan titles (see Antey/RA-11367)
UN 11373	An-12BP (+)	02348304	Sold or leased to Ak-Kanat in 1999
UN 11374	An-12B (+)	3341501	Sold or leased to Ak-Kanat in 1999
CCCP-11377	An-12B (+)	?	
UN 11395	An-12B (+)	402508	Basic Aeroflot c/s with Kazakstan titles
08 Blue	An-12A (+)	1340209	
12 Red	An-12B (+)	402212	
19 Red	An-12B (+)	3340905	Recoded, previous code unknown
79 Red	An-12BP (+)	5342909	
93 Red	An-12BK-PPS	?	No insignia

• **Miras Air [–/MIF]** leased 'military' An-12BP RA-93913 (c/n 4342609) and 'military' An-12B RA-93915 (c/n 4342103) from Atran – Aviatrans Cargo Airlines in 2002-04. Both aircraft wore full Atran livery with 'Operated for Miras Air' stickers on the forward fuselage.

• **Varty Pacific Airlines [–/MDO]** based in Almaty and Karaganda operated two An-12s – 'military' An-12BP UN11005 (c/n unknown) and 'civil' An-12BP UN 11006 No.1 (ex-Tyumen' Airlines RA-12960, c/n

Kazakstan Air Force An-12B '19 Red' (c/n 3340905) is operated by the 603rd Air Base at Almaty. The unusually light grey, almost silver finish is noteworthy.

9346602). The latter aircraft was sold to Inter Trans Avia in December 2001, becoming EX-12960

• Yet another An-12 registered UN 11006 (No.2, c/n unknown) appeared in August 2002. 'Military' An-12BP UN 11008 (c/n 4342505) was seen in December 2004; their operators are likewise unknown at the time of writing.

KENYA

• **African Airlines** leased An-12BP 4K-AZ30 (c/n 5343410) from Silk Way Airlines in March 2003/February 2004.

• Nairobi-based **Astral Aviation Ltd. [–/ACP]** operated An-12BP EK-12148 (c/n 4341906, named *Albatros*) in 2005; later this aircraft passed to Phoenix Aviation (see Kyrghyzstan). In 2006 Astral Aviation wet-leased An-12BP UR-CEM (c/n 3340908) from Veteran Airlines. The aircraft flew humanitarian missions under the UN World Food Programme.

KYRGHYZSTAN

• **British Gulf International Airlines [–/BGI]** is listed as a Kyrghyz airline but home-based at Sharjah, UAE. Originally the airline's aircraft were registered in São Tomé & Principe; however, they were transferred to the Kyrghyz register in late 2002, receiving three-digit registrations under the current standard. Later aircraft had Kyrghyz numeric registrations from the start. Seven aircraft have been reported.

Registration	Version	C/n	Notes
S9-BOS	An-12BP (–)	01347704	Ex-RA-11102, bought 12-00, named *Julia*. Leased to Sarit Airlines. Became, see next line
EX-163			Named *Julia*
S9-BOT	An-12BP (+)	5343305	Ex-D2-FDT, bought 2001. Leased to Sarit Airlines. Became, see next line
EX-161			Named *Fatima*
S9-CAQ	An-12B (+)	3341408	Ex-Savanair D2-FRT, bought 2001; all-white c/s, named *Akula* (= 'shark' in Russian). Became, see next line
EX-162			Reregistered 11-05, named *Akula*
EX-045	An-12A (+)	2340602	Ex-Russian Air Force (previous identity unknown), bought 2004; named *Igor*
EX-160	An-12BP (+)	401901	Ex-S9-CDB, bought 1999; named *Irena*
EX-164	An-12BP (+)	5343703	Ex-RA-11002, bought 2002, named *Alex*
EX-165	An-12BK	00346908	Ex-Russian Air Force '42 Red', bought 2006

Above left: An-12BP EX-164 'Alex' is one of seven operated by British Gulf International Airlines which, despite the name, is a Kyrghyz airline.
Above: An-12BP ER-AXD is operated by the Kyrghyz carrier Inter Trans Avia, despite being Moldovan-registered.

• **Click Airways [4C/CGK]**, also based at Sharjah, had three An-12s.

Registration	Version	C/n	Notes
EX-029	An-12BK	8345607	Ex-XU-395 No.1; also reported as ex-EK-12555 which is same c/n); leased to Expo Aviation?
EX-031	An-12BP (+)	8346006	Ex-EK-12333, bought 2004, basic Bright Aviation Services c/s
EX-042	An-12BK	00347107	Converted An-12PP! Ex 4R-AIA

• **EX Aero Fret Business**, a sister company of the Congolese airline Aero Fret Business, operated An-12BK EX-124 No.1 (ex-TN-AGZ, c/n 8345403) in mid-2006; see below.

• **Inter Trans Avia Ltd. [YS/ITD]** based at Bishkek-Manas bought a single 'civil' An-12BP, EX-12960 (ex-Varty Pacific Airlines UN 11006, c/n 9346602), in 2001. In 2003 the aircraft was placed on the Moldovan register as ER-AXD.

• The fleet of **KAS Air Company [KW/KSD]**, also based at Manas airport, likewise consists of just one *Cub* – 'military' An-12BP EX-11001 (c/n 6344104). (An-12 registrations have a way of being re-used time and time again; there were four different An-12s registered 11001.)

• Sharjah-based **Phoenix Aviation [–/PHG]**, a division of the Phoenix Free Zone Enterprise, operated An-12B EX-11760 (c/n 4342404) which had previously flown with Trans Air Congo as TN-AGH. The machine was sold to Congo-Kinshasa as 9Q-CVG.

• **Reem Air [V4/REK]** founded in 2004 and based at Sharjah, UAE, operates two *Cubs* bought in 2005 – An-12PS EX-096 (ex-Russian Navy '15 Yellow', c/n 6344608) and 'military' An-12B EX-098 (ex-PMT Air 3X-GDM, c/n 401912). The former aircraft was sold to Gomelavia in June 2006 to become EW-245TI.

• The following An-12s were operated by as yet unidentified Kyrghyz carriers.

Registration	Version	C/n	Notes
EX-084	An-12BK	8345807	Ex-4K-AZ36, bought 2005. Sold to Mango Airlines 2006 as S9-PSK
EX-085	An-12TA	2340801	
EX-086 No.1	An-12BP (+)	5343006	Ex-4L-12004. Became, see next line
EX-092			
EX-119	An-12AP?	?	Ex-4L-TAS; c/n reported as 00347408 but if this is indeed an An-12AP and ex-7P-ANA as advertised, it should be 2340709! Sold as ER-ACV
EX-124 No.2	An-12BK	02348107	Ex-Russian Air Force '50 Red', converted An-12BK-PPS

LESOTHO

Anton Air International [–/ANP], a sister company of Aviakompaniya Pilot (see Russian section), leased all three of its An-12s in 1997.

Registration	Version	C/n	Notes
7P-ANA	An-12B (+)	2340709	Demilitarised. Ex-RA-11038, leased from Aviakompaniya Pilot ?-97
7P-ANB	An-12BP	4342404	Ex-RA-11760, leased from Aviakompaniya Pilot ?-97. To Trans Air Congo as TN-AGH
7P-ANC	An-12BP	9346608	Ex-RA-11658, leased from Aviakompaniya Pilot ?-97
TN-AGF	?	?	Operated in 1998

LIBERIA

• **Air Cess [–/ACS]** based at Sharjah operated four An-12s.

Registration	Version	C/n	Notes
EL-AKN	An-12A (+)	1901706	Ex-von Haaf Air D2-FVD, bought ?-95, named *Flying Cat*; transferred to Air Pass 1998 as 3D-SKN
EL-AKR	An-12BP (+)	9346801?	Ex-Special Cargo Airlines RA-11321?, bought ?-96; sold to Pamir Air same year as YA-PAA
EL-AKV	An-12A (+)	1340107	Ex-Aviastar RA-48971, named *Voyager*; transferred to Air Pass 9-98 as 3D-AKV
EL-RDL	An-12B (+)	2340809	Ex-RA-11734, named *Lastochka* (Swallow); transferred to Air Pass 11-98 as 3D-RDL

• **Flying Dolphin**, another Sharjah-based cargo airline, (later rebranded **Santa Cruz Imperial [–/SCI]**, operated nine An-12s.

Santa Cruz Imperial An-12BP EL-ALJ languishes in non-airworthy condition at Sharjah.

Registration	Version	C/n	Notes
EL-ALA	An-12BP (–)	00347405	Ex-RA-12991, bought ?-96; sold to Atlas Air ?-99 as 3C-ZZD
EL-ALB	An-12B (+)	402108	Ex-Special Cargo Airlines RA-12116, bought ?-96
EL-ALD		?	
EL-ALF	An-12BP (+)	9346801?	Ex-Pamir Air YA-PAA, bought ?-96
EL-ALJ	An-12BK	8346202	Ex-Pamir Air YA-PAB, re-equipped with ROZ-1 radar; bought ?-97
EL-ANB		?	
EL-ASA	An-12A (+)	3340909	Ex-Special Cargo Airlines RA-11890, bought 8-10-97. Leased to Savanair; crashed Luanda 2-2-99
EL-ASC	An-12B (+)	3341206	Ex-Southern Cross 3D-ASC, ex-Amuraviatrans RA-11831, bought ?-97
EL-ASS	An-12B (+)	?	Reported as ex-RA-11890 in error; reregistered EY-ASS (!) 27-7-98

• **ACS Air Charter Service [–/ACH]** leased 'civil' An-12BP UR-LTG (c/n 00347201) from Volare Aviation Enterprise in April 2000. The aircraft wore full Volare colours – except for the tail logo, which was that of ACS! The scenario was repeated in late 2002 when An-12BK UR-UCK (c/n 9346905) was leased from Ukrainian Cargo Airways, operating from Amsterdam-Schiphol as a temporary base; this time the aircraft also gained 'www.aircharter.co.uk' titles on the tail.

LIBYA

Kallat el-Saker Air [–/KES] operates a 'civil' An-12BP, ER-ADG (c/n 00347109), leased from Grixona in November 2005.

MACEDONIA

Avioimpex [M4/AXX] leased a demilitarised An-12B, LZ-SFL (c/n 4342101), from Air Sofia in June 1995; the aircraft was reregistered Z3-AFA. In mid-1996, however, it was returned to the lessor, regaining its former identity.

MALDIVES

Air Cargo Maldives leased 'military' An-12BP LZ-SFE (c/n 5342708) from Air Sofia in 1992.

MALI

Transair Mali leased 'civil' An-12BP CCCP-12981 (c/n 00347104) from Aeroflot's Noril'sk UAD in 1992.

MALTA

Air Malta [KM/AMC] operated 'civil' An-12BP CCCP-12965 (c/n 9346409) wet-leased from Aeroflot (Rostov-on-Don UFD) between 19th May and 19th July 1992.

MOLDOVA

• **Aeriantur-M [–/MBV]** has a single 'military' An-12BP, ER-AXI (ex-Avial' RA-11339, c/n 6344310), bought in February 2005. The aircraft retains basic Avial'/Russian Postal Service colours.

• **Aerocom [–/MCC]** which, like most Moldovan airlines, is based in Kishinyov (Chisinau), operated five An-12s.

Registration	Version	C/n	Notes
ER-ACI	An-12BP (+)	6343707	Ex-ICAR Airlines UR-PWH, bought ?-99
ER-ACP	An-12B (+)	3341108	Ex-DQ-FBS, bought ?-01, named *July Morning*. Sold to Vega Avia 2003 as 9XR-MK?
ER-ADE	An-12A (+)	2340503	Ex-D2-FCU, bought ?-00
ER-ADT	An-12A (+)	2340605	Ex-Renan, bought ?-98. Crashed Honiara 16-10-01
ER-AXA	An-12BP (–)	01347907	Ex-Avial'-NV RA-11112 (or ex-Bright Aviation Services LZ-BRW?), bought 2-02. Operated for Air Bridge Group

• **Air Bridge Group** operated An-12BK ER-AXE (previous identity unknown, c/n 7345201) in early 2003. By December 2006 it had been sold to Armenia as EK-12201.

• **Airline Transport, Inc. [–/RIN]** has two An-12BKs – ER-AXY (ex-Air Sofia LZ-SFT, c/n 9346904) and ER-AXZ (ex-Ukrainian Air Force '03 Blue', c/n 8346106) bought in 2004. The aircraft are operated in an anonymous red/white colour scheme.

• An airline called **Grixona [–/GXA]** operates two 'civil' An-12BPs – ER-ACY (ex-RA-12992, c/n 00347306) and ER-ADG (ex-Magadan-

East meets West. Many Moldovan *Cubs* are anonymous-looking, and An-12BK ER-AXZ (seen here making an interesting contrast with United Parcel Service Airbus Industrie A300-622F N149UP) belongs to Airline Transport, Inc.

avialeasing RA-12984, c/n 00347109) leased in 2005. The latter aircraft was sub-leased to the Libyan airline Kallat el Saker.

• In March 2006 **ICS-Air** acquired a single 'civil' An-12BP registered ER-ACS (ex-Avial'-NV RA-12994, c/n 00347401).

• The small fleet of **JetLine International [–/MJL]** whose aircraft are Moldovan-registered but based in the Ukraine includes a single An-12BP, ER-AXK (c/n 00347005), bought in 2004.

• Originally known as **Mikma [–/ITL]** and renamed **Tiramavia [–/TVI]** in 2000, the flying division of the Mikma electronics industry enterprise operated at least 15 An-12s.

Seen here visiting Sharjah, An-12BP ER-AXE of Air Bridge Group was operated for the United Nations Peace Forces and still wears white UNPF colours.

Registration	Version	C/n	Notes
ER-ACA	An-12BK	00347102	Ex-Soviet Air Force? Bought ?-00. Sold to Azerbaijan by 8-03 as 4K-AZ35
ER-ACB	An-12A (+)	2340608	Ex-Soviet Air Force CCCP-10231. Sold to Angolan Air Force 2004 as D2-MBD
ER-ACD*	An-12B (+)	402605	Ex-Algerian Air Force 7T-WAC/514, bought ?-95. Sold to ALADA by 1998 as D2-FAW
ER-ACE*	An-12B (+)	402812	Ex-Algerian Air Force 7T-WAG/591, bought ?-95. Lst Aerotropical, Lda; shot down Lukapa, Angola, 27-2-96
ER-ACG	An-12BP (–)	9346504	Ex-Special Cargo Airlines RA-12972. Sold to Congo Brazzaville as TN-AGK No.1
ER-ACH	An-12BP (+)	4342209	Ex-Slovak Air Force '2209 Black'. Sold to Angolan Air Force by 9-01 as T-309
ER-ACJ	An-12BP (–)	01347909	Ex-National Commuter Airlines D2-FDC, bought by 5-01. Sold to Space Cargo, Inc ?-01 as 3C-QRI
ER-ACL	An-12A (+)	0901306	Bought by 5-98. Sold to Aero Fret Business by 2004 as TN-AHA
ER-ACO	An-12BP	5343204	Ex-Uzbekistan Airways UK 11372, bought 2005, basic Uzbekistan c/s
ER-ACR	An-12BP	6343810	Ex-Uzbekistan Airways UK 11369, bought 2005, basic Uzbekistan c/s
ER-ACZ	An-12BK	7345403	Ex-RA-93922. Sold to Trans Air Congo as TN-AGZ
ER-ADB	An-12TB	402007	Ex-CCCP-11532. Sold to Angolan Air Force 2003 as T-306
ER-ADC	An-12B	1340206	Ex-Atlant UR-11501, bought 2000; sold to Air Fret Business ?-04 as TN-AGY
ER-ADO	An-12B	8346105	Ex-Busol Airline UR-11347, bought 2004; sold to Sudan 2006
ER-ADL	An-12BP (+)	4342610	Ex-D2-FBD. Crashed Monrovia 15-2-02
ER-ADM	An-12BP (+)	5343405	Ex-NAPO-Aviatrans RA-12388. Sold to Angolan Air Force by 1-01 as T-301
ER-ADN	An-12B (+)	3341606	Ex-NAPO-Aviatrans RA-11328, bought ?-99; opf DHL. Sold to Air Sofia by 2006 as LZ-SFI
ER-AXG	An-12BK	00347407	Ex-Soviet Air Force '12 Yellow', bought 2003; operated for DHL

* ER-ACD and ER-ACE were reported for Velocity Airlines in some sources.

• **Pecotox-Air [–/PXA]** operated An-12AP ER-AXM (ex-Air Sofia LZ-SFN, c/n 2340806) leased in October 2003. The aircraft was returned in mid-2005, regaining its Bulgarian registration.

• The cargo airline **Renan [–/RAN]** had three An-12s.

Registration	Version	C/n	Notes
ER-ACK No.1	An-12BP (–)	8345503	Ex-Ural Airlines RA-12952. Sold to Burundi ?-00 as 9U-BHO
ER-ADD	An-12AP (+)	2340403	Ex-Soviet Air Force CCCP-11961
ER-ADT	An-12AP (+)	2340605	Ex-RA-11382. Also reported as ER-ADI; opf Air Bridge Group. Sold to Aerocom

• **Sud Aerocargo** had at least one An-12BP, ER-AXB (ex-Avialeasing UK 11418, c/n 7344705) bought in 2001. In January 2002, however, the aircraft was sold to an unknown owner as 3C-QRN.

• The fleet of **Tepavia Trans [–/TET]** includes An-12BP ER-ADK (ex-Varty Pacific UN11005, c/n 5342802) and An-12BK ER-AXL (c/n 8345809) purchased in November 2003 and June 2004 respectively.

• **Valan International Cargo Charter Ltd. [–/VLN]** acquired a single An-12BK, ER-AXC (former tactical code unknown, c/n 7345209), in 2001. In 2002 it was sold to AZZA Air Transport of Sudan as ST-DAS. However, in 2003 the carrier acquired An-12BP '661 Black' (c/n 5343208) from the Russian Air Force; this aircraft became ER-AXH.

• Some Moldovan *Cubs* were/are anonymous-looking and the operators remain unknown. Such aircraft include 'military' An-12B ER-ACC (ex-Algerian Air Force 7T-WAB, c/n 402606), An-12TA ER-ACK No.2 (ex-11383, c/n 2340604; sold to ALADA (?) as D2-FBV), ER-ACT (version and c/n unknown) reported in 1999, An-12AP (?) ER-ACV (ex-EX-119), An-12BK ER-AXQ (ex-'96 Red' and '17 Red', c/n 8345805) and An-12BK ER-AXX (ex-Air Ukraine UR-11314, c/n 8345604) registered in 2006. ER-AXQ was sold to Africa West Airlines as UN 11376 that year.

MOZAMBIQUE

The **Mozambique People's Air Force** (FPA – *Força Popular Aérea de Moçambique*) had at least two An-12s serialled 011 and 012 (c/ns unknown). Both were apparently on lease from the Soviet Air Force (or masqueraded in FPA markings for appearance's sake) and were eventually returned to the USSR

MYANMAR

The **Myanmar Air Force** has four Shaanxi Y8Ds on strength delivered between September 1992 and November 1994. These wear a civil-style colour scheme and are serialled 5815 through 5818 (c/ns 080803, 080804 (?), 090801 and 090802).

Like some other Polish Air Force aircraft, its two An-12BPs were periodically leased by LOT Polish Airlines. Here SP-LZB is seen at rest wearing LOT tail colours and appropriate titles; the aircraft should have had a white belly and a different cheatline with huge LOT titles at the front in keeping with the 1977 standard.

NEW ZEALAND

Air New Zealand [NZ/ANZ] wet-leased 'military' An-12BP LZ-SFL (c/n 4342101) from Air Sofia between August and 5th December 1997.

NIGERIA

• **Dasab Airlines** operates 'military' An-12B 9XR-MK (c/n 3341108?) jointly with Rwandan carrier Vega Avia which owns the aircraft.

• **Fresh Air Cargo [–/FRR]** based at Sharjah, UAE, operates a single 'civil' An-12BP, 5N-BCN (ex-RA-12965, c/n 9346409), leased from Aeroflot-Don in May 2001. In 2004 the aircraft was reregistered 3X-GDR; its operator at the time is unknown.

• **Harco Air Services [–/HCO]** based in Kaduna leased 'civil' An-12BP RA-11114 (c/n 01347909) from Komiavia in August 1992. The aircraft was also operated for Nigeria Mails at the same time.

PAKISTAN

Royal Airlines [R0/RPK] based in Karachi leases *Cubs* from British Gulf International as required. In May 2005 it leased 'military' An-12BP EX-164 (c/n 5343703).

PERU

In 1991 **Compania de Aviación Peruana** operated two *Cubs* leased from the Soviet Ministry of Aircraft Industry's Moscow UFD/201st Flight – An-12BK OB-1448 (ex-CCCP-11868, c/n 9346310) and 'civil' An-12BP OB-1449 (ex-CCCP-12990, c/n 00347304). Both aircraft were returned in 1992, regaining their original identities.

POLAND

For several years the Polish Armed Forces had to rely on Big Brother to provide aircraft for landing major airborne assaults. For instance, in May 1963 the troopers of the 6th Airborne Division (6. PDPD) made use of Soviet Air Force An-8s and An-12s to take their training. On 26th October 1965 a group of 6. PDPD paratroopers was air-dropped over the Erfurt training ground in East Germany during the Warsaw Pact exercise *Oktyabr'skaya grozah* (October Storm).

In 1966, however, the **Polish Air Force** (PWL – *Polskie Wojsko Lotnicze*) got its own strategic airlift capability, taking delivery of two

An-12BPs which were serialled '50 Red' (c/n 6344307) and '51 Red' (c/n 6344308). The *Cubs* equipped a squadron of the 13th Transport Regiment (13. PLT – *Pulk Lotnictwa Transportowego*) which was based at Kraków-Balice.

The PWL put the type to good use, participating in various WarPac exercises. Real-life airlift missions were also performed; for example, in November-December 1973, as related in Chapter 7, the *Cubs* airlifted the Polish contingent of the United Nations Peace Forces to the Middle East to help maintain peace in the days after the Yom Kippur War. The contingent largely consisted of 6. PDPD personnel.

The first such mission was flown on 13th November when a PWL An-12 delivered ten officers, three GAZ-69 jeeps with drivers and various items of equipment to Cairo-West. Starting on 16th November, a steady stream of Polish servicemen doing the first tour of UNPF duty poured into Egypt, accompanied by all the necessary materiel and supplies – right down to firewood for the stoves! The non-stop flights took them from Kraków through Budapest, Skopje and Crete; the flights lasted an average of 5 hours and 20 minutes. The last sortie was flown on 12th December.

The PWL's transport element was regularly used in the interests of civilian organisations and the An-12s were leased to **LOT Polish Airlines [LO/LOT]** several times, receiving civil registrations and an appropriate colour scheme; the aircraft flew cargo charters to Astrakhan' (USSR), Hanoi, Cairo, London, Benghazi, Rome, Tokyo etc. Thus, '50 Red' was registered SP-LZA from 8th June to 17th July 1967 and on 27th September 1972; unfortunately on 13th May 1977 it crashed on approach to Beirut. '51 Red' was registered SP-LZB from 8th June to 17th July 1967, from 29th May 1968 to 24th July 1972 and on 9th October 1972; on 2nd July 1993 it made its final flight in Polish service and was withdrawn from use at Kraków-Balice. Fortunately this was not the end of the road yet; on 10th February 1995 the aircraft was sold to Air Sofia as LZ-SFS.

PORTUGAL

Air Luxor [–/LXR] leased An-12B LZ-SFG (c/n 3341605) from Air Sofia in late 1997 or January 1998. Unfortunately, on 4th February 1998 the aircraft was lost in a crash at Lajes in the Azores.

RUSSIA

• **Aerofreight Airlines** (aka Aerofrakht) [–/FRT] founded in 1998 operated seven An-12s. On 2nd September 2002 the airline's operating licence was revoked after one of its aircraft was found to be overloaded by 50% (!).

Registration	Version	C/n	Notes
RA-11115	An-12BP (–)	01348003	Lsf Aeroflot-Don; basic Aeroflot c/s, Aeroflot-Don logo/Aerofreight Airlines titles
RA-11116	An-12BP (–)	01348006	Leased from Tesis
RA-11124	An-12BP (–)	02348106	Leased from Tesis
RA-11408	An-12B (+)	3341209	Ex-Aviaobshchemash, full c/s. Sold to Silk Way Airlines 7-04 as 4K-AZ56
RA-11529	An-12BP (+)	6344109	Leased from Aviastar, basic Aviastar c/s
RA-12974	An-12BP (–)	9346506	Leased from Aeroflot-Don. To Avial'-NV
RA-12992	An-12BP (–)	00347306	Ex-Avial'-NV, bought ?-02
RA-12994	An-12BP (–)	00347401	Leased from Aeroflot-Don by 8-01. To Avial'-NV
RA-48984	An-12B (+)	402913	Ex-Ukraine Air Alliance UR-48984; leased from VASO. Transferred to Vim Airlines ?-03

Registration	Version	C/n	Notes
RA-11813	An-12B (+)	3340908	Ex-Ukraine Air Alliance UR-11813. Sold to Veteran by 2005 as UR-CEM
RA-11831	An-12B (+)	3341206	Sold to Southern Cross ?-97 as 3D-ASC
RA-11886	An-12A (+)	2340302	Sold to Noril'sk Air Enterprise 22-12-95
RA-11890	An-12B (+)	3340909	Sold to Special Cargo Airlines 16-8-97
RA-13341	An-12BP (+)	9346904	Demilitarised. Sold to Solis Aviation ?-01 as LZ-SAA

• **Antares Air [–/ANH]** bought demilitarised An-12BP RA-11013 (c/n 6344002) from KiT in 1995, operating it in basic Aeroflot colours with no titles or logo. On 14th August 1996 the aircraft was cancelled from the Russian register and sold to São Tomé & Principe, becoming S9-CAN on 13th October 1997.

• **Aero-Nika** leased 'military' An-12A RA-11790 (c/n 1400302) from the Yermolino Flight Test & Research Enterprise on 11th September 1994. Unfortunately the aircraft crashed in Ust'-Ilimsk on 29th October that year.

• An airline called **Airstars** (or, in Russian, Aerostars) **[–/ASE]** leased An-12BK RA-13392 (c/n 00347210) from KAPO-Avia (see below) in June 2001. The aircraft was in basic KAPO-Avia colours with Airstars (to port)/Aerostars (to starboard) titles; in 2003 it was repainted in full Airstars colours. In 2006 Airstars leased 'military' An-12BP RA-11529 (c/n 6344109) from Aviastar.

• An airline called **Alfa 92** operated An-12BP RA-11311 (c/n 1400201) in 1996.

• **Amuraviatrans [–/AAX]**, the flying division of the Amur Shipbuilding Plant in Komsomol'sk-on-Amur operated five An-12s.

• **Antey [–/TEY]**, the flying division of the Omsk 'Polyot' Aircraft Production Association (OAPO – *Omskoye aviatsionnoye proizvodstvennoye obyedineniye 'Polyot'*, ex-MAP aircraft factory No.166), had

Registration	Version	C/n	Notes
RA-11301	An-12PP	00347107	Ex-Ukrainian AF '71 Red', converted to freighter, refitted with ROZ-1 radar. Sold to Inter Trans Air as LZ-ITD
RA-11302	An-12BP (+)	8346004	Demilitarised. Crashed Colombo 24-3-00
RA-11303	An-12BK	00347604	Sold to Veteran Airlines
RA-11367*	An-12BP (+)	8345607	Sold to Daallo Airlines 2003 as EK-12555
RA-11368†	An-12BP (+)	8346006	Sold to Inter Trans Air ?-00 as LZ-ITB
RA-11369‡	An-12BP (+)	00346909	
RA-11665	An-12BP (+)	6343903	

RA-11301 was the most unusual among the aircraft operated by Antey, being a demilitarised An-12PP. Note that the Initsiativa-4-100 radar has been replaced by an ROZ-1 radar in a small radome.

An-12BP RA-11339 belonging to Avial'-NV was operated for the Russian Postal Service as a mailplane, wearing this striking colour scheme with *Pochta Rossii* titles and a 'double eagle' on the tail in addition to the owner's titles. It is seen here at Moscow-Sheremet'yevo.

seven An-12s (see table on previous page). The plant performs An-2 to An-3 conversions, manufactures the An-74 STOL transport and is to build the An-70 heavy STOL transport.

Notes:

* The registration was originally worn by demilitarised An-12B CCCP-11367 (c/n 402901) and – concurrently with RA-11367 – by 'military' An-12B UN 11367 (c/n 3341201)!

† The registration was previously worn by An-12B CCCP-11368 with unknown c/n and An-12BP EW-11368 (c/n 4342010).

‡ The registration was concurrently worn by demilitarised An-12BP UK 11369 (c/n 6343810)!

• **Antex-Polyus [–/AKP]** based at Yermolino industrial airfield near Moscow bought An-12TA RA-11098 (c/n 2340801) from the defunct Yermolino Airlines in 2002. The aircraft was eventually sold to Azerbaijan as 4K-AZ59.

• The **Arsen'yev 'Progress' Aircraft Production Association** (AAPO – *Arsen'yevskoye aviatsionnoye proizvodstvennoye obyedineniye 'Progress'*, ex-MAP aircraft factory No.116), had two 'military' An-12BPs – RA-11650 (ex-CCCP-11650 No.2, ex-Iraqi Air Force I.A.F.685, c/n 6344305) and RA-98102 (ex-CCCP-98102 No.2, c/n 5343005). Both were eventually sold to Gromov Air (see below). The plant manufactured the Mil Mi-24 attack helicopter, the Mi-34 light utility helicopter, as well as Yak-50 and Su-26 competition aerobatic aircraft; now it builds the Kamov Ka-50 Black Shark attack helicopter and the Yak-54 aerobatic aircraft.

• **Atlant-Soyuz Airlines [3G/AYZ]** established on June 8, 1993 operates scheduled and charter passenger and cargo services from Moscow (Sheremet'yevo-2 and Domodedovo) and Chkalovskaya AB, mostly with aircraft leased from other carriers and the Russian, Belorussian and Ukrainian air forces as required. These included numerous *Cubs* which came and went, so to say.

Atlant-Soyuz is known as 'the Moscow Government airline' – for more than one reason. Firstly, the Moscow Government has a stake in

Registration	Version	C/n	Notes
RA-11049	An-12BP (+)	8346109	Demilitarised. Lsf Yermolino Flight Test & Research Enterprise
RA-11113	An-12BP (–)	01347908	Ex-CCCP-11113 No.2.* Derelict Moscow-Vnukovo by 8-01
RA-11125	An-12B (+)	3341006	Demilitarised, Aeroflot polar c/s. Lsf Komsomol'sk-on-Amur Aviation Production Association 1996
RA-11356	An-12BP (+)	7345206	Lsf Yermolino Flight Test & Research Enterprise 3-99
RA-11516	An-12BP (+)	4341909	Lsf Yermolino Flight Test & Research Enterprise 1997
RA-11666?	An-12BP (+)	?	Seen Luxembourg 9-01; registration confirmed but operator unconfirmed!
RA-11916	An-12AP (+)	2400901	Lsf Yermolino Flight Test & Research Enterprise 1997. Basic Aeroflot colours, no titles
RA-12984	An-12BP (–)	00347109	Lsf Magadanavialeasing 1998. Ex-Magadanaerogrooz; white overall, MAG Cargo Services (Magadanaerogrooz) stickers

the airline; secondly, Moscow Mayor Yuriy M. Luzhkov and other government officials often made use of the airline's aircraft during trips in Russia and abroad. Hence some Atlant-Soyuz aircraft wear additional Cyrillic 'Aviakompahniya pravitel'stva Moskvy' titles, much to the amusement of spotters. No An-12s remain in the fleet as of now.

* CCCP-11113 No.1 was a grey-painted 'military' An-12BP.

• **Avia (Yuriy Petrov's Airline) [–/AWL]**, a private enterprise based at Novosibirsk-Tolmachovo, operated 'civil' An-12BP RA-11122 (c/n 02348104) and 'civil' An-12A RA-11131 (c/n 2400702) purchased from Klyuch-Avia. Despite lacking a tail gunner's station, the latter aircraft was originally a military communications relay version with an extra APU in the aft fuselage.

• Aviacor [–/VCR], the flying division of the Samara aircraft factory of the same name, operated two 'civil' Cubs – An-12BP RA-11110 (ex-CCCP-11110 No.2, c/n 01347902) and An-12B RA-11117 (c/n 5402707) from Samara-Bezymyanka airfield. The former aircraft was written off in a landing accident at El Fasmer, Sudan, on 7th August 1993; the other one was sold to Etele Air by October 1998.

• Starting in 1992, the Moscow cargo airline **Avial' Aviation Company Ltd. [–/RLC]** operating from Domodedovo, Sheremet'yevo-1 and Zhukovskiy operated twelve An-12s. In 2000 the name was changed to **Avial'-NV**.

Registration	Version	C/n	Notes
RA-11112	An-12BP (–)	01347907	*Ex-Tyumen' Airlines. White overall, no titles. Sold to Aerocom 2-02 as ER-AXA*
RA-11128*	An-12BP (–)	02348203	*Ex-Tyumen' Airlines; full c/s. Sold to Veteran Airline 2004 as UR-CEN*
RA-11130	An-12BP (–)	02348205	Ex-Sakha Avia, bought by 2006
RA-11324*	An-12B (+)	2340805	*Demilitarised, full c/s. Sold to Showa Airlines by 7-03 as 9L-LDW?*
RA-11339	An-12BP (+)	6344310	*Ex-Penza Air Enterprise; ex-CCCP-11339 No.2.† Demilitarised, full c/s; later Russian Postal Service c/s. Sold to Aeriantur-M 2-05 as ER-AXI*
RA-11345	An-12B (+)	401801	*Ex-Sakha Avia. Demilitarised, full c/s. Leased to Air Armenia 9-03 to 6-04 as EK-12001. Sold to Air Sofia by 1-05 as LZ-SFR*
RA-11766	An-12B (+)	401605	*Lst/jointly operated with East Line (1998); basic Aeroflot colours, large East Line titles; sold to Etele Air ?-00*
RA-11899*	An-12B (–)	402601	*Full c/s; sold or retired by 2002*
RA-11906	An-12AP (+)	2340802	Ex-Noril'sk Air Enterprise
RA-12974	An-12BP (–)	9346506	In service 12-05
RA-12992	An-12BP (–)	00347306	*Lst/jointly operated with East Line (1998); basic Aeroflot colours, no titles; sold to Aerofreight Airlines by 2002*
RA-12994	An-12BP (–)	00347401	*Ex-Aerofreight Airlines, in service 2005. Sold to ICS-Air 3-06 as ER-ACS*
RA-69314	An-12BP (+)	5343004	*Ex-Aviast, bought 2004. Sold to ATMA as UN 11003 No.2*

* Aircraft thus marked originally wore full livery with Avial' titles (without the 'NV' suffix).

† CCCP-11339 No.1 was a Voronezh-built An-12A (c/n 2400505).

• The Troitsk-based cargo carrier **Aviaobschchemash [–/OBM]**, also referred to as **AOM Air Company** (not to be confused with the French AOM – Air Outre Mer), operated eight An-12s in Aeroflot colours. As the name implies, Aviaobschchemash was the flying division of the former Ministry of General Machinery (Minobschchemash).

Registration	Version	C/n	Notes
RA-11327	An-12A (+)	1400104	Ex-Russian Air Force. Damaged Bryansk 8-11-97
RA-11408	An-12B (+)	4341209	Blue/white tail. Sold to Aerofreight Airlines ?-00
RA-11532	An-12B (+)	402007	
RA-11756	An-12BP (+)	4342208	Sold to Aviast
RA-11795	An-12A (+)	8900704	Ex-CCCP-11795 No.2*
RA-11830	An-12B (+)	4342210	
RA-11851	An-12TB (+)	402003	Crashed Nizhnevartovsk 2-11-96
RA-98116	An-12A (+)	9901101	

* CCCP-11795 No.1 was a demilitarised An-12A (c/n 1400103) which crashed on 25th March 1986.

• **Aviaprima Sochi Airlines [J5/PRL]** briefly leased 'civil' An-12BP RA-11959 from Samara Airlines in May 1994.

• An airline called **Aviast [–/VVA]** operated four An-12s.

Registration	Version	C/n	Notes
RA-11756	An-12BP (+)	4342208	Bought from Aviaobschchemash, grey/white c/s
RA-11962	An-12BP (+)	5343007	Bought from Trans Aero Samara, demilitarised, full c/s
RA-69314	An-12BP (+)	5343004	Leased from Aviastar 2001, basic Aviastar c/s. Sold to Avial'-NV 2004
RA-48494	?	?	In service by 2-07
RA-48984	An-12B (+)	402913	Leased from VASO by 7-06

• Looking rather smart, demilitarised An-12BP RA-93913 of Atran Cargo Airlines sits on the east apron at Moscow-Domodedovo on 20th August 2002. Sister ship RA-93915 visible beyond wears additional 'Operated for Miras Air' titles. Note the difference in the style of the Atran titles.

• The fleet of the **Aviastar Joint-Stock Company [–/FUE]** included two 'military' An-12BPs – RA-11529 (c/n 6344109) and RA-69314. The two aircraft were eventually sold to Airstars and Avial' respectively by December 2004. Aviastar is the post-Soviet name of the Ul'yanovsk Aircraft Production Complex (UAPK – *Ool'yah*novskiy *aviatsi*onnyy *proiz*vod*stvennyy* **kom***pleks*) building the An-124 Ruslan heavy transport and the Tu-204 medium-range airliner.

• **Aviatrans Cargo Airlines [V8/VAS]** established in 1992 (formerly the 201st Flight of MAP's Moscow UFD) operated eight *Cubs* from Moscow-Domodedovo and Moscow-Myachkovo. On 1st January 1997 the airline was renamed **Atran – Aviatrans Cargo Airlines**.

Registration	Version	C/n	Notes
RA-11868	An-12BK	9346310	Full c/s
RA-11901	An-12A (+)	1340103	Basic Aeroflot c/s; WFU Myachkovo by 8-98, used for spares
RA-12990	An-12BP (–)	003437304	Full c/s
RA-93912	An-12B (+)	4341709	Full c/s
RA-93913	An-12BP (+)	4342609	Full c/s, c/n falsely painted on as 3442609!; lst Miras Air by 8-02
RA-93915	An-12B (+)	4342103	Full c/s, c/n falsely painted on as 4132103!; lst Miras Air by 8-02. Sold to AeroVis 2005 as UR-CEX
RA-98117	An-12B (+)	402301	
RA-98118	An-12BP (+)	6344304	Demilitarised. Basic Aeroflot c/s. Sold to AeroVis 2005 as UR-CEZ

• **Baikal Airlines [X3/BKL]**, alias **Baikalavia**, was the successor of the East Siberian CAD's Irkutsk UAD. Its fleet included six An-12s. The airline's financial position was shaky in the late 1990s and plans of a merger with Chita-Avia in the hope of improving things were announced in April 1998. However, the 17th August 1998 bank crisis ruined these plans and Baikal Airlines filed for bankruptcy in September. Operations were restarted on a small scale in the spring of 1999

but the company terminally vanished soon afterwards; the fate of its aircraft is mostly unknown.

Registration	Version	C/n	Notes
RA-11032	An-12BP (–)	7345004	
RA-11034	An-12BP (–)	7345010	
RA-11116	An-12BP (–)	01348006	Sold to Tesis
RA-11124	An-12BP (–)	02348106	Sold to Tesis
RA-11996	An-12B (+)	402504	
RA-12988	An-12BP (–)	00347206	Basic Aeroflot colours, no titles. Sold to Flight JSC

• **CNG Transavia [–/CGT]** based in Voronezh had An-12BK RA-98103 (c/n 00347003) and 'military' An-12BP RA-98119 (c/n 7344801). They were leased to Sharjah-based subsidiary KNG Transavia Cargo as 3C-AAL and 3C-AAG respectively.

• The **Chelyabinsk Air Enterprise** (*Chelya*binskoye *a*viapred*priyah*tiye) **[H6/CHB]**, formerly **Chelal** (Chelyabinsk Airlines), operated a single 'civil' An-12BP (RA-12987, c/n 00347202) in basic Aeroflot polar colours without titles but with the old Chelal 'bird' nose logo. The aircraft was sold to ALADA as D2-FRG in July 1998.

• Moscow-based **Dobrolyot [–/DOB]** was an airline with a famous name. The original Dobrolyot was a passenger carrier, the precursor of Aeroflot, and ceased operations in 1922. Reborn 70 years later as a cargo airline, the new Dobrolyot was the flying division of the Soyuz Production Association (NSA Soyuz), an aerospace industry company. Its fleet included An-12B RA-11240 (c/n 402706).

• **Donavia Joint-Stock Co.** (*Donskiye a*vialini*i* – Don Airlines) **[D9/DNV]** was established in August 1993 as the successor of the North Caucasian CAD/Rostov-on-Don UAD. Its fleet included five late-production 'civil' An-12BPs. In 1998 the debt-ridden airline came under outside management and, after a period of negotiations with

Still wearing the original Donavia titles, An-12BP RA-11115 is seen here visiting Dubai.

An-12B RA-11766, one of several operated by East Line over the years, 'cleans up' as it climbs away from Moscow-Domodedovo.

Aeroflot Russian Airlines, was absorbed as the Rostov division, changing its name to **Aeroflot-Don** in 2000.

Registration	C/n	Notes
RA-11115	01348003	Full colour scheme. Leased to Aerofreight Airlines
RA-12960	9346602	Full colour scheme. Sold to Varty Pacific as UN 11006
RA-12965	9346409	Leased to Fresh Air Cargo 5-01 as 5N-BCN
RA-12974	9346506	
RA-12994	00347401	

• Established at Moscow-Domodedovo in 1993, **East Line [P7/ESL]** grew into a major airline with a wide network of cargo services; passenger services were added later. Originally the carrier had no fleet of its own, and its An-12s were leased from other airlines as required – often in the owner's colours with East Line titles.

In December 2004 the airline division of East Line Group was renamed **Roosskoye Nebo/Russian Sky**. No An-12s were operated under this trading name.

Registration	Version	C/n	Notes
RA-11112	An-12BP (–)	01347907	Lsf/jointly operated with Avial' (1998); white overall, partial UN titles
RA-11766	An-12B (+)	401605	Lsf/jointly operated with Avial' (1998); basic Aeroflot c/s, large East Line titles
RA-12992	An-12BP (–)	00347306	Leased from/jointly operated with Avial' (1998); basic Aeroflot colours, no titles
RA-13392	An-12BK	00347210	Leased from KAPO-Avia, basic KAPO colours, East Line titles
UR-BWM	An-12BK	00347004	Demilitarised. Leased from Volare Aviation Enterprise, returned by 5-02
UR-LAI	An-12BP (–)	8345505	Lsf Volare Aviation Enterprise by 11-99; basic Volare colours, East Line titles
UR-LIP	An-12BK	9346405	Lsf Volare Aviation Enterprise by 11-99; basic Volare colours, East Line titles
UR-SVG	An-12BP (+)	4342309	Demilitarised. Leased from Volare Aviation Enterprise by 11-99, returned by 10-01; basic Volare colours, East Line titles, Russian flag

• **Elf Air [E6/EFR]**, the commercial flying division of avionics designer NPO Vzlyot, operates a mixed bag of passenger and cargo aircraft from Zhukovskiy, including grey-painted 'military' An-12A RA-13321 (c/n 2340301), a former avionics testbed. The aircraft retained the overall grey finish and Aeroflot titles it had worn when operated by the Soviet Air Force. It was retired in 1997.

• **Etele Air [–/ETO]** bought 'civil' An-12B RA-11117 (c/n 5402707) from Aviacor in 1998. In 2000 it was joined by demilitarised An-12B RA-11766 (c/n 401605) purchased from Avial'-NV; unlike RA-11117 which retained the basic Aviacor livery, this aircraft wore all-white UN World Food Programme colours. RA-11117 was also seconded to the UN in late 2002, wearing UN tail titles, the legend 'United Nations Humanitarian Air Service' and revised titles (*operated by* EteleAIR *for WFP*). When Etele Air folded in 2003 the two aircraft were sold – allegedly to Congo, but soon surfaced as UR-CDB and UR-CBZ respectively.

• **Eurasia Airlines [UH/EUS]** based at Moscow-Vnukovo leased An-12BPs RA-11324 and RA-11339 from Avial'-NV in the spring of 2002. In 2003, however, the Russian CAA unearthed grave breaches affecting safety and withdrew Eurasia's operating licence in October 2003.

• The **Exparc [–/EPA]** 'airline' was formed in 1992 for providing logistical support of the Russian polar research stations under the EksPArk programme (*Ekspeditsiya 'Parashooty nad Arktikoy'* – 'Parachutes over the Arctic' Expedition) so as not to depend on the Air Force or GosNII GA from which aircraft had to be leased. Apart from two IL-76TDs of its own, it briefly leased 'military' An-12A RA-11734 (c/n 2340809) from the Russian Air Force and An-12B RA-11892 (c/n 402501) from Sakha Avia in 1994.

• **Far Eastern Cargo Airlines** (*Dahl'nevostochnyye groozovyye avialinii*) [–/FEW] based in Khabarovsk leased An-12s from other carriers as required.

• **Flight Joint-Stock Co.** (*Aviakompahniya Flayt*) [–/FLV] based at Astrakhan'-Narimanovo had two *Cubs* – ex-SPAir demilitarised An-12BP RA-11003 (c/n 5343704) and ex-Baikalavia 'civil' An-12BP RA-12988 (c/n 00347206). The former aircraft was sold to Air West in 1998 as ST-AWM.

Above: Another sight to be seen no more – An-12BP RA-11339 is pictured here at Moscow/Vnukovo-1 in the colours of the defunct Eurasia Airlines. The cheatline is a remnant of the Avial' livery.

• The **Flight Research Institute named after M. M. Gromov (LII)** in Zhukovskiy operated a variety of *Cubs* – both as testbeds and for regular transport duties. The transport-configured aircraft were operated by LII's first air transport subsidiary, **Volare Air Transport Company** (*Aviatrahnsportnaya kompahniya Volare*) *[OP/VLR]* founded in 1992. (This is not to be confused with Volare Aviation Enterprise [F7/VRE] (see Ukrainian section) and the Italian airline Volare Airlines SpA [8D/VLE, later VA/VLE].)

In 1997 Volare ceased operations and the aircraft were transferred to LII's new airline, Gromov Air [–/LII, later –/GAI]. In late 2005 the airline was renamed **Moskoviya** (Muscovy).

Registration	Version	C/n	Notes
RA-11309	An-12BP (+)	00347510	Leased from Irkut ?-03, basic Irkut c/s
RA-11650	An-12BP (+)	6344305	Ex-BF Cargo LZ-BFG, bought 2000; all-white c/s with titles. Sold to Almaty Aviation 11-02 as 11650 (later UN-11650)
RA-11813	An-12B (+)	3340908	Basic Aeroflot polar c/s
RA-12108	An-12TBK	9346308	Ex-BF Cargo LZ-BFE, all-white c/s; sold to AZAL Cargo 9-01 as 4K-AZ18
RA-13331	An-12BK	6344510	Ex-'10 Red', ex-CCCP-48974 No.2, former de-icing systems testbed; grey c/s, no titles. Sold to Start in 1994
RA-48984	An-12B (+)	402913	Leased from VASO 2005, returned same year
RA-98102	An-12BP (+)	5343005	Demilitarised. Ex-BF Cargo LZ-BFD, ex-CCCP-98102 No.2, ex-Soviet AF '29 Blue'; basic Aeroflot polar c/s. Sold to Almaty Aviation 11-02 as UN-98102)
43 Red	An-12BK	8345902	An-12M-LL ejection seat/APU testbed

• **GosNII GA** (the State Civil Aviation Research Institute located at Moscow/Sheremet'yevo-1) **[–/ISP]** operated one 'civil' An-12BP (RA-11101, c/n 01347703) and two demilitarised An-12BPs – RA-11530 (c/n 6344503) and RA-11531 (c/n 6344506) which were former An-12BPTs Tsiklon 'storm chasers'. The aircraft were operated jointly with the **Flight-Chernobyl' Association** (*Polyot-Chernobyl'*) **[–/FCH]** in Aeroflot colours. RA-11101 crashed in Lukapa, Angola, on

6th October 1996; RA-11531 was sold to Air Nacoia as D2-FVG No.1 that same year, the fate of the third aircraft is unknown.

• Impulse-Aero [–/IMR] based at Moscow/Vnukovo-3 had a single An-12BK with the non-standard registration RA-13357 (c/n 8345604). The aircraft was sold to Air Ukraine in 1996 to become UR-11314.

• **Irkut-Avia [–/UTK]**, the flying division of the Irkutsk Aircraft Production Association (IAPO – *Irkootskoye aviatsionnoye proizvodstvennoye obyedineniye*), had four ex-VTA *Cubs* – An-12BP RA-11309 (c/n 00347510), An-12BP RA-11310 (c/n 4342601), An-12B RA-12162 (ex-CCCP-12162 No.2, c/n 3341509) and An-12BP RA-13391 (c/n 5342805). The transports wear an eye-catching three-tone blue/white livery.

• **KAPO [–/KAO]** (*Kazahnskoye aviatsionnoye proizvodstvennoye obyedineniye* – Kazan' Aircraft Production Association named after Sergey P. Gorboonov (MAP aircraft factory No.22) which builds the Tupolev Tu-22M and Tu-160 bombers, the Tu-214 medium-haul airliner and is set to build the Tu-334 short-haul airliners and Tu-330 civil/military medium transport, has a single demilitarised An-12BK refitted with an ROZ-1 radar. Registered RA-13392 (c/n 00347210), the aircraft wears the smart house colours of blue and white; it was leased to Aerostars as of this writing.

Gromov Air An-12BP RA-98102 is seen here on the south side of Zhukovskiy airfield, its home base, in 2001.

Above: An-12BP RA-11310 undergoing routine maintenance at its home base, Irkutsk-2 airfield, shows off the stylish livery of Irkut.

• The fleet of **KiT Air** (*Kosmos i Trahnsport* – Space & Transport), a division of the Omsk 'Polyot' (Flight) Production Association (in the days when it was an MOM enterprise before resuming aircraft production), included demilitarised An-12BP RA-11013 (c/n 6344002). 'Kit' is Russian for 'whale', and the airline's logo depicted exactly that. The aircraft was sold to Antares Air in 1995.

• The Samara-based airline **Klyuch-Avia** ('Key-Avia') had a single 'civil' An-12A, RA-11131 (c/n 2400702) which was operated for the Samara Metal Works. It was sold to Yuriy Petrov's Airline in 1996.

• **KnAAPO [–/KNM]** (*Komsomol'skoye-na-Amoore aviatsionnoye proizvodstvennoye obyedineniye* – Komsomol'sk-on-Amur Aircraft Production Association named after Yuriy A. Gagarin) has four An-12s. The Association produces single-seat versions of the Su-27 tactical fighter, the Beriyev Be-103 six-seat general-purpose amphibian and the Sukhoi Su-80 utility aircraft.

Registration	Version	C/n	Notes
RA-11125	An-12B (+)	3341006	Demilitarised
RA-11230	An-12BP (+)	5342708	Ex-BF Cargo LZ-BFA
RA-11789	An-12BP (+)	6343905	Ex-BF Cargo LZ-BFB. Demilitarised, blue/white tail, KnAAPO badge on nose, no titles
RA-48978	An-12PP	9346410	Converted to freighter. Basic Aeroflot colours, KnAAPO badge on nose, no titles

• **Komiavia [–/KMA]** (to be specific, the airline's main division in Syktyvkar), later renamed Komiaviatrans, operated a number of An-12s. After the reorganisation of the airline in 1998 these were transferred to the Syktyvkar-based **Komiinteravia [8J/KMV]**, a sister company established in 1996, along with all other heavy fixed-wing aircraft. As of this writing, all the *Cubs* have been sold off.

An-12BP RA-13392 operated by KAPO (the Kazan' aircraft factory) looks magnificent during a late afternoon departure from Moscow-Domodedovo.

An-12BP RA-12957, a former Noril'sk Air Enterprise aircraft with a long history of polar support operations, shows its new Kosmos Cargo titles (in a mixed-language rendition) and Kosmos tail colours as it awaits the next flight at Moscow/Vnukovo-1 on 5th September 2001.

Registration	Version	C/n	Notes
RA-11114	An-12B (–)	01347909	Sold to Special Cargo Airlines ?-99
RA-11375	An-12TB (+)	402405	Demilitarised. Crashed Slavgorod 20-8-93
RA-11526	An-12B (–)	02348207	Sold to Angola as D2-FDB
RA-12972	An-12BP (–)	9346504	Sold to Special Cargo Airlines

Registration	Version	C/n	Notes
RA-11002	An-12BP (+?)	5343703	Sold to British Gulf International Airlines 12-02 as EX-164
RA-11102	An-12BP (–)	01347704	Sold to British Gulf International Airlines 12-00 as S9-BOS
RA-11106	An-12BP (–)	01347808	C/n also reported as 01347802
RA-11113	An-12BP (–)	01347908	
RA-11366	An-12B (+)	402808	Demilitarised. Leased to CAT Cargo as TC-KET 3-8-94, never returned
RA-11986	An-12B (+)	401901	Sold to Angola as D2-FCV
RA-12984	An-12BP (–)	00347109	Sold to Magadanavialeasing

• The charter airline **Korsar [6K/KRS]** based at Moscow/Vnukovo-3 operated two demilitarised *Cubs* – An-12B RA-11008 (c/n 402612) and An-12TB RA-11025 (c/n 6344103) – on lease from NPO Energiya, the corporation responsible, among other things, for the Buran (Snow-storm) space shuttle. The aircraft flew in Aeroflot colours – which was probably just as well, because Korsar's own livery was singularly unin-spiring. *Korsar* means 'corsair' in Russian, but the airline's name had nothing to do with pirates; it was derived from the names of its founders, Korovin and Sarzhveladze. RA-11008 was written off in a landing accident at Huambo, Angola, on 22nd November 1995.

• By mid-1996 RA-11025 had been transferred to **Kosmos Aircompany [–/KSM]**, a division of NPO Energiya based at Vnukovo-3, and received a stylish livery with a red/white/blue cheatline and a blue tail featuring a Planet-Earth-cum-orbiting-satellite tail logo. (Some observers have dubbed this colour scheme 'Milky Way', though the 'candy bar' allusion is rather questionable!) By September 2001 it was joined by 'civil' An-12BP RA-12957 (c/n 8345508) which combined a red Aeroflot 'polar' cheatline with Kosmos tail colours and titles.

• **Kumertau Express**, the flying division of the Kumertau Aircraft Production Enterprise (KumAPP) manufacturing the Kamov Ka-27/Ka-32 and Ka-226 helicopters, owned demilitarised An-12A RA-48970 (c/n 2400502). The aircraft was leased to BF Cargo in 1994-96 and temporarily reregistered LZ-BFC for most of the lease. In 1998 it was sold to the Yermolino Flight Test & Research Enterprise (YeLIIP).

• **Magadanaerogrooz** (= Magadan Air Cargo, or Magadan Cargo Airlines) **[–/MGG]** operated seven An-12s until it went out of business in 1998.

• The leasing company **Magadanavialeasing [–/MLZ]** took over the fleet of the bankrupt Magadanaerogrooz, including RA-12984 which it leased to Atlant-Soyuz. In 2004 this aircraft was sold to the Moldovan carrier Grixona as ER-ADG.

• **Moscow Airways** (*Moskovskiye avialinii*) **[M8/MSC]** established in 1991 and based at Sheremet'yevo-2 owned a single demilitarised An-12A, RA-11318 (c/n 401908). In 1996 the airline had its licence revoked because of unsatisfactory operational standards. The *Cub* was sold to the Angolan carrier von Haaf Air as D2-FVG No.2.

• **Mostransgaz**, one of the natural gas industry's (initially) many flying divisions, operated a single demilitarised An-12AP RA-12188 (c/n 1400106) in a striking blue/white colour scheme. In 1997 the airline was absorbed by **Gazpromavia Ltd. [–/GZP]**, the flying division of the powerful Gazprom corporation; two years later the An-12 was sold to United Arabian Co., Sudan, as ST-AQE.

• **NAPO-Aviatrans [–/NPO]**, the flying division of NAPO (*Novosi-beerskoye aviatsionnoye proizvodstvennoye obyedineniye* – Novosi-bisk Aircraft Production Association named after Valeriy P. Chkalov) which produces the Su-34 fighter-bomber, the An-38 regional airliner and is set to build the Su-49 new-generation primary trainer, had six *Cubs*.

Registration	Version	C/n	Notes
RA-11328	An-12B (+)	3341606	Ex-Soviet Air Force '23 Red'. Sold to Mikma ?-99 as ER-ADN
RA-12192	An-12BP (+)	5343305	
RA-12193	An-12BK	9346805	
RA-12194	An-12BK	00347203	
RA-12195	An-12BK	00347410	
RA-12388	An-12BP (+)	5343405	Sold to Mikma ?-99 as ER-ADM

• The **Noril'sk Air Enterprise** (*Noril'skoye aviapredpriyahtiye*), the successor of the Krasnoyarsk CAD/Noril'sk UFD, had six An-12s.

Registration	Version	C/n	Notes
RA-11100	An-12BP (–)	01347702	Also reported as an An-12TB. Retired Noril'sk-Alykel', fuselage used as a warehouse
RA-11816	An-12B (+)	3341003	
RA-11886	An-12A (+)	2340302	Bought from Amuraviatrans 22-12-95. Crashed Pushkin 23-7-98
RA-11906	An-12AP (+)	2340802	Sold to Avial'-NV by 10-04
RA-11989	An-12B (+)	401910	
RA-12981	An-12BP (–)?	00347104	

• **Petrolada**, an airline based in Petrozavodsk, had a single 'military' An-12A registered RA-12187 (c/n 1340201). The aircraft was damaged in a landing accident in Lensk on 19th December 1993.

• **Aviakompaniya Pilot** ('Pilot Airlines') [–/PIL] based in Krasnodar operated three An-12s.

Registration	Version	C/n	Notes
RA-11038	An-12B (+)	2340709	Demilitarised. Ex-ELINT aircraft. Leased to AntonAir International ?-97 as 7P-ANA
RA-11760	An-12BP	4342404	Leased to AntonAir International ?-97 as 7P-ANB
RA-11658	An-12BP	9346608	Leased to AntonAir International ?-97 as 7P-ANC

• **Polyot Russian Airlines** (*Rosseeyskaya aviakompahniya Polyot*) [–/POT] operated two 'military' An-12BPs – RA-11320 (c/n 4342409) and RA-11325 (c/n 5342801). The former aircraft was sold to Hellier International in 1999 as TN-AGE, while the other aircraft went to Ariana Afghan Airlines in 198 as YA-DAB.

• The **Penza Air Enterprise** [–/PNZ] had three 'military' Cubs – An-12Bs RA-11337 (c/n 3341204), RA-11338 (c/n 3341506) and An-12BP RA-11339 (c/n 6344310). The former aircraft crashed on approach to Baku on 14th March 1995. In 2000 RA-11338 was sold to Angola as D2-FRC, while RA-11339 was sold to Avial'-NV.

• **Pulkovo Avia** (originally known as the St. Petersburg Air Enterprise) [Z8/PLK] named after its home base operated seven 'civil' An-12BPs. For years the entire fleet wore Aeroflot colours with or without titles; it was not until 1997 that Pulkovo-Avia introduced its own livery. However, the freighters did not last that long – all of the An-12s had been sold or retired before any of them could be repainted.

Registration	C/n	Notes
RA-11105	01347801	Aeroflot blue/white (later polar) colour scheme. Sold or retired 1997
RA-11108	01347810	Ex-CCCP-11108 No.2.* Lst Global Air 9-92 to 7-93 as LZ-PVK. Sold or retired 1997
RA-11109	01347901	Ex-CCCP-11109 No.2.* Aeroflot polar c/s. Lst UNPF in Bosnia 11-92 as 11109. Sold or retired 1997
RA-11127	02348202	Aeroflot c/s. Lst Global Air 9-92 to 7-93 as LZ-PVL. Damaged Lucapa (Angola) 9-5-95 and repaired
RA-11527	02348208	Aeroflot blue/white (later polar) colours. Sold or retired 1997
RA-12983	00347106	Aeroflot polar c/s. Sold or retired 1997
RA-12995	00347402	Aeroflot polar c/s. Leased to HeavyLift Cargo Airlines 12-96

* These registrations previously belonged to military An-12Bs.

• **RVPP Rostvertol [–/RUZ, later –/REV]**, the Rostov helicopter factory, operated at least two 'military' Cubs – An-12A RA-11976 (c/n 1340106) and An-12B 13387 (no prefix; c/n 402902?). The latter aircraft crashed on approach to Tyumen' on 25th September 1993; RA-11976 remained in service until 1999 when it was sold to Vega Airlines as LZ-VEA.

• The **Russian Air Force** continues to operate the An-12 in substantial numbers; about 600 were reportedly in service in the mid-1990s, though many have now been sold off. The remaining aircraft are in service with the 61st VA (Air Army) into which the VTA was transformed during the merger of the Air Force and the Air Defence Force in 1998. This consists of two airlift divisions, each with four or five regiments. Known An-12 units were based at Ivanovo-Severnyy AB (517th VTAP and 610th TsBP i PLS), Klin-5 AB (978th VTAP), Shadrinsk, Tver'-Migalovo AB, Ul'yanovsk-Vostochnyy, Khabarovsk-Bol'shoy (257th OSAP), Petropavlovsk-Kamchatskiy/Yelizovo (317th OSAP), Levashovo AB near St. Petersburg (128th OSAP), and so on.

A substantial part of the fleet is still quasi-civil; some of these aircraft are listed in the first part of the table. The aircraft wear full 1973-standard Aeroflot colours unless otherwise noted.

Registration	Version	C/n	Notes
CCCP-10228	An-12BP (+)	6343902	Grey c/s. 610th TsBPiPLS, Ivanovo-Severnyy; struck off charge 2001, scrapped by 2006
RA-11037	An-12B (+)	3341103	Based Kaliningrad-Khrabrovo; for sale 5-04
RA-11139	An-12B (+)	3341001	Based Ostaf'yevo
RA-11178	An-12B (+)	?	Grey c/s
RA-11227	An-12B (+)	401911	Preserved Baikonur-Krainiy (formerly Leninsk)
RA-11240	An-12B (+)	402706	Based Ul'yanovsk-Vostochnyy
RA-11241	An-12B (+)	402102	Sold to Lasare Air by 2000 as 4L-11241
RA-11260	An-12B (+)	8346003	
RA-11265	An-12B (+)	6343805	Ex-CCCP-11265 No.2. Based Tver', later to Ivanovo-Severnyy
RA-11266	An-12B (+)	?	
RA-11275	An-12TA (+)	2340803	Based Ostaf'yevo. Sold to Goliaf Air by 1-05 as S9-BOZ
RA-11286	An-12B (+)	6343809	610th TsBPiPLS, Ivanovo-Severnyy; derelict by 6-99, scrapped by 2006
RA-11290	An-12B (+)	?	
RA-11327	An-12A (+)	1400104	Sold to Aviaobschchemash
RA-11343	An-12BK	00347503	Ex-CCCP-11343 No.2, based Tver'
RA-11364	An-12BK	00347601	Based Ostaf'yevo

Reg	Version	C/n	Notes
RA-11393	An-12B (+)	6344309	Based Ulan-Ude/Vostochnyy
RA-11400	*An-12BP (+)*	*5343510*	*Sold to Silk Way Airlines 2006 as 4K-AZ60*
RA-11401	An-12BP (+)	5343402	Based Kaliningrad-Khrabrovo; for sale 5-04
RA-11406	An-12BP (+)	?	Grey c/s
RA-11408	*An-12B (+)*	*3341209*	*Sold to Aviaobschchemash before 1995*
RA-11412	An-12BP (+)	5343301	
RA-11414	An-12BK	9346507	Grey c/s
RA-11420	An-12BP (+)	8346101	
CCCP-11425	An-12B (+)	401807	Based Ostaf'yevo 1994; see next line!
RA-11425	An-12BP (+)?	9346802	Grey c/s; may be An-12BK
RA-11426	An-12BP (+)	4342204	Grey c/s
RA-11428	An-12BP (+)	?	Grey c/s
RA-11432	An-12BP (+)	5343002	
RA-11652	An-12B (–)	402702	226th OSAP, Kubinka AB; communications relay version
RA-11653	An-12B (–)	402703	226th OSAP, Kubinka AB; communications relay version
RA-11654	An-12B (–)	402602	226th OSAP, Kubinka AB; communications relay version
RA-11660	An-12BP (+)	5343209	
RA-11666	An-12BP (+)	?	
RA-11668	An-12BK	?	Grey c/s, strap-on chaff dispensers
RA-11680	An-12A (+)	9900805	
RA-11719 No.1	*An-12BP (+)*	*6344601*	*WFU Chkalovskaya AB by 8-99, c/n painted on as 4601; see next line!*
RA-11719 No.2	An-12BP (+)?	02348110	Could be An-12BK. Ex-Soviet AF '48 Red', seen Chkalovskaya AB 8-02!
RA-11732	An-12BP (+)	?	
RA-11740	An-12BP (+)	6344406	Based Ulan-Ude/Vostochnyy
RA-11742	An-12BP (+)	?	
RA-11755	An-12BP (+)	6343808	Based Tver'
RA-11780	*An-12BP (+)*	*7345102*	*Based Ivanovo-Severnyy; scrapped by 2006*
RA-11786	An-12BP (+)	5343507	Based Orenburg; for sale 5-05
RA-11791	An-12B (–)	402611	226th OSAP, Kubinka AB; communications relay version
RA-11792	An-12B (–)	402701	226th OSAP, Kubinka AB; communications relay version
RA-11803	An-12BK	8345806	
RA-11835	An-12BP (+)	5343604	
RA-11844	An-12BP (+)	?	
RA-11861	An-12BP (+)	?	
RA-11894	An-12B (+)	402708	226th OSAP, Kubinka AB
CCCP-11920	*An-12BP (+)*	*6344303*	*Derelict Ivanovo-Severnyy by 1997*
RA-11924	An-12BP (+)	6344508	226th OSAP, Kubinka AB
RA-11931	An-12B (+)	6344509	
RA-11936	*An-12A (+)*	*2340507*	*Based Ostaf'yevo. Sold to Air Sofia 2003 as LZ-SFW*
RA-11943	An-12BP (+)	5343609	978th VTAP, Klin-5 AB
RA-11945	An-12BP (+)	5343409	Based Ulan-Ude/Vostochnyy
RA-11965	*An-12A (+)*	*2400702*	*Grey c/s. Based Ivanovo-Severnyy; scrapped by 2006*
RA-11969	An-12BP (+)	?	
RA-11995	An-12BP (+)	5343506	
RA-12101	*An-12B (+)*	*402509*	*Based Ivanovo-Severnyy; scrapped by 2006*
RA-12103	*An-12B (+)*	*401903*	*610th TsBPiPLS; derelict Ivanovo-Severnyy by 6-99*
RA-12105	An-12BP (+)	5343404	Leased to NPO Vzlyot; W/O Nar'yan-Mar 11-12-97 in ground collision with Mi-8T RA-24247
RA-12108	An-12BK	9346308	Polar c/s; sold to civil operator by 1995
RA-12115	An-12BP (+)	?	
RA-12121	*An-12B (+)*	*401912*	*Based Ostaf'yevo; sold to NPP Vega-M 10-03 as RA-11372*
RA-12122	*An-12BK*	*402002*	*Based Ostaf'yevo; sold to NPP Vega-M 1-03 as RA-11373*

Reg	Version	C/n	Notes
RA-12124 No.1	An-12B	402505	In service 7-93; see next line!
RA-12124 No.2	An-12BK?	00347507	Based Chkalovskaya AB 2000-01; Aeroflot c/s, no titles
RA-12131	An-12BP (+)	?	
RA-12132	An-12BP (+)	?	
RA-12133	An-12BP (+)	?	
RA-12135	*An-12BP (–)*	*00347002*	*226th OSAP, Kubinka AB. Crashed nr Rzhev 22-5-01*
RA-12137	An-12BK	6344410	223rd Flight, grey c/s w. Russian flag cheatline
RA-12143	An-12BP (+)	?	
RA-12187	An-12BP (+)	1340201	
RA-12330	An-12BP (+)	?	
RA-12574	An-12BP (+)	5343504	978th VTAP, Klin-5 AB

The remainder of the fleet wears the familiar red star insignia and, with a few exceptions, an overall grey colour scheme. Lately it has been livened up by colourful nose art on some aircraft. Since the tactical codes do not tell much, the list is in c/n sequence; a full list cannot be given for reasons of space.

C/n	Version	Tact. code	Notes
8900503	An-12A (+)	27 Blue	GIA, IVATU military college, Irkutsk
2400602	An-12A (+)	47 Red	Based Ostaf'yevo
2400905	An-12TA (+)	20 Blue	
2401006	An-12A (+)	11 Blue	4th VA. Rostov-on-Don
402105	An-12B (+)	21 Red	
402010	*An-12B (+)*	*12 Yellow*	*Sold to NPP Vega-M 10-04 as RA-11374*
402409	An-12B (+)	28 Red	Based Ul'yanovsk-Vostochnyy
402510	An-12B (+)	18	Based Tambov-Vostochnyy
403113	An-12BP (+)	62 Red	
1340208	An-12R	10 Blue	4th VA. Rostov-on-Don
2340601	An-12A (+)	35 Blue	Based Kaliningrad-Khrabrovo
2340602	*An-12A (+)*	*not known*	*Sold to British Gulf International 2004 as EX-045*
2340701	An-12A (+)	18 Red	Also marked 09018; based Levashovo
2340708	An-12A (+)	18 Blue	Ex-CCCP-11898. 4th VA/245th OSAP, Legnica AB, Poland. Became, see next line
		94 Red	16th VA/226th OSAP, Sperenberg AB; became, see next line
		36 Red	4th VA/535th OSAP, Rostov-on-Don
2340710	An-12A (+)	89 Red	16th VA/226th OSAP, Sperenberg AB; to 4th VA/535th OSAP, Rostov-on-Don
3340910	An-12B (+)	16 Red	Based Levashovo AB
3341009	An-12B (+)	17 Red	
3341102	An-12B (+)	93 Red	16th VA/226th OSAP; Sperenberg AB, later Kubinka AB
3341203	An-12B (+)	92 Red	Ex-CCCP-11407. 16th VA/226th OSAP
3341207	An-12B (+)	90 Red	Ex-CCCP-1218.; 16th VA/226th OSAP
3341306	*An-12B (+)*	*12 Red*	*Based Ivanovo-Severnyy; scrapped by 2006*
3341402	*An-12B (+)*	*70 Black*	*Basic Aeroflot c/s, based Ostaf'yevo. Sold to Scorpion Air 11-03 as LZ-MNQ*
3341404	An-12RR	21 Red	Based Levashovo
3341408	*An-12B (+)*	*10 Red*	*Based Almaty. Sold after 1993, to Savanair as D2-FRT*
3341502	*An-12B (+)*	*not known*	*Based Ivanovo-Severnyy; scrapped by 2006*
3341503	An-12B (+)	08 Red	226th OSAP, wfu Kubinka AB; Russian flag on tail instead of star
3341507	*An-12B (+)*	*98 Red*	*16th VA/226th OSAP. Scrapped Kubinka AB*
3341601	An-12B (+)	16 Blue	4th VA/245th OSAP. Became, see next line
		85 Red	16th VA/226th OSAP. Became, see next line
		35 Red	4th VA, Rostov-on-Don; later '35 Blue'
3341602	An-12B (+)	50 Red	978th VTAP, Klin?
4341708	An-12B (+)	98 Red	16th VA/226th OSAP, Sperenberg AB

C/n	Version	Tactical code	Notes
4341905	An-12B (+)	84 Red	Ex-CCCP-11537; 16th VA/226th OSAP
4342203	An-12BP (+)	91 Red	Ex-CCCP-12182; 16th VA/226th OSAP
4342407	*An-12BP (+)*	*99 Red*	*16th VA/226th OSAP; scrapped Kubinka AB*
4342410	An-12BP (+)	95 Red	16th VA/226th OSAP
4342604	An-12RR	11 Red	
4342703	An-12BP (+)	86 Red	16th VA/226th OSAP
4342907	*An-12BP (+)*	*17 Red*	*16th VA/226th OSAP; scrapped Kubinka AB*
5343108	An-12BP (+)	15 Red	16th VA/226th OSAP; wfu Kubinka AB
5343207	An-12BP (+)	97 Red	16th VA/226th OSAP
5343208	*An-12BP (+)*	*661 Black*	*Ex-CCCP-11661, basic Aeroflot c/s. 978th VTAP, Klin-5 AB. Sold to Valan 2003 as ER-AXH*
5343310	An-12BP (+)	34 Red	Based Ostaf'yevo, Woolly Mammoth nose art
5343403	An-12BP (+)	42 Red	Based Kirzhach, Parachute Systems Research Institute test aircraft, wfu 1996. See next line!
5343503	An-12BP (+)	42 Red	Rep. based Kirzhach; clash with previous entry!
5343605	An-12BP (+)	38 Yellow	Based Tambov?
6343802	*An-12BP (+)*	*02 Red*	*Based Tver'. Sold to AeroVis 2006 as UR-CFB*
6343901	An-12PP	85 Red	16th VA/226th OSAP; to 4th VA/535th OSAP
6344102	*An-12BP (+)*	*34 Red*	*Based Ivanovo-Severnyy; scrapped by 2006*
6344302	*An-12BP (+)*	*11 Red*	*Based Ivanovo-Severnyy; scrapped by 2006*
7345104	An-12BP (+)?	34 Red	Could be An-12BK
7345202	An-12BK-IS	15 Red	
7345203	An-12BK-IS	09 Red	257th OSAP, tiger nose art. For sale 2006
8345606	An-12BK	12 Red	Based Levashovo
8345708	An-12BK	21 Red	
8345709	An-12BK	07 Red	257th OSAP; RINT aircraft
8345801	An-12BK	51 Red	Chkalovskaya AB
8345808	An-12BK	15 Red	128th OSAP/1st Sqn, Levashovo AB; Horned Owl nose art
8345907	An-12BP (+)?	not known	Possibly An-12BK
9346209	An-12BK?	95 Red	Ex-'98'
9346303	An-12PP	68 Red	No active jammers (chaff dispensers in tailcone only). Based Chkalovskaya AB
9346305	An-12BK	26 Red	Reported as An-12TBK; based Ostaf'yevo
9346604	An-12BP (+)?	21 Red	317th OSAP; possibly An-12BK
9346605	An-12BK-PPS	90 Red	
9346704	An-12BK	28 Blue	257th OSAP
00346908	*An-12BK*	*42 Red*	*Based Ivanovo? Russian flag on tail. Sold to British Gulf International 2006 as EX-165*
00347007	An-12BK	18 Red	Damaged, stored Chkalovskaya AB
00347009	An-12BK	15 Red	
00347406	An-12BK-PPS	22 Red	
00347605	An-12BP	27 Red	
01347706	An-12BK-PPS	82 Red	
01347707	An-12BK-IS	16 Red	Based Levashovo AB
01347904	An-12BK-PPS	06 Red	1974 version. Later converted to transport
02348107	An-12BK-PPS	50 Red	1974 version. Later converted to transport; sold to Kyrghyzstan 2006 as EX-124 No.2
02348109	An-12BK-PPS	52 Red	1974 version. Later converted to transport;
02348206	An-12BK-PPS	02 Red	
02348301	An-12BK-PPS	40	
02348303	An-12BK-PPS	24 Red	Based Ivanovo-Severnyy. Cvtd to transport
02348309	An-12BK-PPS	39 Red	1974 version. Based Akhtoobinsk

• The Russian Air Force has commercial divisions. The 223rd OSAP, one of the units making up the 8th ADON (*aviadiveeziya osobovo naznacheniya* – independent special mission air division) at Chkalovskaya AB, was transformed into an 'airline' called 223rd Flight Unit State Airline [–/CHD]. Among other things it operated An-12B RA-12126 (c/n 402507) and An-12BK RA-12137 (c/n 6344410).

• The **Russian Naval Aviation (AVMF)** also operated the An-12 in substantial numbers. A few examples are listed below.

C/n	Version	Tactical code	Notes
6344602	An-12PS	14 Yellow	Pacific Fleet Air Arm, blue side flash
6344608	*An-12PS*	*15 Yellow*	*Sold to Reem Air 2005 as EX-096*
7344702	An-12PS	16 Yellow	North Fleet Air Arm, Severomorsk-1 AB, red side flash
7344703	An-12PS	17 Yellow	North Fleet Air Arm, Severomorsk-1 AB, blue side flash
7344704	An-12PS	not known	
1400305	An-12A(+)	36 Yellow	Based Ostaf'yevo
2400501	An-12A(+)	34 Yellow	Based Ostaf'yevo
2400506	An-12A(+)	32 Yellow	Based Ostaf'yevo
402009	An-12B (+)	28 Yellow	Based Ostaf'yevo

• Headquartered in Yakutsk, **Sakha Avia [K7/IKT]** (formerly Yakutavia) was the national airline of the Republic of Yakutia (Sakha) and one of the biggest Russian air carriers. It consisted of several air enterprises, more than one of which operated An-12s; there were 13 of the type on strength. In the late 1990s Sakha Avia suffered from excessive capacity and much of its enormous fleet was put in storage or leased to other carriers. In December 2002 the carrier broke up and the Yakutsk division was rebranded Yakutia (which see).

Registration	Version	C/n	Notes
RA-11130	An-12BP (–)	02348205	Batagai A.E. Leased to Sir Aero ?-00; sold to Avial'-NV by 2006
RA-11234	An-12B (+?)	401907	Retired by 1997
RA-11236	An-12B (+)	402111	Yakutsk A.E. Basic Aeroflot polar colours, Sakha Avia logo, no titles; registration painted on as RA 11Z36. Sold to Natalco Airlines ?-99 as S9-BAN
RA-11345	An-12B (+)	401801	Yakutsk A.E. Demilitarised; sold to Avial'-NV
RA-11354	An-12B (+?)	401812	Yakutsk A.E. Sold or retired by 2002
RA-11403	An-12B	401906	Crashed near Lyudino 24-2-96
RA-11767	An-12B (+)	401909	Yakutsk A.E.
RA-11884	An-12B (+)	401710	Yakutsk A.E.
RA-11892	An-12B (+)	402501	Yakutsk A.E. Sold to Sir Aero ?-96
RA-11991	An-12B (+)	402006	Yakutsk A.E. Demilitarised, basic Aeroflot polar colours, Sakha Avia titles/logo. Sold to Aviostart by 2-00 as LZ-ASY
RA-12953	An-12BP (–)	8345504	Yakutsk A.E. Sold to Coptrade Air Transport by 10-99 as ST-AQF
RA-12955	An-12BP (–)	8345506	Nyurba A.E. Reported for Viliuy Aircompany; crashed near Krasnoyarsk 11-11-98
RA-12959	An-12BP (–)	8345510	Aeroflot polar colours. Sold to Heller International 1999 as D2-FBY

• **Sakhaviatrans [–/SVT]**, a sister company of Atran based in Yuzhno-Sakhalinsk, leases aircraft from Atran as required; these included An-12B RA-98117 leased in 2001-06 and An-12BP RA-98118 leased in 1994-98. The former aircraft wore full Sakhaviatrans colours.

• **SAT – Sakhalinskiye aviatrassy** (Sakhalin Air Routes) **[HZ/SHU]** operated 'civil' An-12BP RA-12992 (c/n 00347306) leased from a leasing company in July 2005 for one year. The aircraft subsequently became ER-ACY with Grixona.

• **Samara Airlines [E5/BRZ]**, one of the biggest Russian regional carriers based at Samara-Kurumoch airport, operated four *Cubs*, all of which have been disposed of (see table overleaf).

Above: An-12BP RA-11049 wearing the colours (but not the titles) of SPAIR Air Transport Corp. comes in to land at Moscow-Domodedovo; the aircraft had probably been sold to the Yermolino flight test centre by the time the picture was taken.

Registration	Version	C/n	Notes
RA-11959	An-12B (+)	402410	Demilitarised. Sold to Rila Airlines ?-98 as LZ-RAA
RA-12954	An-12BP (–)	8345505	Sold to Volare Aviation Enterprise 1999 as UR-LAI
RA-12956	An-12BP (–)	8345507	Sold to Expo Aviation 1998 as 4R-EXC
RA-12986	An-12BP (–)	00347201	Sold to Volare Aviation Enterprise 1999 as UR-12986

• **Sir Aero Joint-Stock Co. [–/SRN]** based in Yakutsk owned two ex-Sakha Avia *Cubs* – 'civil' An-12BP RA-11130 (c/n 02348205) bought in 2000 and 'military' An-12B RA-11892 (c/n 402501) bought in 1996.

• **SPAIR Air Transport Corporation [–/PAR]** (*Aviatrahns*portnaya *korporahts*iya *Spaer*) based at Yekaterinburg-Kol'tsovo airport and mainly concerned with cargo carriage operated four An-12s. The letters SP in the carrier's name were derived from the name of its director, Valeriy Spoornov. The airline ceased operations in 1999.

Although it looks like an An-12BP, RA-11329 seen here landing at Moscow-Domodedovo in the late 1990s is an An-12BK refitted with an ROZ-1 radar and demilitarised after sale to Special Cargo Airlines.

Registration	Version	C/n	Notes
RA-11003	An-12BP (+)	5343704	Demilitarised. Sold to Flight Air Company
RA-11049	An-12BP (+)	8346109	Demilitarised. Sold to Yermolino Flight Test & Research Enterprise
RA-11356	An-12BP (+)	7345206	Sold to Yermolino Flight Test & Research Enterprise
RA-11415	An-12P (+)	401708	Fate unknown

• **Special Cargo Airlines** (*Spetsiahl'nyye groozovyye avialinii*) **[–/SCI]** based at Yermolino south of Moscow operated ten *Cubs* until it ceased operations in 2000. (Note: 'Civil' An-12BP RA-12959 (c/n 8345510; sold to Savanair as D2-FBY) was also reported for Special Cargo Airlines but this is doubtful – see Komiavia!)

Registration	Version	C/n	Notes
RA-11114	An-12B (–)	01347909	Sold to National Commuter Airlines as D2-FDC
RA-11301	An-12PP	00347107	Demilitarised (converted to transport). Sold to Bulgaria as LZ-LTD
RA-11321	An-12BP (+)	9346801	Sold to Air Cess 1-96 as EL-AKR
RA-11329	An-12BK	8346010	Demilitarised and re-equipped with small ROZ-1 radar. Sold to Hellier International ?-98 as D2-FBZ
RA-11863	An-12BP (+)	401905	Basic Aeroflot c/s, no titles
RA-11890	An-12B (+)	3340909	Ex-Amuraviatrans, bought 16-8-97; sold to Santa Cruz Imperial 8-10-97 as EL-ASA
RA-12116	An-12BP (+)	402108	Sold to Santa Cruz Imperial as EL-ALB
RA-12191	An-12BK	401905	Refitted with ROZ-1 radar. Sold to Air Cess as EL-AKW
CCCP-13320	An-12BP (+)	8345407	Demilitarised. Crashed Khatanga 23-9-91
RA-12972	An-12BP (–)	9346504	Ex-Komiavia. Sold to Mikma as ER-ACG

• **Start Air Transport Co.** based in Zhukovskiy had a single An-12BK, RA-13331 (c/n 6344510) bought from LII in 1994. This was a highly non-standard aircraft retaining traces of earlier use as the 'Tanker' de-icing systems testbed (see Chapter 2). Interestingly, the titles were an attempt to combine the Roman (START) and Cyrillic (CTAPT) rendering, and the result was something in between.

• **SVGAL** (*Severo-vostochnyye groozovyye avialinii* – North-Eastern Cargo Airlines) **[–/MGD]** based at Magadan-Sokol (Russia) and Kent International (UK) operated three 'military' An-12Bs until its demise in 1999, whereupon most of the aircraft went to Magadanavialeasing.

Registration	C/n	Notes
RA-11242	3341406	
RA-11421	401711	Ex-avionics testbed. Sold to ALADA as D2-FBJ
RA-12119	402109	

• Cargo carrier **Trans Aero Samara [–/TSL]** based at Samara-Bezymyanka had two demilitarised An-12BPs, RA-11363 (c/n 00347505) and RA-11962 (c/n 5343007). In 1999 the airline ceased operations; RA-11363 was sold to Zapolyar'ye in January 2003 while RA-11962 was sold to Aviast.

An-12BP RA-12973 shows full Tyumen' Airlines colours during a visit to Moscow-Domodedovo.

• The Moscow airline **Tesis [UZ/TIS]** operated at least two 'civil' An-12BPs – RA-11116 and RA-11124 bought from the defunct Baikalavia, leasing them to Aerofreight. By 2006 both aircraft had been sold off (to Brlight Aviation Services as LZ-BRV and to Veteran Airline as UR-CCY respectively).

• **Tyumen' Airlines** (*Tyumenskiye avialinii*) **[7M/TYM]** based at Tyumen'-Roshchino had nine An-12s; only one (RA-12976) remained in service by 2002. The airline was severely hit by the 1998 Russian bank crisis and eventually went bankrupt, ceasing operations on 1st November 2003.

Registration	Version	C/n	Notes
RA-11112	An-12BP (–)	01347907	White overall, partial UN titles. Sold to Avial' ?-98
RA-11128	An-12BP (–)	02348203	White overall, no titles. Sold to Avial' by 8-99
RA-11766	An-12B (+)	401605	Basic Aeroflot colours, no titles. Sold to Avial' 1998
RA-11973	An-12B (+)	401606	Retired Tyumen' by 8-95
RA-12973	An-12BP (–)	9346505	Full colour scheme. Crashed 11-5-98, circumstances unknown (written off)
RA-12976	An-12BP (-?)	9346510	Sold to Air Victory 2004
RA-12980	An-12BP (-?)	00347103	WFU Tyumen' by 2000
RA-12992	An-12BP (–)	00347306	Basic Aeroflot colours, no titles. Sold to Avial' 1998
RA-12998	An-12BP (–)	01347610	Not in fleet list 2002, fate unknown

• The Ulan-Ude Aircraft Production Association (U-UAPO) had a demilitarised An-12B registered RA-12174 (c/n 3341505). The aircraft was sold to Skycabs as 4R-SKL in May 1998.

• **Ural Airlines** (*Oorahl'skiye avialinii*) **[–/URW, later U6/SVR]** operated six An-12s. This airline based in Yekaterinburg (formerly Sverdlovsk) came into being in 1993 when the Sverdlovsk Aviation Enterprise was organisationally separated from Kol'tsovo airport.

Registration	Version	C/n	Notes
RA-11017	An-12BP (+)	6344008	Retired by 1999
RA-11019	An-12BP (+)	6344202	Demilitarised. Aeroflot colours. Retired by 1999
RA-11036	An-12BP (+)	7344810?*	Full colour scheme. Retired by 1999
RA-12952	An-12BP (–)	8345503	Sold to Renan ?-99 as ER-ACK
RA-12975	An-12BP (–)	9346509	Sold ?-00 as 3C-OOZ
RA-12999	An-12BP (–)	01347701	Sold to Vega Airlines ?-99 as LZ-VEB

* There is some confusion concerning RA-11036. Some sources report this aircraft as c/n 7345310 and c/n 7344810 as CCCP-11086.

Above: Volga-Dnepr Airlines An-12BP CCCP-11746 makes a magnificent sight as it sits on a rain-soaked apron beneath a rainbow at Ul'yanovsk.

• The fleet of **VASO Airlines [DN/VSO, later 2Z/VSO]**, the flying division of the Voronezh Aircraft Production Joint-Stock Co. (*Voronezh-skoye aktsionernoye samolyotostroitel'noye obshchestvo*) which produces the Il-96-300 long-haul airliner, included 'military' An-12B RA-48984, which is leased out as required. The aircraft was operated by Ukraine Air Alliance as UR-48984 in 1997; the most recent lessee is Aviast (since mid-2006).

• **NPP Vega-M** (the NIIP avionics house) operated 'military' An-12Bs RA-11372, RA-11373 and RA-11374 (ex-Russian Air Force RA-12121, RA-12122 and '12 Yellow' respectively, c/ns 401912, 402002 and 402010) bought in 2003. All three were sold in mid-2004; the first aircraft became 3X-GDM with PMT Air of Guinea, the second machine was sold to Avialeasing as UK 12002 and the third aircraft to Sudan.

• **Velocity [–/VKT]** (formerly **VIA Viktor Airlines**) operated a single Ukrainian-registered 'military' An-12A, UR-11961 (c/n 2340403), leased from the Antonov OKB in 1995.

• Zhukovskiy-based **Veteran Airlines [–/VTN]**, a sister company of the Ukrainian airline of the same name (see below), reportedly oper-

ated ex-Antey An-12BK RA-11303 (c/n 00347604). The airline suspended operations in 1997 and the aircraft went to the other Veteran Airlines as UR-11303.

• Moscow/Domodedovo-based **Vim Airlines [NN/MOV]**, now strictly a passenger carrier, reportedly operated An-12B RA-48984 on lease from VASO in January 2003 to February 2004. The 'Vim' is actually the initials of the airline's founder, V. I. Merkoolov.

• Established in 1990 as the first non-Aeroflot specialised cargo carrier in the Soviet Union and later Russia, **Volga-Dnepr Airlines [VI/VDA]** operated ten An-12s – mostly on short-term leases.

Registration	Version	C/n	Notes
CCCP-11341 No.2*	An-12BK	00347606	Leased from Soviet Air Force. To Armenia as EK-12222
CCCP-11342	An-12BK	00347607	Ex-Soviet Air Force. Crashed near Skopje 23-7-92
CCCP-11343 No.2*	An-12BK?	00347503	Leased from Soviet Air Force
CCCP-11344 No.2*	An-12BK?	00347409	Lsf Soviet Air Force, grey c/s; became RA-11344 while on lease
RA-11529	An-12BP (+)	6344109	Leased from Aviastar 10-95 to ?-97
CCCP-11746	An-12BP (+)	7345007	Lsf Soviet Air Force 1-92 to ?-??; full c/s
RA-11814	An-12BP (+)	7345008	Leased from Aviastar 10-95 to ?-97
CCCP-11908 No.2*	An-12BP (+)?	6344501	Leased from Soviet Air Force
CCCP-11922	An-12B P (+)	7345005	Leased from Soviet Air Force 8-92 to ?-??
RA-48971	An-12A (+).	1340107	To Azerbaijan Airlines as 4K-48971 around 1995

* CCCP-11341 No.1 was An-12B c/n 401702 which crashed on 17th February 1973; CCCP-11343 No.1 was another An-12B (c/n

An-12BP RA-11768 of the Yermolino Flight Test & Research Enterprise (YeLIIP) soaks up the last rays of the evening sun at Moscow-Domodedovo on 25th November 1998.

401706); CCCP-11344 No.1 was An-12B c/n 401707 (both written off as time-expired); CCCP-11908 No.1 was another Tashkent-built An-12BP (c/n 4342101) which was sold as LZ-SFL.

• **Yakutia Airlines [K7/SYL]** was established in December 2002 as the successor of the defunct Sakha Airlines' Yakutsk division, taking over An-12s RA-11354, RA-11767 and RA-11884.

• The **Yermolino Flight Test & Research Enterprise** (YeLIIP – Yermolinskoye lyotno-ispytahtel'noye issledovatel'skoye predproyahtiye) [–/EFE] operated eight *Cubs* from Yermolino. In 1999 YeLIIP was renamed Yermolino Airlines. The enterprise ceased operations in 2002.

Registration	Version	C/n	Notes
RA-11049	An-12TB (+)	8346109	Ex-SPAIR; demilitarised
RA-11098	An-12TA (+)	2340801	Ex-Soviet Air Force CCCP-11098; grey c/s. Sold to Antex-Polyus
RA-11356	An-12BP (+)	7345206	Ex-SPAIR; reported as an An-12BK
RA-11516	An-12B (+)	4341909	
RA-11768	An-12BP (+)	5343103	Ex-Russian AF '36 Blue', ex-CCCP-11436. Full c/s. Sold to Southern Cargo Airlines (see end of chapter)
RA-11790	An-12A (+)	1400302	Ex-avionics testbed. Crashed Ust'-Ilimsk 29-10-94 while opf Aero-Nika
RA-11916	An-12B (+)	2400901	Basic Aeroflot c/s, titles; ex-avionics testbed
RA-48970	An-12A (+)	2400502	Demilitarised. Ex-Kumertau Express, bought ?-98. Sold to Sierra Leone 2006 as 9L-LFQ

• The airline **Zapolyar'ye** (literally 'regions beyond the Polar circle') based at Noril'sk-Alykel' operates a mixed fleet which includes former Trans Aero Samara An-12BP RA-11363 purchased in January 2003.

• **Zenit [–/EZT]** based in Zhukovskiy operated 'military' An-12B RA-11312 (ex-Soviet AF '87 Red', c/n 3340903) and 'civil' An-12B RA-11992 (c/n 402604, a former Soviet AF communications relay aircraft). RA-11312 was sold to the Angolan Air Force as T-303 in 2001.

• The operators of the following An-12s are unknown.

Registration	Version	C/n	Notes
RA-11010	An-12TB (+)	3341110	Ex-Soviet Air Force CCCP-11010; basic Aeroflot c/s, no titles. Sold to Juba Air Cargo as EX-11010
11383	An-12TA (+)	2340604	Ex-Soviet Air Force CCCP-11383; grey/white c/s, no titles. Sold to Moldova as ER-ACK No.2

RWANDA

Vega Avia operates 'military' An-12B 9XR-MK purchased in 2003; this aircraft may be ex-Aerocom ER-ACP (c/n 3341108). The aircraft was jointly operated with Dasab Airlines.

SÃO TOMÉ & PRINCIPE

• **Goliaf Air** operates three *Cubs* purchased in early 2005 – An-12TA S9-BOZ (ex-Russian Air Force RA-11275, c/n 2340803), An-12B S9-DAF (c/n unknown, named *Principe*) and An-12AP S9-SAT (c/n 2340606) bought from Africa West Airlines.

• **Zanex Airlines** operated an An-12 registered S9-SAT No.1 (c/n unknown). The aircraft was lost in a crash landing at Saurimo, Angola, on 17th December 1998, whereupon the registration passed to another An-12.

• Additionally, four An-12s registered in São Tomé & Principe – demilitarised An-12BP S9-CAN (ex-RA-11013, c/n 6344002), An-12B S9-CDB (ex-D2-FCV, c/n 401901, named *Emmanuel*), An-12BK

Goliaf Air An-12B S9-DAF 'Principe' undergoes maintenance at Sharjah.

Above: Slovak Air Force An-12B '2209 Black' vacates the runway after landing. The outer engines have been shut down already.

S9-DBP leased in 2001 (ex/to Silk Way Airlines 4K-AZ33, c/n 8346201) and An-12 S9-GRC (c/n unknown) – belonged to unidentified operators. The former aircraft was written off in a crash landing at Lukapa, Angola, on 20th January 1999.

SIERRA LEONE

• **Showa Air** operated 'military' An-12Bs 9L-LCR (ex-CCCP-12166, c/n 4341801) acquired in February 2002 and 9L-LDW acquired by July 2003. The latter aircraft was probably ex-Avial'-NV RA-11324 (c/n 2340804) and was operated in the ex-owner's full colours. 9L-LCR was damaged beyond repair when it overran at Goma, Zaïre, on 27th May 2003.

• Sierra Leonean An-12s whose operators are unknown include An-12BP 9L-LEA (ex-Avia-Pusk UN 11001, c/n 5343408) operated in late 2003 and demilitarised An-12A 9L-LFQ (ex-RA-48970, c/n 2400502) seen in mid-2006. The former aircraft became EK-11001 with Air Armenia in December 2003

SINGAPORE

Air Mark Aviation based at Singapore-Seletar operated 'military' An-12P LZ-SFG and An-12B LZ-SFK wet-leased from Air Sofia in 1997. In May 2002 the airline leased An-12BP LZ-SFT from the same carrier.

SLOVAKIA

The Slovak Air Force (Slovenské Vojenské Létectvo) received one of the CzAF An-12s, 2209 Black, after the break-up of Czechoslovakia. However, with just one *Cub* on strength, the same problems were encountered as in neighbouring Czech Republic. Eventually the Slovaks sold the aircraft to Tiramavia as ER-ACH in 1998.

SRI LANKA

• The No.2 Transport Wing of the **Sri Lankan Air Force** (SLAF) based at Ratmalana AB operated three Shaanxi Y8s.

By July 1996 CR-873 had been transferred to the civil register as 4R-HVC in order to facilitate flights abroad.

Serial	Version	C/n	Notes
CP701	Y8D	060802	C/n often reported as 060801 but photoproof exists! Probably directly reserialled to
CR871			Shot down near Palaly AB 18-11-95
CP702	Y8D	060804	Probably directly reserialled to
CR872			Blue/white PLAAF-style c/s. Crashed 5-7-92
CR873	Y8B	070802	Ex-ACA Air Changan Airlines B-3105, leased as a replacement for temporarily unserviceable CR871; was to have been returned 4-95 but retained after loss of CR871

• **Expo Aviation (Pvt) Ltd. [8D/EXV]** has a 'civil' An-12BP, 4R-EXC (ex-RA-12956, c/n 8345507) purchased from Samara Airlines in early 1999. Later, this airline operated a Kyrghyz-registered An-12BK, EX-029 (ex-XU-395 No.1), in 2004-06 – apparently on lease from Click Airways.

• **Skycabs Ltd.** operated four 'military' An-12s.

Registration	Version	C/n	Notes
4R-SKL	An-12B (+)	3341505	Ex-U-UAPO RA-12174, bought ?-98; sold to Inter Trans Air ?-00 as LZ-ITS
RA-11408	An-12B (+)	3341209	Leased from Aviaobschchemash in 1995
RA-12116	An-12B (+)	402108	Leased from Special Cargo Airlines
RA-13357	An-12BK	8345604	Leased from Impulse-Aero ?-95

Gleaming with fresh paint, An-12BP 4R-EXC has just had the new livery of Expo Air applied at Sharjah (note the protective film on the transparencies).

An-12B ST-JUA looks smart in the full colours of Juba Air Cargo

• **Srilankan Airlines [UL/ALK]** wet-leased An-12B LZ-SFK (c/n 4341901) from Air Sofia in the autumn of 2001. This was followed by the lease of An-12A LZ-SFW in May 2004 – May 2005.

• An unidentified Sri Lankan airline acquired demilitarised An-12PP 4R-AIA (ex-XU-355, c/n 01347107) from Air Sofia in March 2002. On 16th August same year the aircraft suffered a landing accident in Karachi.

SUDAN

• **Air West Co. Ltd. [–/AWZ]** has operated several An-12s registered both in and outside Sudan.

Registration	Version	C/n	Notes
ST-AWM	An-12BP (+)	5343704	Demilitarised. Ex-FLight Air Company RA-11003, bought by 12-98, basic SPAir c/s
ST-AWU	An-12BK	8345804	Ex-Russian Air Force, bought ?-99, previous identity unknown
ER-ACW	An-12BP (–)	8345510	Ex-Savanair D2-FBY, bought ?-00; basic Savanair c/s, no titles. Sold to Bright Aviation Services ?-00 as LZ-BRC
RA-11734	An-12B (+)	2340809	Demilitarised; leased 12-94, ex-UNPF white colours
S9-BOT	An-12BP (+)	5343305	Reported for Air West 3-02

• **AZZA Transport Co. Ltd. [–/AZZ]** operated four *Cubs*.

Registration	Version	C/n	Notes
ST-ALV No.2	Y8F-100	?	
ST-AQG	An-12	?	
ST-ARV	An-12BK	8345310	Ex-Dvin Air EK-11028, bought 2006
ST-DAS	An-12BK	7345209	Ex-Valan ER-AXC, bought 2002

• **Coptrade Air Transport** operated 'civil' An-12BP ST-AQF (ex-Sakha Avia RA-12953, c/n 8345504) in October 1999. The aircraft was sold to Trans ATTICO (see below) same year.

• **Data International Aviation Ltd. [–/DTN]** had three An-12s – ST-APG (c/n unknown), An-12A ST-APJ (previous identity unknown, c/n 2400701) and An-12 ST-APU (c/n unknown).

• **El Magal Aviation [–/MGL]** leased 'civil' An-12BP RA-12988 (c/n 00347206) in late 1998. In 2003 the airline bought An-12A UR-48975 (c/n 1400101) from Motor-Sich; this aircraft, which became ST-SIG, crashed in Dalan, Sudan, on 12th May 2004.

• **Forner Airlines** operated 'civil' An-12BP ST-AQF (ex-Mikma ER-ACG, c/n 9346504) in March 2002.

• **Juba Air Cargo [–/JUC]** operated two *Cubs*.

Registration	Version	C/n	Notes
ST-ARN	An-12BK	8346010	Ex-EK-11011
EX-11010	An-12TB (+)	3341110	Ex-RA-11010, in service 2003-04. Became, see next line
EK-11010			Became, see next line
ST-JUA			Reregistered 2005

• An airline called **Kata** has a single An-12BK, ST-AZM (ex-Ukrainian Air Force '05 Red', c/n 00346907) bought in late 2005.

• **Sarit Airlines [–/SRW]** operated ten An-12s.

Registration	Version	C/n	Notes
ST-SAA	An-12BP (+)	5342905	Ex-Soviet Air Force CCCP-11773. Crashed Wau, Sudan, 24-9-03
ST-SAD	An-12BP (+)	5343307	Ex-Soviet Air Force CCCP-11132. Sold to Armenia 2005 as EK-11132
ST-SAE	An-12BP (–)	01347305	Ex/to EK-12777, leased from South Airlines 2004
ST-SAF	An-12BK	00347606	Ex-EK-12222. DBR Gajlij 5-10-04
ST-SAR	An-12B (+)	402102	Ex-Lasare Air 4L-CAA, leased 10-00
ST-SAT	An-12BP (+)	4343502	Ex-Soviet Air Force CCCP-11424
S9-BOS	An-12BP (–)	01347704	Named Julia. Leased from British Gulf International
S9-BOT	An-12BP (+)	5343305	Leased from British Gulf International
EK-11997	An-12BP (+)	6344407	Leased from unknown operator by 2003. Damaged Geneina, Sudan, 3-11-03 and possibly DBR
4K-AZ30	An-12BP (+)	5343410	Leased from unknown airline 11-04, lease ended 2005

• **SASCO Airlines** (Sudanese Air Services Co.) **[–/SAC]** based in Khartoum operated An-12BK EX-022 (ex-3C-QRN, c/n 7344705) in late 2004; by October 2006 the aircraft had passed to a new operator, Sunlight Airlines. In the first half of 2005 SASCO also operated An-12BK EX-034 (c/n 01348005).

• The Sudan Air Force (Silakh al-Jawwiya as-Sudaniya) operated three *Cubs*.

Serial/ registration	Version	C/n	Notes
988	An-12BP (+)	8345908	Ex-Iraqi Air Force YI-AER, bought 2007
ST-ALU No.1	Y8D	070804	*Derelict Wau, Sudan. Registration passed to an An-26 in 1999*
ST-ALV No.1	An-12BP (+)	8345909	*Ex-Iraqi Air Force YI-AEP. Registration later to Y8F-100 (see AZZA Transport)*

Note: Some sources reported that the Sudan Air Force had An-12s serialled 700 (which was actually an An-24RT), 711, 722, 733, 744 and 755; however, recent reports fail to confirm this.

• In 2001 an airline called **Sudanese States Aviation Co. Ltd. [–/SNV]** bought an An-12 registered ST-AQQ (version and c/n unknown).

• **Trans Arabian Air Transport [–/TRT]** operates demilitarised An-12AP ST-AQE (ex-RA-12188, c/n 1400106) on lease from United Arabian. The aircraft retains the faded colour scheme of previous owner Mostransgaz.

• **Trans ATTICO** (African Transport, Trading & Investment Co.) **[–/ETC]** based in Khartoum and Sharjah operated the abovesaid An-12BP ST-AQF and demilitarised An-12BP ST-AQP (ex-TN-AGC, c/n 4342305). ST-AQF was sold to Natalco Airlines of Congo; later, Trans ATTICO bought An-12BK ST-ARN (ex-EK-11011, c/n 8346010).

• The abovementioned An-12AP ST-AQE is operated by **United Arabian Co. [–/UAB]**.

• **Air Pass**, a sister company of Air Cess (Liberia), operated most of the latter carrier's fleet which was transferred to the Swazi register in 1998. 'Pass' is an acronym for Pietersburg Aviation Services & Systems; this was because, though nominally a Swazi company, the airline was based at Pietersburg-Gateway Int'l airport, South Africa. In 1998 Air Pass suspended operations, selling almost its entire fleet to Centrafricain Airlines.

Registration	Version	C/n	Notes
3D-SKN	An-12A (+)	1901706	Ex-EL-AKN, named *Flying Cat*
3D-AKV	An-12A (+)	1340107	Ex-EL-AKV, named *Voyager;*
3D-RDL	An-12B (+)	2340809	Ex-EL-RDL, named *Lastochka*

• An airline called **Southern Cross** bought 'military' An-12B RA-11831 (c/n 3341206) from Amuraviatrans in 1997. The registration 3D-ASC was allocated but possibly not taken up and the aircraft may have been directly resold to Santa Cruz Imperial as EL-ASC.

The **Tanzanian People's Defence Force Air Wing** took delivery of two Shaanxi Y8s in November 2003; the grey-painted aircraft are serialled JW-9034 and JW-9035 (c/ns unknown). Oddly, they have been described as Y8F-200s, though it would be more logical to suppose they are export Y8D-IIs with Western avionics.

• **THY Turkish Airlines (Türk Hava Yollari) [TK/THY]** briefly operated 'military' An-12B LZ-SFK (c/n 2341901) wet-leased from Air Sofia in 1993.

• On 3rd August 1994 **CAT Cargo** leased demilitarised An-12B RA-11366 (c/n 402808) from Magadanaerogrooz; the aircraft was reregistered TC-KET. By 1997 the aircraft had been withdrawn from use at

An-12B TC-KET displays the colours of the defunct CAT CArgo as it sits parked at Istanbul-Ataturk International.

An-12B LZ-BAE was operated by HeavyLift Cargo Airlines in full colours in 1995-96. Here it is seen resting between flights at Manston.

Istanbul-Atatürk International (Yesilköy) airport and was still stored there in 2000.

UNITED ARAB EMIRATES

Aerocomplex, a Soviet/UAE (later Russian/UAE) joint venture, leased freighters from Aeroflot as required. These included red/white 'civil' An-12BPs CCCP-11108 No.2 (c/n 01347810) and CCCP-11118 (c/n 01348002) leased from the Leningrad UAD in the summer of 1990.

UNITED KINGDOM

• **HeavyLift Cargo Airlines [NP/HLA]** operated 'civil' An-12B LZ-BAE (c/n 402001) leased from Balkan Bulgarian Airlines between late 1995 and mid-1996 in full HeavyLift colours. Later in 1996 it was supplanted by a sister aircraft, RA-12995 (c/n 00347402) leased from Pulkovo Avia.

• Veteran Airlines 'military' An-12AP UR-PAS *Andrey* (c/n 2401105) was based at Manston-Kent International at one time, flying cargo charters for **Skyline Aviation**. Its customers included DHL, Rolls-Royce and the Ford Motor Company.

THE UKRAINE

• Rovno-based **AeroVis Airlines [–/VIZ]** had an all-An-12 fleet.

Registration	Version	C/n	Notes
UR-CBF	An-12A (+)	2340507	Ex-Air Sofia LZ-SFW, bought 2005
UR-CBG	An-12BP (+)	6343705	Ex-Atlant-SV UR-11302, bought 11-02
UR-CCP	An-12A (+)	2340505	Ex-Heli Air LZ-CBM, bought 2-04
UR-CEX	An-12B (+)	4342103	Ex-Atran RA-93915, bought 2005, basic Atran c/s, no titles. Sold to Bright Aviation Services \ 2006 as LZ-BRI
UR-CEZ	An-12BP (+)	6344304	Ex-Atran RA-98118
UR-CFB	An-12B (+)	6343802	Ex-Russian Air Force '02 Red', bought 2006

• **Air Ukraine/Avialinii Ukrainy [6U/UKR]**, the original Ukrainian flag carrier, leased at least one An-12BK ('54 Red', c/n 8345702) from the Ukrainian Air Force in December 1996; the aircraft was reregistered UR-11346 for the duration. In 1996 the airline acquired An-12BK RA-13357 (c/n 8345604) from Impulse-Aero; the aircraft was reregistered UR-11314. In December 2006 the machine was sold to Moldova as ER-AXX.

• The Antonov Design Bureau operates a large fleet of assorted aircraft of its own make, including four An-12s. These are operated by **Antonov Airlines [–/ADB]** and wear a smart blue/white colour scheme with the ADB logo and titles.

Registration	Version	C/n	Notes
UR-11315	An-12BP (+)	4342307	Demilitarised. Basic Aeroflot c/s with large 'Antonov 12' titles, later full c/s
UR-11322	An-12A (+)	0901409	Ex-EW-11322, leased from Wings ?-96
UR-11765	*An-12B (+)*	*401705*	*Was leased to Air Sofia 1993-98 as LZ-SFM. DBR in hard landing at Kiev-Gostomel' 2005 and scrapped*
UR-21510	An-12AP (+)	0901404	Ex-CCCP-21510, ex-Soviet Air Force '88 Red'. Grey c/s with large 'Antonov 12' titles, repainted in full c/s by 12-96; retrofitted with non-standard radar (bigger than ROZ-1 but smaller than Initsiativa-4-100)

• **Antonov Airtrack [–/UAP]** operated 'military' An-12BP UR-UAA (previous identity unknown, c/n 6344701) in 1996-98, eventually selling it to Khors Aircompany. There were also plans to add one ex-Soviet Air Force An-12BP and three An-12BKs to the fleet but the aircraft were unserviceable and the reconditioning job dragged on so long that the airline ceased operations before taking delivery.

• Simferopol'-based **Atlant-SV [L4/ATG]** had at least four 'military' *Cubs*. The airline ceased operations in 1997.

Antonov Design Bureau ground crews work on Antonov Airlines An-12B UR-11765 which made a hard landing at Kiev-Gostomel' (the damage to the port main gear unit is evident). Eventually, after damage assessment, the aircraft was declared a write-off and stripped for spares.

Registration	Version	C/n	Notes
UR-11300	An-12B (+)	402211	Ex-Polissyaaviatrans
UR-11302*	An-12BP (+)	5343705	Former code unknown; ASO-2 flare packs; WFU Kiev-Svyatoshino minus insignia by 9-02; sold to AeroVis Airlines 11-02
UR-11357*	An-12BP (+)	5343203	Ex-Polissyaaviatrans; ex-CCCP-11357 No.2*
UR-11501	An-12A (+)	1340206	Sold to Tiramavia ?-00 as ER-ADC

* The registration CCCP-11302 was used before by An-12BP c/n 8346004; CCCP-11357 No.1 was an An-12B (c/n 402802).

• Kiev-based **Busol Airline [–/BUA]** (the name, pronounced *boosol*, is Ukrainian for 'stork') operated three *Cubs*. They retained the standard Air Force grey colours but had Busol Airline titles and a stork superimposed on a Ukrainian flag on the tail. This airline vanished in 1998.

Registration	Version	C/n	Notes
UR-11347	An-12BP	7345208	Sold to Tiramavia 2004 as ER-ADO
UR-11348	An-12BK	7345208	Ex-Ukrainian AF '21 Blue'. To Volare Aviation Enterprise 3-00 as UR-SMA
UR-11349	An-12BK	9346302	Former code unknown; ASO-2 flare packs. To Veteran Airlines ?-00 as UR-YMR

• Khar'kov-based **ICAR Airlines (Independent Carrier) [C3/IPR]** owned a single 'military' An-12BP registered UR-PWH (previous identity unknown, c/n 6343707). The aircraft was sold to Aerocom in 1999 as ER-ACI. Previously it leased An-12BP UR-11819 from the Khar'kov aircraft factory (see next entry).

• The aircraft fleet of the **Khar'kov State Aircraft Manufacturing Co.** (KSAMC, or KhDAVP – *Kharkovs'ke derzhavne aviatsiyne vyrobniche pidpriyemstvo*) included a demilitarised An-12BP, UR-11819 (c/n 6344009), and a 'military' An-12B, UR-11833 (c/n 3341008). The latter aircraft (painted in ex-Air Force grey colours) had been retired by 2002, while UR-11819 was sold to Motor-Sich.

• **Khors Aircompany [X6/KHO, later X9/KHO]** (named after the sun god of the ancient pagan Slavic peoples) operated four An-12s.

Registration	Version	C/n	Notes
UR-11319	An-12BP (–)	4342510	Shot down by UNITA rebels near Cuito-Cuanavale, Angola, 14-12-98
UR-11326	An-12AP (+)	2400802	Sold to Africa West Airlines as S9-DBA
UR-11332	An-12BP (+)	4342202	Ex-Ukrainian AF '84 Blue', transferred ?-97. Lst BIO Air Company ?-00 as T9-CAD
UR-TSI	An-12BP (+)	6344701	Ex-Antonov Airtrack UR-UAA; operated with this registration until mid-1998

• **Motor-Sich [M9/MSI]**, the flying division of the Zaporozhye-based aero engine factory of the same name, operated four *Cubs*.

Registration	Version	C/n	Notes
UR-11316	An-12BK	9346810	Ex-RA-11316 (ex-owner unknown); re-equipped with ROZ-1 radar
UR-13332	An-12B (+)	4341707	Ex-Soviet Air Force '82 Red'
UR-11528	An-12B (+)	3341005	Retired by 1999
UR-11819	An-12BP (+)	6344009	Ex-KSAMC
UR-48975	An-12A (+)	1400101	

• **Polissyaaviatrans** (Poles'ye Air Transport) **[–/POS]** of Zhitomir operated An-12B UR-11300 (c/n 402211) and An-12BP UR-11357 (c/n 5343203). Both were transferred to Atlant-SV in 1997.

• **Shovkovyy Shlyakh** ('silk way' in Ukrainian) purchased An-12TBK 4K-AZ18 (c/n 9346308) in late 2003. After serving with the airline for about three years as UR-CBU the freighter was sold to Silk Way Airlines of Azerbaijan in 2006, becoming 4K-AZ63. Another An-12 operated by Shovkovyy Shlyakh was registered UR-CBW (c/n unknown).

• **Ukraine Air Alliance** (*Ookrayina-Aeroal'yans*) **[–/UKL]** owned three 'military' An-12Bs – UR-11813 (c/n 3340908), UR-UAF (c/n 3341108) and UR-48984 (ex-Voronezh Aircraft Factory RA-48984, c/n 402913, bought in 1997). The first aircraft was sold to Amuraviatrans, becoming RA-11813; UR-UAF was sold to Fiji as DQ-FBS, while UR-48984 (which reportedly carried the c/n at one time as 402603) was sold to Aerofreight, Russia, regaining its previous identity.

• The **Ukrainian Air Force** (UAF, or VPS – *Viys'kovo-povitryany seely*) inherited a substantial number of An-12s from the VTA when the Soviet

Union collapsed. They are based in Kiev, Krivoy Rog, L'vov, Saki and Vinnitsa. However, as mentioned earlier, funding problems and political complications following the break-up of the Soviet Union and the resulting spares shortage have caused many UAF *Cubs* to be cannibalised for spares.

Most Ukrainian An-12s were operated by numerous 'airlines' under UAF management which help the Air Force generate urgently needed cash (though at times it is hard to tell which airline is civil and which is not!). When the ultimate fate of aircraft no longer listed by a given airline is unknown these are assumed returned to the UAF.

C/n	Version	Tactical code/ registration	Notes
1400301	An-12A (+)	83 Blue	Based Sknilov AB, L'vov?
1400304	An-12A (+)	23 Blue	
3341301	An-12B (+)	78 Red	For sale 9-05
3341610	An-12B (+)	69 Red	Based Novofyodorovka AB, Saki? For sale 9-05
4341710	An-12B (+)	61 Blue	Transferred to Ukraine Cargo Airways 2004 as UR-UDD
4342007	An-12BP (+)	77 Red	Based Novofyodorovka AB, Saki? Ex-Soviet Air Force '70'
4342106	An-12BP (+)	79 Red	Based Novofyodorovka AB, Saki?
4342110	An-12BP (+)	83 Red	Based Novofyodorovka AB, Saki?
4342202	An-12BP (+)	84 Blue	Based Sknilov AB, L'vov. Transferred to Khors Aircompany ?-97 as UR-11332
4342306	An-12BP (+)	50 Red	Based Vinnitsa?
4342308	An-12BP (+)	61 Red	Based Novofyodorovka AB, Saki? Ex-Soviet Air Force '72'. Transferred to Veteran Airlines by 8-02 as UR-PLV
4342610	An-12BP (+)	86 Blue	Based Sknilov AB, L'vov. Transferred to civil register as UR-12423 (see below)
5343505	An-12B (+)	72 Red	Based Odessa. For sale 2006
6344301	An-12BP (+)	04 Red	
6344603	An-12BP (+)	?	Based Sknilov AB, L'vov?
6344605	An-12BP (+)	73 Blue	Based Sknilov AB, L'vov? Transferred to Volare Aviation Enterprise 3-00 as UR-LMI
6344607	An-12BP (+)	86 Blue	Based Odessa. For sale 2006
7345208	An-12BK	21 Blue	Ex-Soviet AF '84 Blue'. Transferred to Busol Airline ?-94 as UR-11348
8345702	An-12BK	54 Red	Based Sknilov AB, L'vov? Leased to Air Ukraine 12-96 as UR-11346
8346106	An-12BK	03 Blue	Based Sknilov AB, L'vov? Sold to Airline Transport, Inc. 2004 as ER-AXZ
9346208	An-12BP (+)?	22 Blue	Reported as An-12BP but may be An-12BK. Sold to Dvin Air Cargo as EK-11030
9346309	An-12BK	68 Red	Ex-CCCP-12113. Stored 2002; sold to Scorpion Air 2003 as LZ-MNP
9346405	An-12BK	24 Blue	Transferred to Volare Aviation Enterprise as UR-LIP
9346607	An-12BP (+)?	86 Red	Reported as An-12BP but may be An-12BK
9346802	An-12BP (+)?	?	Based Sknilov AB, L'vov? Reported as An-12BP but may be An-12BK. Sold to a Russian operator by 8-01 as RA-11425
9346809	An-12BP (+)?	87 Red	Based Sknilov AB, L'vov? Reported as An-12BP but may be An-12BK
00346907	An-12BK	05 Red	Based Melitopol'. Sold to Kata by 12-03 as ST-AZM
00347004	An-12BK	20 Blue	Transferred to Volare Aviation Enterprise 5-98 as UR-BWM
00347006	An-12BK	57 Blue	Based Vinnitsa?
00347107	An-12BK	71 Red	Sold to Antey 6-96 as RA-11301
?	An-12BP (+)?	11259	WFU Odessa by 5-02
4341910	An-12BP (+)	UR-11351	Former tactical code unknown. Sold to Dvin Air Cargo ?-97 as EK-11351
401810?	An-12B (+)	UR-11352	ELINT aircraft? Based Vinnitsa?
4342610	An-12BP (+)	UR-12423	Ex-86 Blue. Sold to Angola as D2-FBD

• **Ukrainian Cargo Airways** (UCA, or UATK – *Ookrayins'ka aviatseeyna trahnsportna kompahniya*) [–/UKS] based in Zaporozhye operated four An-12s. UR-UCK was leased to Air Charter Services (Liberia) in late 2002

Registration	Version	C/n	Notes
UR-UCK	An-12BK	9346905	Ex-Veteran Airlines UR-11304
UR-UCM	An-12BK	?	Demilitarised, all-white c/s. Sold 2002
UR-UCN	An-12BK	00347604	Ex-Veteran Airlines UR-11303; leased to Veteran
UR-UDD	An-12B (+)	4341710	Ex-Ukrainian Air Force '61 Blue', Aeroflot-style cheatline

• **Veteran Airlines** [–/VPB] based in Dzhankoy had eight An-12s.

Registration	Version	C/n	Notes
UR-11303	An-12BK	00347604	Transferred to Ukrainian Cargo Airways as UR-UCN; see six lines down!
UR-11304	An-12BK	9346905	Transferred to Ukrainian Cargo Airways as UR-UCK
UR-11305	An-12BK	00347803	Sold to Imtrec Aviation as XU-395 No.2
UR-11306	An-12BK	9346205	
UR-CCY	An-12BP (–)	02348106	Ex-Tesis RA-11124, bought 2006. Operated for UN-WFP
UR-CEM	An-12BP (+)	3340908	Ex-Amuraviatrans RA-11813, bought 2005, operated for UN-WFP. Sold or leased to Astral by 1-06
UR-CEN	An-12BP (–)	02348203	Ex-Avial'-NV RA-11128, bought 2004
UR-PAS	An-12AP (+)	2401105	Named *Andrey*
UR-PLV	An-12BP (+)	4342308	Ex-Ukrainian Air Force '61 Red'
UR-UCN	An-12BK	01347604	Leased from UCA Ukrainian Cargo Airways
UR-YMR	An-12BK	9346302	Ex-Busol Airline UR-11349, transferred ?-00

• Kiev-based **Vitair** [–/VIT] operated An-12BP UR-11819 (c/n 6344009) in 1995.

• **Volare Aviation Enterprise Joint-Stock Company** [F7/VRE] based in Krivoy Rog operated seven An-12s.

Registration	Version	C/n	Notes
UR-BWM	An-12BK	00347004	Ex-Ukrainian Air Force '20 Blue', transferred 4-99
UR-LAI	An-12BP (–)	8345505	Ex-Samara Airlines RA-12954, bought ?-99.
UR-LIP	An-12BK	9346405	Ex-Ukrainian AF '24 Blue'; grey c/s, later full c/s, named 'The Spirit of Cornwall 2'. Crashed near Agadir 7-2-02
UR-LMI	An-12BK	6344605	Ex-Ukrainian Air Force '73 Blue', full c/s
UR-LTG	An-12BP (–)	00347201	Ex-UR-12986, ex-Samara Airlines RA-12986, bought by 9-99. Lst ACS Air Charter Services
UR-SMA	An-12BK	7345208	Demilitarised. Ex-Busol Airline UR-11348
UR-SVG	An-12BP (+)	4342309	Demilitarised. Ex-TN-AGE, ex-RA-11320

• An unidentified Ukrainian airline operated An-12P UR-BYW (ex-UR-11332, c/n 0901409). First seen at Kiev-Svyatoshino in September 2002, the aircraft carried only 'Cargo' titles. In late 2003 the aircraft was refurbished and sold to Scorpion Air as LZ-MNN.

UZBEKISTAN

• **Avialeasing Aviation Company [AD/TWN]**, an Uzbek/US joint venture based at Tashkent-International (Sergheli) airport and Opa Locka (Florida), operated three An-12s which it leased to various airlines.

Registration	Version	C/n	Notes
UK 11109	An-12BP (+)	01348005	Ex-TAPO-Avia
UK 11418	An-12BK	7344705	Demilitarised. Ex-TAPO-Avia. Sold to Sud Aerocargo 2001 as ER-AXB
UK-12002	An-12B (+)	402002	Ex-Vega-M RA-11373, bought 2005; also carries large SRX titles

• 'Military' An-12BP 06105 (c/n 5343606) was operated by an airline called **Mathur Avia** in 1992 (the registration was probably painted on with no prefix, though some sources report it as CIS-06105).

• 'Military' An-12BPs UK 06105, UK 11109 and An-12BK UK 11418 were operated by **Simurg [–/JRP]**, the flying division of the Tashkent Electronics Plant, in 1997 (the name refers to a Bird of Happiness in Oriental folklore).

• Over the years **TAPO-Avia [PQ/CTP, later 4C/TPR]**, the flying division of the Tashkent Aircraft Production Corporation based at

Registration	Version	C/n	Notes
UK 06105	An-12BP (+)	5343606	Sold 2000 as EX-001
UK 11109	An-12BP	01348005	Ex-Soviet Air Force '10'. Full c/s. Sold to Avialeasing
UK 11418	An-12BK	7344705	Demilitarised. Full c/s. Sold to Avialeasing?
UK-11804	An-12A (+)	2400406	Demilitarised. Ex-Uzbekistan Airways
UK 11807	An-12BK	00346910	Full c/s
UK 58644	An-12A (+)	2340303	Full c/s
UK 93920	An-12BP (+)	6344610	Sold to Vega Airlines ?-00 as LZ-VEC

Tashkent-Vostochnyy airfield, operated seven An-12s. Besides acting as support aircraft and generating revenue by carrying commercial cargo, they advertise the factory and the aircraft it builds, wearing a smart livery with Tashkent Aircraft Production Corporation titles.

• The **Uzbekistan Air Force** operated a number of *Cubs*. Some sources say An-12BPs UK 11369 and UK 11372 were also Air Force aircraft and were leased to Uzbekistan Airways.

• **Uzbekistan Airways/Uzbekiston Havo Yullari [HY/UZB]**, the Uzbek flag carrier based at Tashkent-International and Samarkand, operated five An-12s.

Registration	Version	C/n	Notes
UK 11109	An-12BP	01348005	Leased from Avialeasing in 1998, returned by 2002
UK 11369	An-12BP (+)	6343810	Demilitarised; ex-Soviet Air Force CCCP-11818, bought 1997. Full c/s. Sold to Tiramavia 2005 as ER-ACR
UK 11372	An-12BP (+)	5343204	Ex-Soviet Air Force CCCP-12130, bought 1997. Full c/s. Sold to Tiramavia 2005 as ER-ACO
UK 11418	An-12BK	7344705	Demilitarised; leased from Avialeasing ?-00, returned by 2002
UK-11804	An-12A (+)	2400406	Demilitarised. Sold to TAPO-Avia after 1996

SOUTH YEMEN (PEOPLE'S DEMOCRATIC REPUBLIC OF YEMEN)

The **South Yemen Air Force (PDRYAF)** operated at least four 'military' An-12s registered 7O-ABH, 7O-ABM, 7O-ACI and 7O-ACJ. The latter two aircraft also wore PDRYAF serials 625 and 626. No c/ns are known.

YUGOSLAVIA

The **Yugoslav Air Force** (JRV – *Jugoslovensko Ratno Vazduhoplovstvo*) took delivery of two An-12BPs in November-December 1971. The aircraft wore dual markings, carrying the civil registrations YU-AIC (c/n 01348007) and YU-AID (c/n 01348010) as well as the JRV serials 73311 and 73312 respectively. Curiously, the aircraft were

Resplendent in the house colours of the Tashkent Aircraft Production Association, An-12B UK 58644 leaves a smoky trail as is climbs away from Moscow-Domodedovo.

built in unarmed commercial configuration; another unusual feature was that a Collins DME set had been integrated at the customer's request.

Little is known about the operational use of the Yugoslav *Cubs*. On 12th December 1988 YU-AID crashed on approach to Yerevan while making an earthquake relief flight. The surviving example had a chance to participate in the civil war in Yugoslavia before it was sold to SiGi Air Cargo as LZ-SGA in 1991.

ZAIRE (NOW DEMOCRATIC REPUBLIC OF CONGO)

• **Adala Airways** bought An-12BK '11 Yellow' (c/n 7345410) from the Belorussian Air Force in October 2001; the aircraft was registered 9Q-CEN. By mid-2005 the aircraft had become military once again, being sold to the Angolan Air Force as T-311.

• **ATO – Air Transport Office** briefly leased 'civil' An-12BP RA-11101 (c/n 01347703) from GosNII GA in December 1993.

• **Mango Airlines** bought 'military' An-12B 9U-BHN No.2 (c/n 3341506) and 'civil' An-12BP 9U-BHO (c/n 8345503) from Air Vitoria in 2005. On 20th March 2006 the aircraft were reregistered 9Q-CVT and 9Q-CVM respectively. Regrettably on 13th July that year 9Q-CVT crashed en route from Goma to Kisangani, DRC. The most recent addition is An-12BK S9-PSK (ex-EX-048, c/n 8345807).

• 'Military' An-12BP EX-001 (c/n 5343606) is operated by the **Congolese Presidential Flight** since mid-2006.

• A 'military' An-12B registered 9Q-CVG (ex-Phoenix Aviation as EX-11760, c/n 4342404) was operated in the DRC in 2005; quite possibly it, too, belonged to Mango Airlines. This aircraft was also lost in a crash on 25th May 2005.

One more 'military' An-12B belonging to an unknown operator was registered 9Q-CIH (ex-Skylink 9L-LEC, c/n 4341803). It crashed in Bukalaza, Uganda, on 5th January 2005.

OPERATORS FROM UNKNOWN NATIONS

• **Africa West Cargo** operated four An-12s.

Registration	Version	C/n	Notes
EK-11304	An-12A (+)	0901304	Leased from Dvin Avia 6-99
S9-DAF	An-12AP (+)	2340606	Ex-Kazan' Aircraft Production Association RA-12971, in service 2004. Sold to Goliaf Air
S9-DBA	An-12AP (+)	2400802	Ex-Khors Airlines UR-11326
UN 11376	An-12BK	8345805	Ex-ER-AXQ, bought 2005. Sold to Fab Air 2006

• **Air People International** operated demilitarised An-12BK 3C-QRN (ex-ER-AXB, c/n 7344705) in January 2003.

• A former Tyumen' Airlines 'civil' An-12BP (c/n 9346510) saw service with an outfit called **Air Victory** under the consecutive identities of RA-12976, EX-025 (both in May 2004) and 4L-IRA.

• 'Military' An-12BP RA-11908 (c/n 6344501) was noted with **ANV** titles in November 2004; the meaning of these titles is unknown.

• **Camp Aviation Services** leased 'military' An-12BP CCCP-11343 (c/n 00347503) from the Soviet Air Force in 1992.

Yugoslav Air Force An-12BP Yu-AID was occasionally used for what its registration implied (aid and relief missions) – and was lost during one of these missions in 1988.

• **Dynami Aviation** leased 'civil' An-12BP LZ-SFA (c/n 02348007) from Air Sofia in late 2006 and added LZ-SFS (c/n 6344308) early in 2007. The aircraft are based in Marseilles for relief flights to Somalia.

• **Fab Air** operated the abovementioned An-12BK UK 11376 in late 2005/early 2006.

• 'Civil' An-12BP RA-11526 (c/n 02348206) of Komiavia was leased by **GAZ Airways** in June-August 1991.

• **Pnac Cargo** purchased An-12BP EK-11351 (c/n 4341910) from Ararat-Avia by May 2004.

• **RPS Air Freight Co.** operated 'civil' An-12BP UN 11007 (ex-3C-OOZ, c/n 9346509). On 31st March 2005 the machine crashed while taking off from Al-Rayyan, UAE.

• **Southern Air Group** leased An-12BP RA-11339 (c/n 6344310) from the Penza Air Enterprise in 1995.

• **Southern Cargo Airlines** operated 'military' An-12BP RA-11768 (c/n 5343103) bought from the defunct Yermolino Airlines in 2006. Shortly after the purchase the aircraft was placed on the Georgian register as 4L-12008. Some sources, however, list it as being with Global Georgian Airways.

• 'Military' An-12BP UK-06105 (c/n 5343606) was operated by **Sunlight Airlines** in 2004. By October 2006 it had been replaced by An-12BK EX-022 (c/n 7344705).

• An airline called **TASCO** leased demilitarised An-12PP RA-11301 (c/n 00347107) from Antey in 1998-99. The aircraft was in basic Antey colours without titles.

• 'Civil' An-12BP RA-12984 (c/n 00347109) was operated by a carrier called **The Atlantic Airlines** (! – *Auth*.) in 1995.

• The abovementioned An-12BP RA-11526 was also operated by **Victory Airlines** in May 1996.

• **Westrac Air Cargo** leased demilitarised An-12TB RA-11025 (c/n 6344103) from NPO Energiya in 1995.

137

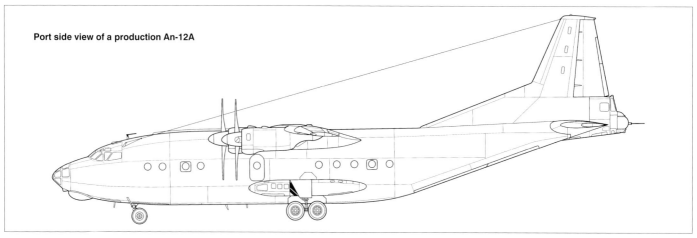

Port side view of a production An-12A

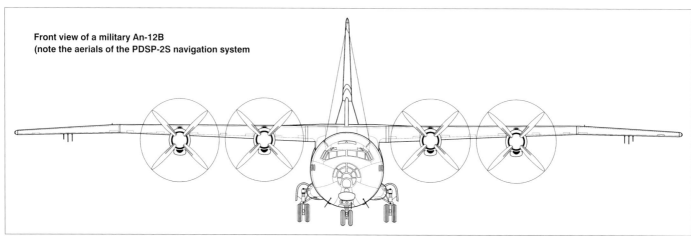

Front view of a military An-12B
(note the aerials of the PDSP-2S navigation system

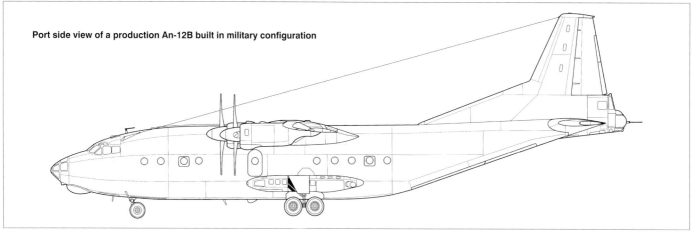

Port side view of a production An-12B built in military configuration

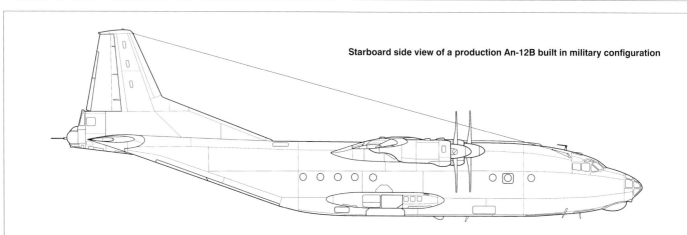

Starboard side view of a production An-12B built in military configuration

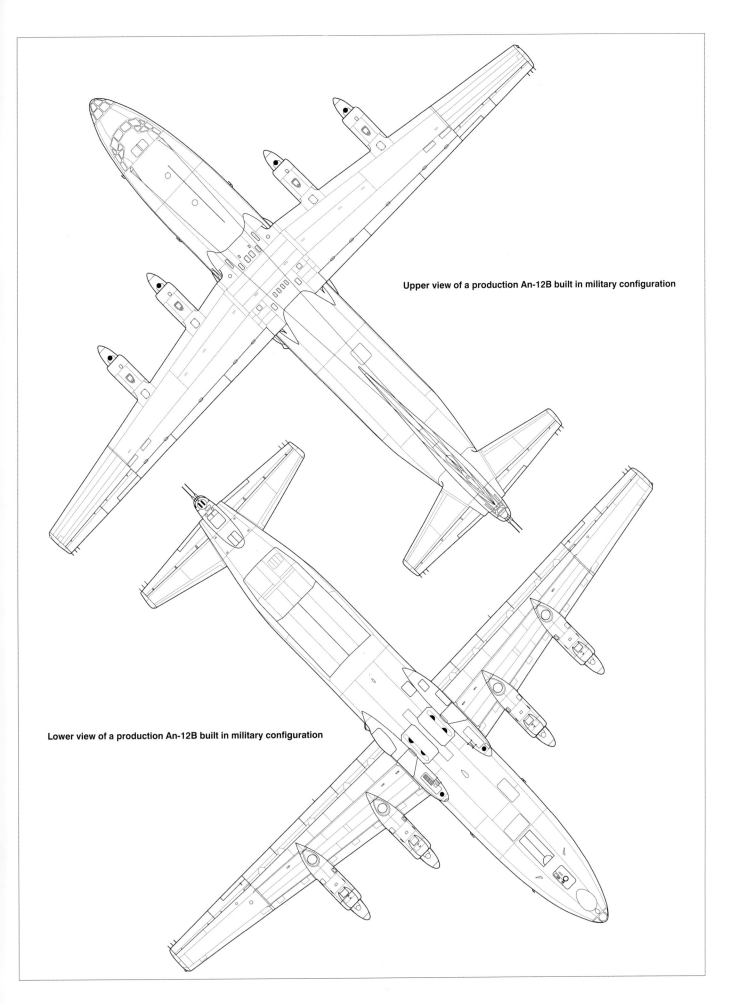

Upper view of a production An-12B built in military configuration

Lower view of a production An-12B built in military configuration

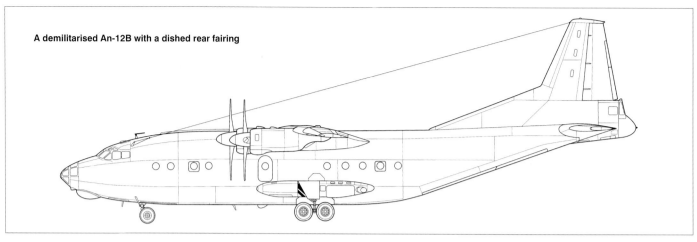

A demilitarised An-12B with a dished rear fairing

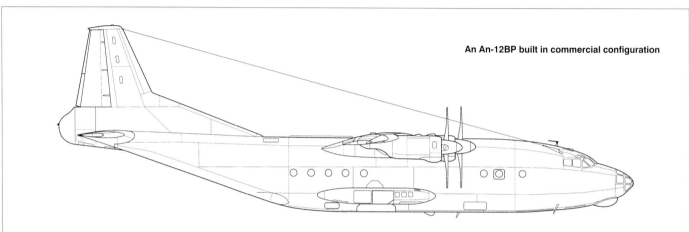

An An-12BP built in commercial configuration

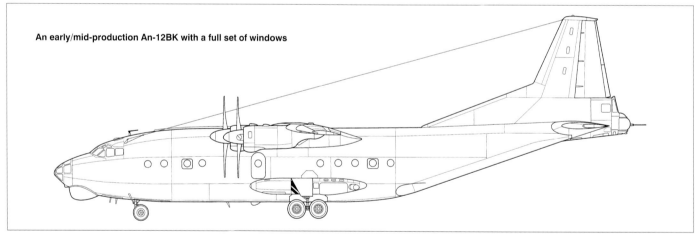

An early/mid-production An-12BK with a full set of windows

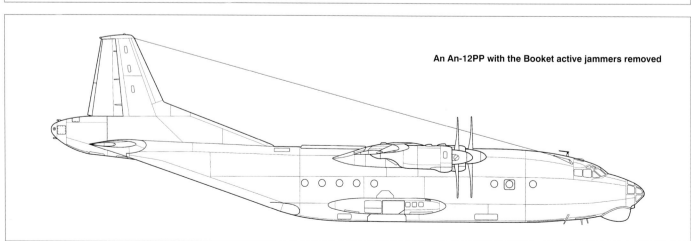

An An-12PP with the Booket active jammers removed

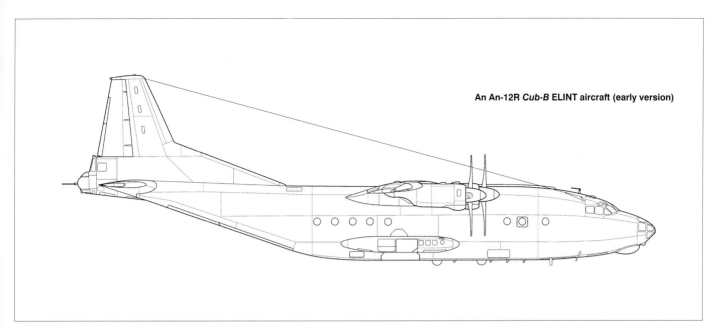

An An-12R *Cub-B* ELINT aircraft (early version)

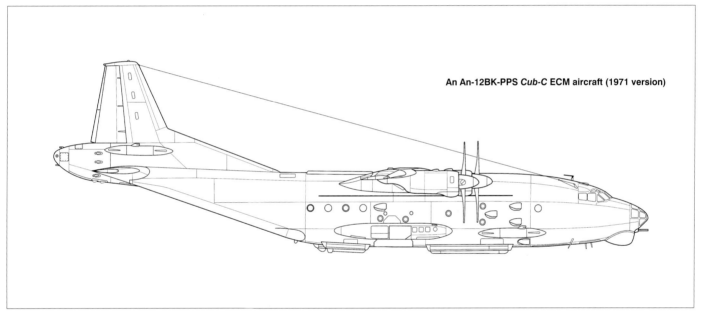

An An-12BK-PPS *Cub-C* ECM aircraft (1971 version)

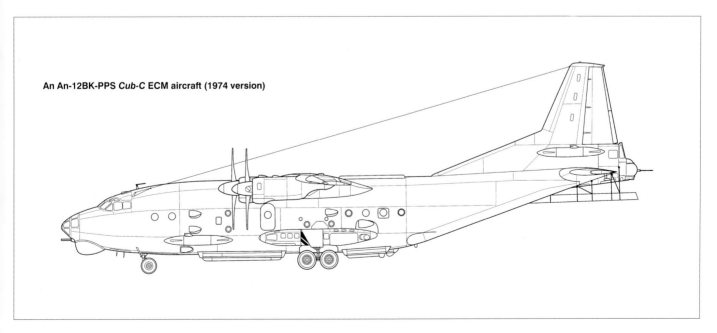

An An-12BK-PPS *Cub-C* ECM aircraft (1974 version)

Russian Air Force An-12BK '28 Blue' (c/n 9346704)
1st VA/257th OSAP, Khabarovsk-Bol'shoy, 2000

Russian Air Force An-12BK '28 Blue' (c/n 9346704)
1st VA/257th OSAP, Khabarovsk-Bol'shoy, 2000

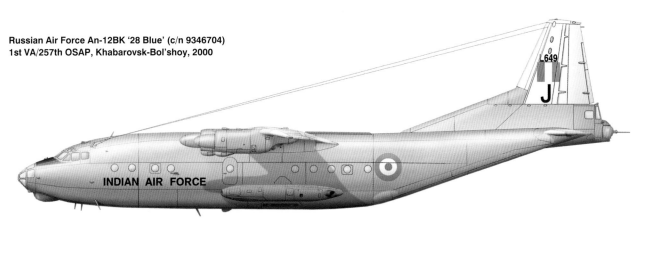

Russian Air Force An-12B '93 Red' (c/n 3341102)
16th VA/226th OSAP, Kubinka AB, 1994

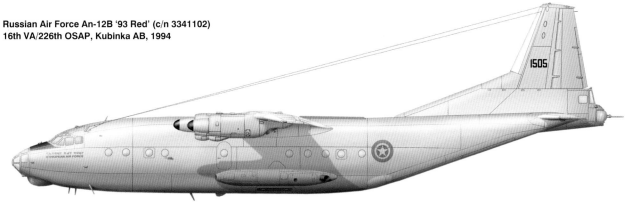

Indian Air Force An-12BP L649/'J' (c/n 6344209)

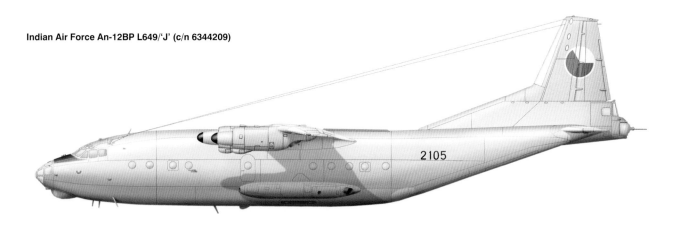

Ethiopian Air Force An-12BP '1505' (c/n 5342907)

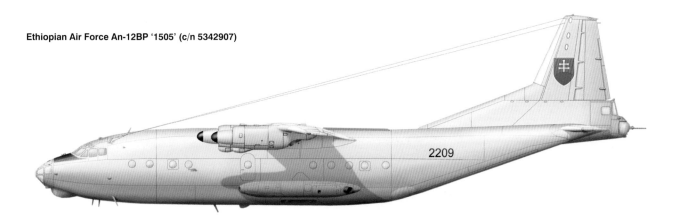

We hope you enjoyed this book . . .

Midland Publishing titles are edited and designed by an experienced and enthusiastic team of specialists.

We always welcome ideas from authors or readers for books they would like to see published.

In addition, our associate, Midland Counties Publications, offers an exceptionally wide range of aviation, military, naval and transport books and DVDs for sale by mail-order worldwide.

For a copy of the appropriate catalogue, or to order further copies of this book, and any other Midland Publishing titles, please write, telephone, fax or e-mail to:

Midland Counties Publications
4 Watling Drive, Hinckley,
Leics, LE10 3EY, England
Tel: (+44) 01455 254 450
Fax: (+44) 01455 233 737
E-mail: midlandbooks@compuserve.com
www.midlandcountiessuperstore.com

US distribution by Specialty Press – see page 2.

Earlier titles in the series:

Vols 1, 3 to 16 are still available
Vol.17: Early Soviet Jet Bombers
Vol.18: Antonov's Heavy Transports
Vol.19: Soviet Heavy Interceptors
Vol.20: Soviet/Russian UAVs
Vol.21: Antonov's Jet Twins
Vol.22: Mil's Heavylift Helicopters
Vol.23: Soviet/Russian AWACS Aircraft
Vol.24: Tupolev Tu-144
Vol.25: Ilyushin IL-12 & IL-14

Red Star Volume 26
RUSSIA'S MILITARY AIRCRAFT IN THE 21st CENTURY

Yefim Gordon

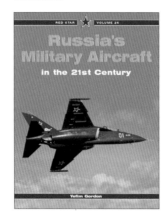

While the large new aircraft programmes of the Cold War era are a thing of the past, military aviation in Russia is not standing still. This volume looks at programmes like the new Mi-8MTKO and Mi-24PN night-capable helicopters, the latest Sukhoi upgrades such as the Su-24M2, Su-25SM and Su-27SM, new and more capable missiles for the Tu-95MS and Tu-160 bombers and the revamping of the training fleet with the Yak-130.

Softback, 280 x 215 mm, 128 pages
269 full colour photographs,
plus line drawings
978 1 85780 224 5 **£19.99**

Red Star Volume 27
LISUNOV Li-2
The Soviet DC-3

Y Gordon, S and D Komissarov

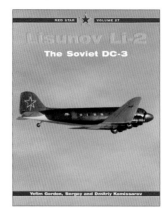

When they bought a manufacturing licence for the DC-3 in 1936, Soviet decision makers had no way of knowing the place the Douglas airliner would come to occupy in aviation's hall of fame. Adapted to employ Russian engines and materials, the DC-3 entered production as the PS-84; later redesignated Li-2. This addition to the series explores what is probably the least-known aspect of the history of one of the world's best-known airliners.

Softback, 280 x 215 mm, 128 pages
235 b/w photographs, plus
12 pages of colour
978 1 85780 228 3 **£19.99**

Red Star Volume 28
BERIEV'S JET FLYING BOATS

Yefim Gordon, Andrey Sal'nikov and Aleksandr Zablotskiy

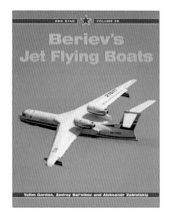

Established during the 1930s, Beriev is one of the less well known of the Soviet design bureaux. Their forte lay in the development of flying boats. Whilst these have been powered by both piston and jet engines, this book focuses on those jet-engined aircraft produced from the late 1960s onwards, including the Be-10, A-40 and Be-200. These aircraft were intended for a variety of roles, such as passenger transport and maritime rescue operations.

Softback, 280 x 215 mm, 128 pages
206 b/w photos, 16 pages of colour,
plus 12 pages of drawings
978 1 85780 236 8 **£19.99**

Red Star Volume 29
KAMOV -27/-32 FAMILY

Yefim Gordon and Dmitriy Komissarov

An in-depth study of this family of helicopter designs with their distinctive contra-rotating rotors. The Kamov Ka-27 helicopter was first produced for the Soviet navy in 1973. Several variants including the Ka-29 and Ka-31, were later built. This aircraft was followed in 1980 by a civilian version, the Ka-32. This was in turn followed by several variants including those for transport and shipboard utility purposes.

Softback, 280 x 215 mm, 128 pages
230 b/w photos, 22 pages of colour,
plus line drawings
978 1 85780 237 5 **£19.99**

Red Star Volume 30
SOVIET ROCKET FIGHTERS

Yefim Gordon

Fighter designers had always tried to make their aircraft go faster. To achieve this some Soviet designers used liquid-propellant rocket motors. The first attempt was the BI, which made its first powered flight on 15th May 1942. Projects from Polikarpov and Mikoyan, the latter based on captured German research, followed before Iliya F Florov's 4302 programme was cancelled at the end of 1947 in favour of turbojet-powered fighters.

Softback, 280 x 215 mm, 128 pages
257 black/white photographs,
plus 54 drawings
978 1 85780 245 0 **£19.99**

Red Star Volume 31
TUPOLEV Tu-114

Yefim Gordon and Vladimir Rigmant

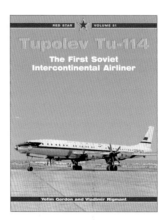

Based upon the earlier Tu-95 strategic bomber, the Tu-114 was the largest airliner constructed to that time. It carried up to 220 passengers at speeds approaching those of a jet; the speed record it set for turbo-prop aircraft still stands today. Aeroflot employed a fleet of 31 on its long-range domestic and international routes, the last being withdrawn in 1975. Some examples were later converted as Tu-126 'Moss' AWACS aircraft for the Soviet Navy.

Softback, 280 x 215 mm, 128 pages
194 b/w, 51 colour photographs,
plus 11 drawings
978 1 85780 246 7 **£19.99**

Red Star Volume 32
LAVOCHKIN'S LAST JETS

Yefim Gordon

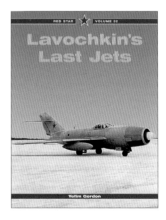

Although one of the less well known Soviet aircraft design teams, the Lavochkin bureau was at the forefront of the Soviet supersonic jet fighter programme from the late 1940s. Its La-15 was a contemporary of the MiG-15, less successful albeit more technically advanced. The elegant long-range, high-altitude La-250 'Anakonda', which appeared in 1956/57, was an impressive interceptor that lost out in competition to the even bigger Tu-28.

Softback, 280 x 215 mm, 128 pages
171 b/w photos, 3 pages of colour,
plus 19 pages of drawings
978 1 85780 253 5 **£19.99**